Blaming the Victims

V

Blaming the Victims

Spurious Scholarship and the
Palestinian Question

Edited by

EDWARD W. SAID

and

CHRISTOPHER HITCHENS

VERSO

London · New York

First published by Verso 1988
Second impression 1988
Third impression 1989
This edition published by Verso 2001
© The individual contributors except as follows:
'Palestine' by G. W. Bowersock and
'Michael Walzer's *Exodus and Revolution:*
A Canaanite Reading' by Edward W. Said
were first published in *Grand Street.*
Copyright © 1984 and 1986 by Grand Street
Publications, Inc. Reprinted by permission.
'Conspiracy of Praise' and 'The Essential Terrorist' by Edward W. Said were first
published in *The Nation.*

10 9 8 7 6 5 4 3

Verso
UK: 6 Meard Street, London W1F 0EG
USA: 180 Varick Street, New York, NY 10014–4606

Verso is the imprint of New Left Books

British Library Cataloguing in Publication Data
A catalogue record for this book is available from the British Library

ISBN 1–85984–340–9

US Library of Congress Cataloging in Publication Data
A catalog record for this book is available from the Library of Congress

Typeset by Columns of Reading
Printed and bound in Great Britain by Biddles Ltd
www.biddles.co.uk

Contents

Introduction

The conflict over Palestine is unusual in many different ways, principally of course because Palestine is not an ordinary place. An almost mythological territory saturated with religious ideology and endowed with overwhelming cultural significance, Palestine has been weighed down with historical as well as political meanings for many generations, peoples, and traditions. During the past century, however, it has been a site of actual all-out conflict between the Zionist movement and the non-Jewish native inhabitants of Palestine, who call themselves (Muslim or Christian) Palestinian Arabs. Yet even though the conflict between the two peoples has always been about possession of and sovereignty over the land, the struggle has also been intense in the public, international world a good distance from the Eastern Mediterranean. This world has comprised international diplomacy, the various mass information systems that include representations in radio, print, journalism, television and film, the domain of scholarship (history, sociology, cultural studies, political science, demography, economics, anthropology, philosophy, archaeology), and of course, the immensely combative, not always edifying, rhetorical interchange often referred to as propaganda. It is by no means an exaggeration to say that the establishment of Israel as a state in 1948 occurred partly because the Zionists acquired control of most of the territory of Palestine, and partly because they had already won the political battle for Palestine in the international world in which ideas, representations, rhetoric, and images were at issue.

1

Since that time, Israel has expanded in size and in power. In 1967 it militarily acquired, and still holds, vast amounts of Arab land and people, including the entire mass of historical Palestine. Yet military occupation and the continued domination of a subjugated non-Jewish population could not have gone on for two decades without considerable outside support. Until World War Two, Europe was the main outside arena for the struggle over Palestine; after World War Two the site shifted to the United States, where Israel has acquired an astonishing, but far from uncontested dominion. Proportionate to its population, Israel is the recipient of more US aid than any foreign state in history. It is estimated that every Israeli citizen today is subsidized by the US at roughly $1,400 per annum; each member of the Israeli military is underwritten by the US at about $9,750 per year. Along with these munificent sums (which incidentally far exceed the US federal subvention to many of its own disadvantaged citizens) has gone the equally significant US political support, whose symptoms are unswerving solidarity with Israel in any international forum of significance, the agreement on strategic co-ordination (which to a large extent explains the structure of covert organization in what has come to be called Iran- or Contra-gate), and the way in which most candidates for elected office in the US feel that it is required for them to declare unqualified support for Israel in order to be, and to remain, elected. As a whole, US support for Israel is necessary for the Jewish state's functioning, which has become almost totally dependent on the US.

Such facts are dramatic. Moreover, they have all sorts of implications not immediately evident. For one, violence against the Palestinians who are the direct victims of Zionist theory and Israeli policy, is both enabled and fueled. When the US Congress stipulates that because Israel is 'our ally' and the only 'stable democracy' in the Middle East, it also goes on to fund Israel at increasing levels year after year; this in turn tightens the grip of the occupation, allows the Israeli government to create more illegal and deeply provocative settlements to be established on the Occupied Territories of the West Bank and Gaza (the total exceeds 120), allows more Palestinian houses to be destroyed, more Palestinians to be jailed, killed or deported, allows more Palestinian land to be expropriated, and allows Israel to make Palestinian life more difficult, more unliveable. For another, because attention to Israel has been institutionalized and because its valence is so positive in Western public life, there has been a tendency, in the US especially, to associate resistance to Israel not simply with 'terrorism' and 'communism,' but also with anti-Semitism. As the arguments for Israeli democracy increase in intensity they have also tended to expand in sheer volume, so that the place of Palestinians in such public locales as the American television screen, the daily newspaper, the commercial film, shrinks to a few stereotypes – the mad Islamic zealot, the gratuitously violent killer of innocents, the desperately irrational and savage primitive.

None of these things are facts of nature, so to speak, nor are they inevitable. They are the result of effort and a great deal of hard work, in which many sometimes co-ordinated, sometimes contradictory, processes are involved, in which men and women commit themselves to political goals both in Israel and abroad, where, as I noted above, support for Israel is absolutely crucial.

The main thing about this today is not that it takes place, but that it takes place with considerable resistance and increasing difficulty. We must now do an abrupt *volte face* and bring to the front another, far less well-known set of processes: the resistance, both cultural and political, to Zionist success. In the main, the resistance has its source in Palestinian efforts to retain contact with their land and to survive furious onslaughts against Palestinian life. Elsewhere in the world, movements of colonial settlement envisaged both a subordinate and exploitative role for the natives; the Zionists were novel in that they saw the Palestinians as subordinates but excluded them from a meaningful existence: they were considered to be inconsequential nomads who 'neglected' the land before 1948. After Israel was established as a state for 'the Jewish people' and not as the state of its citizens, Palestinians were juridically relegated to the status of 'non-Jews'. Thus to be a Palestinian during the first two decades of Israel's existence either meant exile for the 780,000 Palestinians who were driven out in 1948, or it meant an indecent subaltern existence within Israel for the remnant of 120,000 who managed to stay on. The horrifying details of that life were first revealed to the world in Sabri Jiryis's pioneering *The Arabs in Israel* (1976), which was complemented in 1979 by Elia Zurayk's *The Palestinians in Israel: A Study in Internal Colonialism* (1976). Both men, it is worth noting, are themselves products of life as members of the Palestinian minority. A moving personal analogue to both works is Fouzi al-Asmar's *To Be an Arab in Israel* (1975).

Here we must backtrack still further. Almost from the moment that the state of Israel came into being in 1948 – and although the preparations were made well before that time – the West was deluged with a whole series of narratives and images that acquired the solidity and the legitimacy of 'truth'. In spite of the presence of a comfortable 67 per cent majority of Palestinian Arabs who owned over 90 percent of the land in 1948 (this was after decades of Jewish immigration and settlement) the world heard of an 'empty' territory whose inhabitants brutishly opposed Jewish settlement in Zion even after the Holocaust had occurred. Thereafter the myths proliferated and formed a system which, in the West at least, it became inordinately difficult to deny. The 'Arabs' left Palestine because their leaders told them to; the Arabs were out to destroy the Jewish state, and since they were already in league with Hitler, their opposition to Israel was essentially racist and facist; Israel was a democracy whose 'right' to existence was religious, was morally correct (since no one had suffered more than the Jews), was historically inevitable (since the whole world had promised empty Palestine to these enlightened Jewish liberals from Europe), was, above all, politically attractive since it seemed to embody every conceivable cliché about pioneers, ingenious scientists, intrepid humanitarians, and noble fighters; Israel was the target of terrorist attacks which far exceeded in number and savagery anything it inflicted upon its enemies both before and since 1948; and Israel has stood for progress and peace whereas its Arab enemies are medieval Muslim fanatics, irrational murderers, contemptable hypocrites. To these notions there came to be added such extensions or elaborations of the main system as: the Palestinians do not exist, Jordan is really Palestine, the Arabs use the Palestinians as a way of hating Jews or of being gratuitously nasty.

Yet there was always plenty of evidence to refute most, if not all these myths, myths whose principal purpose was not only to gain support for Israel, but also to conceal the appalling human cost to the Palestinians of Israel's successes. There were always real, live Palestinians; there were census figures, land-holding records, newspaper and radio accounts, eyewitness reports, and of course the sheer physical traces of Arab life in Palestine before and after 1948. Anyone who was interested in finding out whether the Palestinians fled because their leaders told them to could have verified the claim by consulting the record, or by actually quoting a documented source on a specific day. Neither exercise seemed necessary. Similarly, it would have been possible to check and see if Arabs had made declarations about peace or not, or whether Arab 'terrorism' could compare in results either with the terrorism of the Stern Gang, the Haganah, and the Irgun, or with Israeli claims of 'purity of arms', whether in fact it was correct, just, or historically inevitable that land owned by one people could be promised over to, and then taken militarily by, another people, the enlightened West applauding the conquerors, and blaming or ignoring the victims almost entirely.

Somehow the myths have led a life of their own. Today, they appear more sublimely absurd than they did four decades ago, and still they keep appearing. Consider for example an adulatory piece on David Ben-Gurion by Shimon Peres, Prime Minister of Israel at the time. Writing in the *New York Times Magazine* 5 October 1986, Peres still can find it in himself – despite history, despite the presence of nearly five million Palestinians – to speak of Palestine and the Palestinians as if they and their land were discovered by the incoming Zionists:

> The land to which they came, while indeed the Holy Land, was desolate and uninviting; a land that had been laid waste, thirsty for water, filled with swamps and malaria, lacking in natural resources. And in the land itself there lived another people [note that Peres does not even feel the need to name that people]; a people who neglected the land, but who lived on it. Indeed, the return to Zion was accompanied by ceaseless violent clashes with the small Arab population [note here how the Palestinians have become 'a small Arab population' instead of what in fact they were: the overwhelming majority in Palestine right up until the founding of Israel in May 1948, whereupon hundreds of thousands of them were forcibly compelled to leave] with the small population in Israel [note how Peres speaks of Israel, not Palestine, despite the fact that at the time Israel did not exist] and with the Arab states that incited them and fought alongside them.

Note here that the Prime Minister of Israel has entirely transformed the people of Palestine into the mere tool of 'the Arab states' who incited them, as if to say that on their own the Palestinians would either have left or would not have resisted the incoming Zionist settlers.

As ideological weapons, such notions had the effect early on of reducing reality in Palestine for Western audiences and policy-makers to a simple binary system. On one side stood the gallant Zionists who were like 'us', on the other a mass of undifferentiated natives with whom it was impossible for 'us' to identify. With the Zionists there came to be associated not just the good, the true and the beautiful, but a definite human image of the White settler hewing civilization out of the wilderness, an image that itself drew upon cultural sources in American puritanism (with its strong philo-Semitic biases), in the nineteenth-century adventure narratives by Europeans about Africa and Latin America, and in the great modernist epics of the self-made or self-fashioned hero. The extraordinary success of popular films like *Exodus*, tied to innumerable episodes of underdog Israelis overcoming immense odds, fostered the astonishing idea more or less prevalent nearly everywhere in the West, that the real victims of the Middle East were the Israeli Jews, whose good-humored ingenious pluck gained them respite from continued Arab threats to 'throw the Jews into the sea'. It was lost, alas, on every Western pundit in 1982 that the *Palestinians* were being driven into the sea as they exited Beirut, and that it was Palestinians not Israeli Jews who were being massacred in miserable refugee camps. But by then the world had begun only very slowly to take notice of the reality of Palestinian resistance (and Israeli brutality) even though the narrative of Palestinian history was still largely underground.

This, I think, is a very important point. The story of Zionist achievements in Israel has a steady, reassuring pulse to it. It is continuous, it is peopled with recognizably human figures who are themselves tied to justly great and justly famous Jews in the West (Einstein, Freud, Chagall, Rubinstein, and so on), it can have a universal validity imputed to or felt in it. The people who speak the narrative represent a world the average Westerner knows. Zionist history as incarnated in the narrative of modern Jewish achievements in short is official, or semi-official. Only a native or an alien terrorist and troublemaker will feel uncomfortable with it. And indeed most Palestinians speaking their history are unlikely to be *of* (however much they may be *in*) the West. Their language is Arabic, their religion Islam or Eastern Christianity, their culture decidedly un-Western. Whereas for the Israeli Jew it has long been possible to describe the agonies of the Holocaust and the restitution provided by the return to Zion, for the Palestinian there is no vast historical tragedy of apocalyptic proportions to draw on, and certainly no vindicated return. The Palestinian disaster (or *nakba*) is human: the destruction of a society, the dispossession and painfully secular, mundane exile that followed, the loss to Zionism of the right even to have a history and a political identity. Most of all the Palestinian has suffered because he or she has been unknown, an unacknowledged victim, and worse, a victim blamed not only for his or her disasters, but for those of others as well.

But even though the Palestinians underwent difficult and, it may confidently be said, maddeningly unjust times, the people did not disappear, nor in all the intermittent defeats did they cry 'enough' or give up on being Palestinian. During the first years after 1948 the so-called remnant who were Israeli citizens attempted to forge links with progressive movements in Israel, and they established organizations like al-'Ard (the Land) to foster Palestinian culture and traditions, in minority opposition. For their part the exiles in the Arab world joined Nasserism; they became Baathists, or Communists, or they went underground and started Palestinian organizations that fought Arab states and Israel alike. The slow emergence of a post-1948 Palestinian literature began its course in the 1960s with the first important works by Mahmoud Darwish, Fadwa Touqan, Ghassan Kanafani, Jabra Jabra, Samih al-Kassem, and others.

We are only now beginning to fathom the massive upheavals in the Arab world, Israel, and the West that followed upon the June 1967 War. But for the Palestinians, 1967 meant the Israeli conquest of the West Bank and Gaza, and therefore the loss of the whole of historical Palestine. Yet 1967 spurred the unmistakable rise of an independent Palestinian national movement, and with that in the realm of culture and ideology, the beginnings of a fully-fledged Palestinian discourse. All these things coincided with the new power of the Palestine Liberation Organization, established in 1964, but after 1967 taken seriously as a major force in regional and international politics. Although in the wake of its clashes with host states (Jordan and Lebanon) the PLO left behind it a tragic legacy of civil war, destruction and resentment, it also had the paradoxical effect of uniting the variously dispersed and dispossessed Palestinian people for the first time in their history. In 1974 at the Rabat Arab Summit, the PLO was declared the sole legitimate representative of the Palestinian people; after a decade and a half of more devastation and dissension, the PLO nevertheless won the acknowledgement and unprecedented support of the people, as signified by the convening of the 1987 Palestine National Council in Algiers. Today, the PLO is recognized by over a hundred governments throughout the world, and with the exception of the US and Israel, it is universally considered not only to represent Palestinians but also to be an essential partner in any meaningful peace between the Arabs and Israel.

The June War led to the October War of 1973, as well as the Camp David agreements of 1979, and the invasions of Lebanon in 1978 and 1982. Elsewhere in the region, the Islamic Revolution in

Iran and the Iran-Iraq War provided more evidence of what 1967 truly portended: that both the state structure established by the great colonial powers after World War One, and the politics in the region by which the West essentially ruled the Middle East, were beginning either to dissolve or to spill over borders. Islamic Iran and Zionist Israel have emerged as transnational powers, curiously dependent upon the Western economy, intransigently independent of Western tutelage at the same time. Similarly, the Palestinian movement has also acquired a powerful international dimension, associated with the kind of liberationist nationalism embodied in the great anti-imperialist movements of Africa, Asia and Latin America. As for the Arab state system, one could perceive in it a host of mediocre and/or corrupt authoritarian regimes, incapable of protecting their borders, sullenly reliant upon internal security forces to quell their native populations and suppress their democratic rights, unable either to handle their oil revenues or later their dwindling resources, and stagnating in dependence upon the US which for its part ignored their protestations while it despised their aspirations in favor of Israel's.

Even this rapid sketch of recent political history provides enough background for understanding the new complex and highly mobile dialectic between Israel and the Palestinians. Whereas before 1967 it had been possible for Israel and its supporters to ignore the Palestinians as so many incidental obstacles to its progress, after 1967 the new chorus of official Israeli and Zionist denials, of spurious scholarship, of rewritten histories takes on a grotesque, almost parodistic garishness, completely at odds with the realities. For in fact the latest confrontation between Israel and the Palestinians was conducted simultaneously on two levels: on the ground so to speak, it was the contest between an openly colonialist movement (which Zionism had always been; now the colonialism was finally and ironically exposed to view before a post-colonial world) and a nationalist insurgency. On the second level, in ideological, political and cultural terms it was a struggle between a movement stripped of its promise and now mired in interminable problems of economic dependence, colonial occupation, increasing militarization, and sheer holding on, and on the other side, a burgeoning revolutionary block directly affiliated with numerous Third World Liberation Movements, coming to consciousness and its own history in all sorts of new ways.

Without wishing to change these formulations, I hasten to add, however, that some thoughtful Israelis and Palestinians who groped for humane modalities of co-existence did come together after 1967, despite the tyranny of the overall contest. And many realized that even though the Zionists followed the pattern of earlier colonizers, Israeli Jews were not in fact white South Africans, or French Algerians. Israel was a real state with a real society. The dawning awareness all around was of two peoples locked in a terrible struggle over the same territory, in which one, bent beneath a horrific past of systematic persecution and extermination, was in the position of an oppressor towards the other people, whose claims were hastening the polarization and desperation of every member of the community. Consider what it now means, that an entire generation of Palestinians and Israelis has only known direct military occupation or, in the case of many among the group of exiled Palestinians, life as stateless refugees, subject to the vagaries of Arab politics, great power cynicism, and the murderous intent of their enemies.

I have remarked the dominance of the Zionist viewpoint in Western cultural discourse: now we must describe the inflections and pressures of that dominance in more detail, at the same time noting the gradual diminishments and restraints imposed upon it by a spirited Palestinian resistance to its spurious, often flagrantly preposterous arguments. One or two things stand out. First is the extraordinary discrepancy between official Zionist discourse (as spun out by institutions, designated spokespersons, apologists and polemicists) and unofficial Zionist work. Some of the young Israeli revisionist historians who have emerged in the mid-eighties (Tom Segev, Benni Morris and so on) are Zionists, but their work is done with a genuine will to understand the past; what they say about the horrors of 1948 they say openly without a desire to lie or conceal the past. Their counterparts in the establishment still operate with the old scruples; for them, Palestinians are 'Arabs', that is, they are either terrorists when they resist or menials when they don't. In any event, the old myths about 1948 are for them to be maintained regardless.

Even more striking, however, is the discrepancy between American and Israeli Zionist discourse. There is a great deal more debate, more freedom of discussion among Israelis than among American Zionists, whose shameless adulation of Israel is almost limitless. Moreover, during the 1980s as the Reagan presidency has embarked on a series of retrograde adventures throughout the world, increasing its aid to dictatorships and right-wing insurgencies, finding a 'terrorist' under every bush and signs of 'the empire of evil' wherever the US did not reign supreme, American Zionists swung sharply to the right. Doubtless there are similar divagations to be observed in the United Kingdom and Western Europe generally, but what makes the American case so notable is of course the unrivalled power and relevance of US support for Israel.

In effect then, the American Zionist community of support for Israel was transformed by the mid-1970s into a uniquely disciplined and tactically superb actor on the American political scene. During the Reagan years, 'The Lobby' as it was called by Edward Tivnan, the author of a 1987 book by that name, could call on virtually the entire Congress to support, or oppose, given pieces of legislation. Major figures in the Senate and the House (Cranston, Inouye, Specter, Kasten, Leahy, Sanford, Fascell, Levine, Obey, Feighan, Wolpe, and many others) were indebted to money from Jewish PACs (see the two long articles on congressional funding activities of the Israeli lobby in the *New York Times*, 6 and 7 July 1987); others, like Kennedy, Moynihan, D'Amato, Dodd, and Solarz, in addition to presidential contenders (Cuomo, Biden, Kemp, Dole), were unswerving adherents of the essentially right-wing Zionist vision of things. Their tenets were that Israel was always right no matter what it did, that the Palestinians were negligible, that terrorism was the major issue in the Middle East. Insofar as these simplistic and incoherent formulas meant that Israel could continue with practices on the West Bank and Gaza that were routinely condemned as barbarism, apartheid, or totalitarianism elsewhere (in Afghanistan and South Africa for instance), then so be it. The honorable exceptions to these scandals of conscience and minimally honorable politics are Jesse Jackson and a tiny handful of Black or genuinely liberal, elected officials.

This sort of concentrated power in American political society has also radiated influences onto civil society, with noteworthy results. The more powerful the lobby grew in America since 1967, the more it drew attention to itself, the more resistance it fostered. So that as such organizations as the Anti-Defamation League (ADL) and the American-Israeli Public Affairs Committee (AIPAC) tried to crush any dissent on Israel in American public life, the more dissent appeared. A pioneering work on Zionist attempts to control opinion and discussion was Alfred Lilienthal's *The Zionist Connection*, which appeared in 1978. The book's merit was to expose instances of suppression and falsification by which publishing houses, journals, newspapers, radio and television stations succumbed to pressure and refrained from disseminating anything that might detract from Israel's faultless reputation as a model state. Although Lilienthal's book named names and gave facts and figures, it was largely ignored in the mainstream press, which preferred not to take up the challenge to its own flaunted independence represented by Lilienthal's book. Yet Lilienthal's fate did not stop others, who have considerably increased in number. Recent exposés of the Zionist lobby at work have been Noam Chomsky's *The Fateful Triangle* (1983) and Paul Findley's *They Dared to Speak Out* (1985), while the magnitude of American Jewish dissonance with the Zionist centre has steadily amplified.

It is now possible to see clearly the established pattern by which supporters of Israel do two things when they write and organize: they reproduce the official party line on Israel, or they go after delinquents who threaten to disturb the idyll. There is a dialectical opposite to this pattern, however. Critics and opponents of the Zionist lobby in civil society take as their tasks first to decode the myths, then to present the record of facts in as neutral a way as possible. Although I shall return to these critical tasks in a moment, the point I want to make here is that nothing – literally nothing – about Palestine can go without proof, contention, dispute and controversy in American civil society: it is as if even the narrative of Palestinian history is not tolerable, and therefore must be told and re-told innumerable times. The starkest example of the attack on the notion of a Palestinian identity has been Joan Peters's book *From Time Immemorial*, a work deluged with praise in the US, yet almost completely ignored in Israel. Peters's argument, that the Palestinians are really Arabs from neighbouring states who came to Palestine between 1946 and 1948 because they were attracted by the prosperity of Zionist settlement, dissolves the Palestinians as a people into a cloud of historical fantasy. Awarded a prize by the Jewish Book Society, it was hailed as a historical event by professional historians (such as Barbara Tuchman) and important luminaries (such as Saul Bellow) even when the book was shown to be riven with plagiarism, misquotations, and massive distortions of fact and figures.

Peters's book and the vogue of works on terrorism have as their immediate source the 1982 Israeli invasion of Lebanon. For the first time in the twentieth-century West, Israel and its supporters were embarrassed by the extraordinary spectacle furnished by the siege of Beirut, displayed in all its gory detail on the evening television news. The subsequent massacres at Sabra and Shatila, the gradual breakdown in US Lebanese policy, the surprising resilience of the Palestinians (whose nationalism, according to General Sharon, was to be smashed once and for all in Beirut and elsewhere), the defeat of Begin: all these exacerbated the political and cultural excesses of the Zionist organizations. AIPAC and ADL both published enemies-lists and handbooks for combating anyone whose criticism of Israel seemed to be getting too much attention; some of the Zionist groups went after the media (the *Washington Post* and NBC in particular) for their alleged anti-Semitic biases in coverage of the Lebanon war. Gradually, and as if by co-ordinated prior agreement, two major themes began to emerge in the Zionist polemic: one, that criticism of Israel was nothing less than a resurgence of classical anti-Semitism; and two, that armed or cultural resistance to Israel conducted by Palestinians was in essence terrorism and only terrorism.

Underlying these intransigently unrealistic notions is, I think, the perhaps more unpalatable reality that official Zionism, as embodied in Israeli state policy and in the discourse of its loyalists in the West, has no military option against the Palestinians, who seem destined to remain irritatingly before Israel, challenging Zionist settlements, vociferously protesting and fighting the abrogation of their rights, popping up in precisely those places (the West Bank, Gaza, and Lebanon, for instance) where they were supposed to have been defeated. But there is a deeper problem. The rhetorical, as well as ethical, concomitant of this apparent impasse is that the 'ideals' of classical Zionism, which had seduced the West and a great many Jews with their promise, seemed now at best to deliver only verbal assurances to a shrinking, less credulous audience. Far from being a light among the nations, Israel had become – along with the United States – an international pariah, trafficking with South Africa, the Shah's Iran, Somoza's Nicaragua, Marcos's Philippines, and every retrograde regime in the Third World. Intellectuals who might claim to be progressive in their support for Israel now have to submit their arguments to extraordinary contortions in order to maintain the fiction that Israel is still a liberal cause. One example of this special form of the *trahison des clercs* is Michael Walzer, the American 'left' political theorist who along with other progressives (Alan Dershowitz, Irving Howe, Martin Peretz) excused Israel for actions condemned everywhere else. Thus you could be against preventive detention, collective punishment, colonialism, pre-emptive war, racist immigration laws, oppressive rental and housing laws everywhere in the world, but be for them in Israel. All this was justified as intimacy and solidarity with one's community.

Roughly the same sort of suppleness is applied in dealing with 'terrorism' and religious enthusiasm. Because Israel is manifestly a state run on largely religious theses, and because it is perfectly true that many of the ugliest aspects of modern atavism are presided over by priests and mullahs as well as rabbis, it proved to be a wise Zionist rearguard tactic to attack Islamic fundamentalism and excuse the others. Rabbi Kahane has proved a convenient whipping boy for these cautious progressives: he can be attacked publicly as an aberration, whereas many of the ideas he proposes now (e.g. forced expulsion of Arabs) have been canonical dogmas of Zionist thought and practice for many decades. As for 'terrorism', it too has proven a handsome device. Writing in *Le Monde Diplomatique* in February 1986, Amnon Kapeliouck notes that as Palestinian nationalism acquired regional and international credibility in the mid-1970s, Israeli officials consciously adopted the policy of characterizing it as 'terrorism'. No one would deny that criminal violence existed, nor that the deliberate killing of innocents is an appalling crime. The problem is that use of the word 'terrorism' was a political weapon designed to protect the strong (and eliminate from memory exploits of 'former' terrorists like Begin and Shamir who now run Israel) as well as to legitimize official military action against innocents. So unmistakable has the Israeli imprint been on the word 'terrorism' that in the *New York Times* of 11 July 1987, reporter Stephen Engelberg described President Reagan as having been greatly influenced by the Benjamin Netanyahu collection on terrorism; this is the book published in 1985 that connected terrorism with Islam, the Palestinians, and the KGB, even to the extent of learning from the book's pages how other presidents had bypassed the Congress to pursue private initiatives of their own.

Let us return now to the oppositional work done by critics of Israeli Zionist policy. I have been saying that dominance has accrued to the Zionist viewpoint in Western, and especially, American cultural discourse; I have also been saying that because the viewpoint itself has been always, if not with convenient enough visibility, contested by Palestinians, its peculiar blindnesses, its ideological weaknesses to say the least, its outrageous falsifications, have come under increasing attack, again under the aegis of Palestinian resistance. Here we must distinguish between the scholarly and the popular. In general it is true to say that prevalent Western modes of scholarly writing about the Middle East have always been part of the politics of the region, particularly so far as the links between American scholarship and policy have been concerned. Today it is reasonable to argue that many – but certainly not all – of the specialists who deal with the Middle East in any of its aspects, are adversely affected by the Zionist-Palestinian conflict. Most of the traditional Orientalists tend to have been carried by the Zionist worldview, so long as the view prevailed on the ground and in Washington. There was a kind of discretely reflective symmetry in the fact that the Arabist officials of the Israeli military occupation have been graduates of university departments of Oriental Studies, in Israel and the West. Therefore – again I generalize – books or articles that suggested the reality and independent validity of an Arab-Islamic culture, that recognized the human rights of the Arabs as a people, that therefore sympathized with the Palestinian side of the conflict were extremely rare in the West. Among the few exceptions were the studies of A.L. Tibawi and Albert Hourani, highly respected academic historians whose work was done in England; in America their counterpart was Philip Hitti.

Things began to change after 1967. Let us put aside the question of whether sources available in Arabic were suddenly more accessible in London, Paris, or New York. As I suggested earlier, it is still difficult for an Arab poet or novelist to get his or her work translated into English because Arabic is considered by most Western publishers to be a 'controversial' language. The same law applies to Arabic scholarly or journalistic work. Some work on the Palestinians was available in English before 1967. We must remember that the crucial issue for any discussion of Palestine has to be 1948, or rather what happened in 1948. Yet few books or articles that discussed 1948 from the Arab perspective circulated easily in the Western archive, even though a few very good ones were available but unused before 1967, e.g. George Antonius's *The Arab Awakening* and Sami Hadawi's *Bitter Harvest*. Two important inaugural works in the post-1967 period, done with impeccable scholarly distinction, appeared as edited by Ibrahim Abu-Lughod: the first, in 1969, a dissenting Arab view of 1967 (*The Arab Israeli Confrontation of 1967*), the second, a fastidiously documented study by many hands, *The Transformation of Palestine* (1971). Both were published by Northwestern University Press, a fact which of course meant that they had a chance of reaching a wider Western audience.

The post-1967 period produced a number of Arab-American organizations whose declared purpose was advancing the Arab and Palestinian viewpoint in Western culture. Similar organizations sprang up in Western Europe. In some cases this meant that translated works from Arabic and Hebrew originals began at last to appear; in others, it meant making suppressed or unfamiliar Zionist texts available as negative evidence of what Israeli apologists had concealed for so long; in still others it meant providing a forum for dissenting or unorthodox scholars both to speak and to meet each other. Most of the time the new organizations – the Association of Arab-American University Graduates chief among them – organized the expatriate Arab communities of the West and enabled them to support academic and popular work that in effect 'produced' the Arab and Palestinian as creatures of secular history for the first time in the West. In addition, a whole generation of Palestinian and Arab writers became known in the West – Mahmoud Darwish, Emile Habiby, Tawfik Zayyat, Ghassan Kanafani, Emile Touma, Sahar Khalife, Sadek al-Azm, Elias Khoury, and many others – thanks to these efforts. *Arab Studies Quarterly*, *The Journal of Palestine Studies*, the AAUG *Newsletter*, along with *MERIP Reports*, the *Review of Middle East Studies* (published in England), *Gazelle*, the *Link*: all these were part of the general critique of Zionist hegemony, and the platforms for new positive and critical work on the Arab and Palestinian realities. In addition, following in the line of Judah Magnes, the great critical efforts of non- or anti-Zionist Jews like Elmer Berger, Israel Shahak, Noam Chomsky, Maxime Rodinson, Livea Rokach, I.F. Stone, many of them sponsored or directly encouraged by Arab efforts in the West, made such things as the Sharett papers, Dov Yermiya's *1982 War Diary*, Kapeliouck's profound study of Sabra and Shatila, as well as a whole mass of 'unknown' documents from the Zionist archive, visible in the clear light of day, forever dismissing the myth of Zionist innocence.

For a time these counter-archival works encountered debate and a much-hoped-for engagement with 'the other side'. This seemed to be required so long as the PLO had a strong base in Beirut, so long as the Palestinian issue remained central to policy discussions in the West about the future of the Middle East. Since 1982, the beginnings of the Iran-Iraq war, and indeed since the Reagan presidency and the establishment of 'terrorism' as the US's favorite policy target, there has been a retreat. Debate is avoided; discussion muted or forbidden; serious attention diverted. Whereas it was once a valid Zionist enterprise to do textual analyses of documents like the Palestinian National Covenant or Resolutions of the Palestine National Council, the shoddier alternative now is to rely on slogans like 'the Palestinian terrorist organization' and on outright defamation whenever intellectual engagement with the Palestinians is unavoidable. Frequently, instead of replying to an argument or attempting to refute facts, the Zionist mouthpiece simply attacks one's ethnic identity ('He's a Palestinian – or a self-hating Jew – after all') or one's general political tendency ('He's a well-known Left apologist').

A description of the post-1982 period would not be complete without some account of how the dismal slide into sectarianism and provincial nationalism in the Arab world has negated the achievements of earlier post-colonial generations. Internationally, the Arab states have been in almost total disarray as a result. Many have adopted a supine even cringingly obeisant attitude to the US; the nadir, in symbolism and reality, of all such postures was the funding of the Nicaraguan Contras by Saudi Arabia. Most Arab regimes have given up entirely on the idea of Arab unity, with dire consequences for Palestine. In some instances they have adopted astringent local measures against Palestinians (Egypt, Jordan, Tunisia, Morocco), in others they directly colluded with Israel and the religious Right (Jordan, Syria, Lebanon). It is generally true, I think, that the underlying tension between the potential catholicity of Palestinian-Arab nationalism and Arab regime nativism has flared up more consistently after 1982 than before. One tiny example gives a flavor of the atmosphere. A profile of 'the Palestinian people' commissioned by the United Nations in 1983 (and included in this collection of essays) was blocked by a number of Arab states because, they alleged, the profile's premises were too 'extraterritorial'; the only Palestinians acceptable to these regimes are those on the West Bank and Gaza. The rest are to be forgotten.

But as the dispersed and complex realities of Palestinian life forced themselves upon the world, and as the official Israel position seemed embarrassing or vacant, the Cold War and its reconstituted ideology furnished ready all-purpose substitutes for thought, especially in the US. Happily these did not get in everyone's way. A new generation of scholars actually learned the relevant languages, read the texts, were interested in the people of the Arab Middle East. Orientalist dogmas were beginning everywhere to be under rigorous attack: the new critical methodologies, and their attendant political attitudes, made short shrift of such lazy platitudes as the Arab mind or Islamic society. Marxism, feminism, hermeneutics, deconstruction and cultural theory rendered old habits obsolete; novel structures appeared all across the humanistic and social science disciplines. Finally, it began to be acceptable to regard the conjunction between power and knowledge as a reality to be confronted and examined, not something to be hidden beneath egregious guild politesse.

In this invigorated context the center was held by discussion of the Palestinian issue, albeit not always explicitly. If, for instance, the theoretical ground was a general discussion of recovered history, of suppressed narratives and outlawed or marginal peoples, many made the direct connection between the general subject and one of its most striking instances. Thus it became a source of embarrassment for intellectuals who opposed the Contras and supported the Sandinistas, who organized against nuclear proliferation and for disarmament, who preached divestment in South Africa and disengagement with 'authoritarian' as well as 'totalitarian' clients, who spoke up for women's rights everywhere in the world, that they continued to ignore Palestinian rights and Israeli behavior, to by-pass no peace issue except the bitter conflict between Palestinian Arabs and Israeli Jews, to suggest that any critical and honest discussion of Israel would lose important Jewish support for major progressive stands.

Thus an invigilated discussion slowly opened up, although it often took oppositional forms and was conducted in counter-institutional places. Student and university lecture platforms, church meeting halls, consciously anti-establishment publications were the main venues, since there has been very little change in the mainstream media or in the principal officially sanctioned cultural sites. As I said above, one of the main foci has been the imperative to restore history to the Palestinians, something they have been doing for themselves all along, but in which Western scholarship has been lagging behind. There is still an extraordinarily remarkable shortcoming in this new and generally excellent scholarship, namely, the relative absence of Arab sources incorporated into the disciplinary discourses. For at least 15 years there has been, for example, a burgeoning of material, some of it both valuable as documentary evidence and first-rate as literature, on Palestinian society around and during 1948 (the work of Bayan al-Hout, Elie Sanbar, Nafez Nazzal, Elias Shoufani, the memoirs of various important personages, the development here and there of people's narratives, and so on.) In addition, the Palestine Research Center – whose archives were carted off (and later returned) by the Israeli army from West Beirut in September 1982 – has compiled geographical, political, sociological and demographic material on pre-1948 Palestinian society. Its journal *Shu'un Filastiniya* brought out a rich series of interviews, autobiographical reflections, oral testimonies, all of them by actors, some important some modest, in the various dramas of Palestine. Very little of all this material in Arabic seems either to be known or used; this suggests that the prevailing research norms that require Western witnesses as the only dependable or credible evidence continue largely unchallenged.

Apart from that, however, the advances are considerable on a very wide front. A great deal is now known about late nineteenth-century Arab Palestine. Skillful use of Ottoman, British and Zionist archives confirms the presence in Palestine of a flourishing and relatively politicized society. The old and much-urged notion, that Palestinian nationalism was created out of the encounter with Zionism, has long been put to rest, as has the idea that Palestinian identity was never anything more than an undifferentiated component in the Ottoman Empire and/or the early Arab nationalist movement. Good research on the importance of the Palestinian issue within the Arab world well before it became a rallying cry for governments, has brought order to the disorder that once ruled, in which Zionist and Orientalist scholars were charging that Palestine was a trumped-up issue used by governments for their own cynical purpose. In fact, Palestine was a popular issue forced upon unwilling or impotent governments who had to respond to mass pressures from below. None of this would have had the basic force it now has without fundamental research on the demographic and land-holding statistics of Palestine. Here too, important research by such scholars as Janet Abu-Lughod, Justin McCarthy, and Alexander Schulch has firmly established the consistent pattern of majority Arab settlement in Palestine many generations before the Zionist influx during the late nineteenth and early twentieth centuries.

It is also important to note that there have been significant Palestinian-sponsored efforts to take research into the Western metropolis itself; these efforts are a sustained counterpoint to research into the Palestinian and Arab past. The Institute of Palestine Studies in Washington, for example, has published a weighty volume, written by Lee O'Brien, *American Jewish Organisations and Israel* (1986), that meticulously studies all the great American Jewish organizations. Similarly, the International Center for Research and Public Policy, also in Washington, has produced an invaluable series of monographs on international public opinion and the Palestine question (the results are startling since it is now quite clear that even in America the consensus is solidly in favor of Palestinian self-determination), on Israeli

Arabism, on Israeli state terrorism, and the like. And as more is discovered about the Palestinians, more is uncovered about Israel. We should note a series of new studies, beginning with Jane Hunter's monthly publication *Israeli Foreign Affairs*, whose documentation of Israeli history and politics lifts the last veils off the hidden past. Simcha Flapan's important book *The Birth of Israel: Myths and Realities* (1987) is a major monument by the recently deceased Zionist socialist; Benjamin Beit-Hallahmi's *The Israeli Connection* (1987) is another work of contemporary history certain to activate much debate and disenchantment.

A huge amount of work obviously remains to be done, and as the Israeli occupation of the West Bank and Gaza enters its third decade one realizes that the magnitude of liberation required can only be accomplished by great and concerted effort. The thing to be remembered, however, is that nothing – and certainly not a colonial 'fact' – is irreversible. There are greatly encouraging signs of a notable change of attitude in numerous Israelis, and some of their Jewish and non-Jewish Western supporters. The Palestinians have since 1974 premised their political work and organization on the notion of joint community for Arabs and Jews in Palestine; as more Zionists see the wisdom of that option, as opposed to continued militarization and inconclusive war, there will have to be more joint political and scholarly work by like-minded people. This collection of essays is presented in advancement of that goal.

Edward W. Said
New York, July 1987

PART ONE

The Peters Affair

1

Conspiracy of Praise

Edward W. Said

Joan Peters's book, *From Time Immemorial: The Origins of the Arab-Jewish Conflict Over Palestine*, was published by Harper & Row in the spring of 1984. Its jacket was covered with endorsements from Barbara W. Tuchman, Saul Bellow, Angier Biddle Duke, Philip M. Hauser, Elie Wiesel, Lucy Dawidowicz, Paul Cowan, Barbara Probst Solomon and Arthur J. Goldberg. Each endorsement testified to the book's immense importance: Tuchman described it as 'a historical event in itself', and Bellow modestly stated that 'millions of people the world over, smothered by false history and propaganda, will be grateful for this clear account of the origins of the Palestinians.' After eight hardcover printings, Harper & Row has now issued a paperback edition of the book, bearing all these endorsements (minus that of Barbara Probst Solomon) plus a new one from Theodore H. White.

With only two exceptions, *From Time Immemorial* received favorable reviews in the American press. (Though as we shall see, its reception in Britain and Israel was almost uniformly negative.) Everyone – except for those two reviewers and Robert Olson, who dismissed the book in *American Historical Review* – commented on Peters's astonishingly thorough scholarship and her unprecedented findings. That assessment was made by relative amateurs (Walter Reich in *The Atlantic* and Timothy Foote in *The Washington Post*), as well as by seasoned pros (Daniel Pipes in *Commentary*, Ronald Sanders in *The New Republic* and John Campbell in *The New York Times*). The general impression was that Joan Peters had at last done all the work necessary to settle one of the most vexing and persistent problems of the twentieth century. No longer could a scholar or propagandist argue that 'the Palestinians' (Peters entitled everyone to enclose the designation of a people in the quotation marks of suspicion) were in fact a real people with a real history in 'Palestine'. Her book asserted that their national as well as actual existence, and consequently their claims on Israel, were at best suspect and at worst utter fabrication. In other words, *From Time Immemorial* relieved Israel and its supporters of responsibility for the refugees created by the establishment of the Jewish state in 1948, and for the subject people of the West Bank and the Gaza Strip.

Although *From Time Immemorial* is clearly relevant to the contemporary debate about the Middle East in the United States, its peculiar distinction is to present itself as a full-scale history *ab origine* of the Palestine problem, which ventures to prove that the Palestinians are and have always been propaganda. How that strikes those of us who have memories of communal life in Haifa, Jerusalem, Safad, Jaffa and Nazareth before 1948 I shall leave to the reader's imagination. Peters claims that a careful rereading of demographic evidence shows that the British (and of course 'the Arabs') suppressed evidence about the number of illegal Arab immigrants in Palestine before 1948. She argues that most of the 1948 refugees were in reality people who had not come to Palestine until 1946 and who therefore cannot possibly be considered true inhabitants of Palestine 'from time immemorial'. In any case, she says, their number has always been inflated for propaganda purposes – a fairly routine Israeli claim in the 1950s and 1960s, now discarded.

As for the tiny handful of 'real' Arab inhabitants in 'uninhabited' Palestine, they did a lot of what Peters calls 'in-migrating', moving from place to place in Palestine, and were therefore little more than nomads. Given the history of Arab hatred of Jews, which Peters rehearses in much detail, she concludes that 'the Palestinians' – who had been attracted by Jewish prosperity to those parts of Palestine from which they were later evicted – are a trick foisted on Israel and the rest of the gullible world merely to expedite the malevolent designs of Arab and Moslem anti-Semitism. Besides, she says, since many Jews expelled from the Arab world came to Israel after 1948, there was, at the very least, parity in the movements of dispossessed people in and out of Palestine.

Nor is this all. Peters tell us that her research was carried out in a spirit of sympathy with the Arab refugees, that she visited them in their miserable camps and studied their history, culture and leaders at close range. That protestation was made much of by reviewers who found that it gave her conclusions the credibility of a genuine discovery arrived at by compassionate research. So obviously well-intentioned a person could have been converted only by the factual evidence she has so dutifully unearthed. (Peters doesn't mention in the body of the text that she wrote an article, 'An Exchange of Populations', in the August 1976 issue of *Commentary*, where her notions about inveterate Arab anti-Semitism are trundled forth, along with the exchange-of-Arabs-for-Jews idea, all in a prose quite free of sympathy for the poor Arab refugees.)

From Time Immemorial bolsters its appearance of legitimacy by including an impressive list of mentors and scholarly authorities, whom Peters thanks profusely. This list of worthies (Peters implies they are virtually her collaborators) includes famous Orientalists like Elie Kedourie, Bernard Lewis and P.J. Vatikiotis. Not one of those men is known for his Arab sympathies, which is probably why not a single one has made any attempt to dissociate himself from her or her ideas even though evidence of her numerous errors and falsifications has been circulating for some time. Besides, their respectability hasn't been threatened, so why should they bother about so trivial a question as the scholarly truth of Peters's book?

For someone with no academic credentials, and with only the sketchiest foreign policy and press background, Joan Peters has now become something of an authority on Arab-Jewish matters for the media (nonfiction's answer to Leon Uris). Interviews with her dot newspapers and magazines across the country, and she has been a guest on numerous radio and television talk shows. *From Time Immemorial* has received, according to Peters, '200 to 300' favorable reviews and has also won a prize in the Jewish Book Council's Israel category.

The two exceptions to this quite extraordinary outpouring of praise were an article in the 11 September 1984 issue of *In These Times*, by Norman Finkelstein, a graduate student at Princeton University, and a review in the Fall 1984 *Journal of Palestine Studies*, by Bill Farrell, a law student at Columbia University. In what I shall now relate, both young men played courageous roles, and if I speak more about Finkelstein it is to note his amazing persistence despite odds that would have deterred almost anyone else. Finkelstein showed that Peters's work was what he called a 'hoax': her evidence was unsound in all sorts of ways; her demographic statistics were inconsistent, mathematically impossible, wildly exaggerated; and, most important, in all the cases he was able to check, she either plagiarized Zionist propaganda sources or deliberately tampered with quotations so as to change their meaning entirely. Much of one chapter, for example, is lifted – mistakes and all – from Ernst Frankenstein's *Justice For My People*, published in 1942. In one place illegal Arab immigration is suggested as 'at least' 200,000; in another, 370,000; in a third, 1,300,000; in a fourth, 3,700,000. Taking the same approach Farrell came up with similar results. When, for example, Peters quotes from the *Hope Simpson Report* of 1930, she transforms the phrase 'Egyptian labor is being employed in certain individual cases' to 'According to that Report, evidence of Arab immigration abounded; "Egyptian labor is being employed." ' Where the Anglo-American *Survey of Palestine* (1945-6) says that in October 1942 'as a matter of emergency' 3,800 laborers were brought into Palestine from Syria and Lebanon, Peters says: 'What the official Anglo-American *Survey* of 1945-6 definitively disclosed . . . is that . . . tens of thousands of "Arab illegal immigrants" [were] *recorded* as having been "brought" into . . . Palestine'. And so on and on.

Since the core of Peters's case was based on a (mis)reading of demographic evidence, both Farrell and Finkelstein took pains to check and recheck her findings, which they found unacceptable. What neither of them noted, however, is that the last census for Palestine was done under British mandate in 1931. No population estimates of twentieth-century Palestine can avoid its findings, which show a vast native Arab majority. Peters totally ignores that census, just as she ignores the authoritative demographic work of Janet Abu-Lughod, Justin McCarthy and others, whose conclusions are diametrically opposed to her own. Instead she relies on Ottoman statistics for the 1890s, compiled by Professor Kemal Karpat of the University of Wisconsin, and on the impressions of a nineteenth-century French traveler, Vital Cuinet. These do little more for her case than add a lot of numbers to what is already a tiresomely shrill text dotted with embarrassing errors, such as the use of medieval historian Makrizi as an eye-witness source about nineteenth-century Palestine. (To his credit, Bernard Gwertzman noted the book's offensive tone in his review for *The New York Times*, on 12 May 1984.)

Despite undercurrents of suspicion about Peters's book set off by Finkelstein, only two publications have followed up on his evidence and printed anything systematically critical of *From Time Immemorial*'s major points. In *The Guardian* and *The Nation* respectively, Noam Chomsky and Alexander Cockburn described what Peters and her ecstatic reviewers were up to, but no one else has paid much attention. At one point, Colin Campbell of *The New York Times* expressed some enthusiasm for writing an article like the one he had done on the David Abraham case, but then he dropped the matter.

When the book appeared in Britain in spring 1985 it received a vastly different set of reviews. It is worth citing a passage from one of those reviews to give some sense of the startling difference between Britain and the United States when it comes to discussion about the Middle East. *The Observer* assigned *From Time Immemorial* to Albert Hourani of Oxford University, probably the world's foremost authority on modern Middle Eastern history. Not incidentally, no scholar of stature was granted the privilege of reviewing Peters in the United States, nor was the book entrusted to someone *not* already known for his or her unqualified support for Israel. The single exception to this pattern may be *The New York Review of Books* which assigned *From Time Immemorial* to Yehoshua Porath, the leading Israeli authority on Palestinian nationalism, an eminent historian and a man known for his moderate views about the Palestinians. (Porath's article is discussed on p. 62.)

At any rate, here is the concluding part of Hourani's review in the 5 March issue of *The Observer*:

Ms. Peters has found, or been provided with, a large number of documents, but most are well-known, and many of them she misunderstands or quotes out of context. She denounces British policy because she believes it broke the promise of the Balfour Declaration and the Mandate that Palestine 'east and west of the Jordan river' should become a 'Jewish homeland'. But the Declaration carefully avoided saying that Palestine should become a 'Jewish homeland'; and the British decision to set up an Arab princedom in Transjordan, and exclude it from the area in which a Jewish national home should be created, was in accordance with the terms of the Mandate.

Her argument that enormous numbers of Arabs came illegally into Palestine also has no basis. One of her few pieces of evidence is a statement made by an obscure Syrian official in 1934 that more than 30,000 Syrians had entered Palestine and settled there during a few months. The Permanent Mandates Commission asked a British representative for his opinion of this, and he said it was 'grossly exaggerated'. Ms Peters quotes the statement by the Syrian official but not the British reply; on the next page the statement becomes 'verified by an official international document'; a little later it has become 'hard evidence', in the light of which British statements to the contrary can be dismissed as fallacious.

The whole book is written like this: facts are selected or misunderstood, tortuous and flimsy arguments are expressed in violent and repetitive language. This is a ludicrous and worthless book and the only mildly interesting question it raises is why it comes with praise from two well-known American writers.

In their 8,000-word essay for *The London Review of Books*, Ian and David Gilmour went painstakingly through *From Time Immemorial*, recording a huge number of its inconsistencies and falsifications, among them Peters's suppression of the fact that no Jewish leader of note until, and even after, 1948 denied the presence of the native Arab Palestinian majority. The Gilmours note that Peters misleadingly bandies about population figures for 'Jewish settled areas' but does not reveal that those areas amounted only to 4 or 5 per cent of the whole country, or – a slightly more subtle tactic – that figures for Christian Arabs are simply left out. Peters's revival of the *canard* about the Arabs leaving voluntarily is also dispatched by the Gilmours, as is her ludicrous contention that British policy encouraged Arab immigration into Palestine.

Similar reviews turned up in *The Times Literary Supplement*, *The Spectator* (which compared *From Time Immemorial* with Clifford Irving's 'autobiography' of Howard Hughes), *Time Out* and *The Sunday Times*, although Peters, whose contact with fact seems tentative, has described the British reviews as 'excellent'. But perhaps the most revealing thing about this strange book was its reception in Israel, also in 1985. Most notices of the book were perfunctory and dismissive; *Davar's* full-length review on 29 March treated it with unmistakable contempt. According to the reviewer, *From Time Immemorial*'s main defect was its embarrassing use of discredited Israeli *hasbara* ('propaganda'). It should be noted that most of Peters's earthshaking evidence about the nonexistent Palestinians had already been used by official and semi-official Israeli information agencies during the 1950s and 1960s, and that it is now quite commonplace for Israeli government representatives to warn against re-using this worthless stuff. One had the impression that Israel had written the book off when Peters appeared in the country to reap the glory of her personal, uniquely American *hasbara* effort. Hence, she was kept out of the public eye; she returned to the United States, just in time to receive her Israeli award in New York.

There are several curious facets to this egregious book. Many passages contain disconnected items all pressed into making the same point. The impression you get is of one team of experts tossing file cards into large folders labeled 'Jews, Arab hatred', or 'Palestinians, myths of', and another team pasting them onto more or less consecutive pages. That Peters has nothing to say about the immense amount of Arab, or for that matter Israeli, material on Palestine, all of it easily enough available, is testimony to how narrowly focused, how dry and single-minded, is her effort. During the past five years alone there have been several volumes of original Arab documentation of Palestinian life in Palestine. (Scholars and reviewers interested in assessing Peters's book may also consult two very recent works, Walid Khalidi's fine *Before Their Diaspora: A Photographic History of the Palestinian 1876-1948*, and Basheer K. Nijim and Bishara Muammar's *Toward the De-Arabization of Palestine-Israel, 1945-1977*. Such works prove that a native Arab community once flourished in Palestine, and that it was not simply the illegal, temporary presence of a small, shifty population of nameless vagrants sneaked in by rascally anti-Semitic British officials acting in cahoots with a worldwide network of Arab fanatics. Peters touches on none of this, nor does she refer to the large bibliography of scholarly Western works on the history of Palestine, many of which give the lie to her preposterous thesis.

Granted that Peters is an inept writer, a bad propagandist and a hopelessly incompetent historian, how is it that virtually no criticism of her work has appeared in the United States? Let us grant also that Harper & Row continues to ignore evidence of her falsfications and plagiarisms. Why do normally competent editors, historians, journalists and intellectuals go along with the fiction that *From Time Immemorial* is a wonderful work of historical discovery? Peters's factual distortions and innumerable mistakes have been exhaustively documented by Norman Finkelstein, yet no one paid attention to him, no one followed his leads. No one paid the slightest heed to the British reviews, or to those in Israel. Worst of all, no one has demanded that Peters and her supporters respond to the huge list of accusations that her book has collected in the eighteen months since it appeared. She still gives interviews to American journalists, cheerfully asserting the complete acceptance of her work.

I speak here less as a Palestinian who wants to keep saying 'but we exist and always have and will', than as an American intellectual disgraced by the shoddiness of our present so-called life of the mind. The Peters case is not just a matter of poor work.

It is, after all, a case of orchestrated compliance by which the history and actuality of an entire people are consigned to nonexistence. Where are all those guardians of intellectual morality who, in a chorus led by the Conor Cruise O'Briens and the Leszek Kolakowskis, whine about Communist and Third World disinformation and propaganda, who stalwartly defend American freedom of expression and healthy debate, who invoke Orwell and denounce totalitarianism? Has it come to this, then: an unconsciously held ideology that permits the most scandalous and disgusting lies – execrably written, totally disorganized, hysterically asserted – to pass as genuine scholarship, factual truth, political insight, without any significant challenge, demurral or even polite reservation?

The sad truth is that where discussion of Israel is concerned, the United States is well below Israel itself in norms of truth and methods of debate. Here then is a perfect illustration of Richard Hofstader's 'paranoid style' in American political life. This is not, alas, a matter of the left being better than the right. The young progressives who publish *Radical History* conscientiously avoid discussion of the Palestinians. Those who know better are cowed by the Israeli lobby. It is true that the American-Israeli Political Action Committee has been criticized in the press for its campus campaigns against those who have dared to speak out against Israel or to support Palestinian rights; yet how many deans and faculty members have raised their voices against the censorship and blackmail still applied by AIPAC against 'enemies' on the nation's campuses?

To read Peters and her supporters is, for Palestinians, to experience an extended act of ethnocide carried out by pseudo-scholarship. Tom Sawyer attends his own funeral as a kind of lark, whereas we are being threatened with death before being permitted birth. And we are told to stay out of the whole thing. The irony of this occurring in the United States at a time when so many effusions about Middle Eastern peace are perpetually stymied by US and Israeli actions designed to keep Palestinians out should not be difficult to detect. In this way – democratically – do intellectuals and the state synchronize their efforts to sweep the small people of this world under the rug.

The one thing I still cannot grasp is how people can be so foolish as to believe *From Time Immemorial*'s contention that the Palestinians are something made up or imaginary, like the unicorn or the tooth fairy. Why do Barbara Tuchman and Saul Bellow, for example, expect that 4 million of us, scattered everywhere, can be made to repeat the lie of our existence for 35 years? Do they imagine that all of us get instructions from a central propaganda office? And, toughest question of all, how have we been as successful as Peters implies in uniting most of the Arab, Islamic, Third World, European and socialist community in our cause if we are no more than a myth? Surely it would have been a lot less trouble for us simply to get a Palestinian state!

2

Disinformation and the Palestine Question: The Not-So-Strange Case of Joan Peters's *From Time Immemorial*

Norman G. Finkelstein

> Turnspeak – the cynical inverting or distorting of facts, which, for example, makes the victim appear as culprit.
>
> *From Time Immemorial*, p.173

Few recent books on the origins of the Mideast crisis have evoked as much interest as Joan Peters's study, *From Time Immemorial* (Harper and Row, 1984).[1] Virtually every important journal of opinion printed one or more reviews within weeks of the book's release. Harper and Row reported that scarcely eight months after publication *From Time Immemorial* went into its seventh printing. Author Joan Peters reportedly had two hundred and fifty speaking engagements scheduled during 1985.

Reviewers have differed in their overall assessment of the book. But they have almost uniformly hailed the research and the demographic findings that are at the core of Peters's study. Jehuda Reinharz, the distinguished biographer of Chaim Weizmann, acclaimed Peters's 'valuable synthesis' and 'convincing . . . new analysis' in the *Library Journal* (15 April 1984). Walter Reich, in his *Atlantic* review (July 1984), wrote that if Peters's 'arguments, especially the demographic one, are confirmed, they will certainly change [our] assumptions about the Arab-Israeli conflict'. Ronald Sanders, author of a monumental study of the Balfour Declaration, likewise opined in *The New Republic* (23 April 1984) that Peters's demographics 'could change the entire Arab-Jewish polemic over Palestine'. In *Commentary* (July 1984), Daniel Pipes threw all caution to the wind in his appraisal of Peters's findings –

her 'historical detective work has produced startling results which should materially influence the future course of the debate about the Palestinian problem'. Martin Peretz, again in *The New Republic* (23 July 1984), suggested that there wasn't a single factual error in the book, and that, if widely read, it 'will change the mind of our generation. If understood, it could also affect the history of the future.' Timothy Foote, in the *Washington Post* (24 June 1984), acclaimed *From Time Immemorial* as 'part historic primer, part polemic, part revelation, and a remarkable document in itself'.

The accolades continued. Nazi holocaust scholar Lucy Dawidowicz congratulated Peters for having 'brought into the light the historical truth about the Mideast'. Barbara Probst Solomon called *From Time Immemorial* 'brilliant, provocative and enlightened'. Barbara Tuchman ventured that the book was a 'historical event in itself'. Saul Bellow predicted that 'Millions of people the world over, smothered by false history and propaganda, would be grateful for this clear account of the origins of the Palestinians'. Moralist Elie Wiesel promised that Peters's 'insight and analysis' would shed new light on our understanding of the Mideast conflict. Arthur Goldberg, Paul Cowan and others added their voices – and names – to the chorus of praise.

That a scholarly work meets with critical acclaim would hardly be news were it not for the fact that *From Time Immemorial* is among the most spectacular frauds ever published on the Arab-Israeli conflict. In a field littered with crass propaganda, forgeries and fakes, this is no mean distinction. But Peters's book has thoroughly earned it.

The fraud in Peters's book is so pervasive and systematic that it is hard to pluck out a single thread without getting entangled in the whole unravelling fabric. To begin with, the fraud falls into two basic categories. First, the evidence Peters adduces to document massive illegal Arab immigration into Palestine is almost entirely falsified. Second, the conclusions Peters draws from her demographic study of Palestine's indigenous Arab population are not borne out by the data she presents. To confound the reader further, Peters resorts to plagiarism.

Daunting Hercules

Peters purports to document massive illegal Arab immigration into the Jewish-settled areas of Palestine during the British mandate years (1920-48). Her thesis is that a significant proportion of the

700,000 Arabs residing in the part of Palestine that became Israel in 1949 had only recently settled there, and that they had emigrated to Palestine because of the economic opportunities generated by Zionist settlement. Therefore, Peters claims, the industrious Jewish immigrants had as much, if not more, right to this territory than the Palestinian 'newcomers'.

Peters begins by recalling that Palestine's Arab population expanded at a remarkable rate during the years of the British mandate. She is skeptical of the generally accepted opinion – scholarly, official British, even mainstream Zionist[2] – that 'natural' increase accounts for by far the greater part of the growth in Palestine's Arab population in this period. Peters writes that 'the so-called "unprecedented" rate of "natural increase" among the non-Jews was never satisfactorily broken down or explained' (p. 223). She takes special exception to the findings of the 'population expert' (her phrase) A.M. Carr-Saunders in his 1936 study, *World Population*. In her version of his conclusions (p. 224), Peters first alleges that Carr-Saunders 'contradicted' himself by, on the one hand, claiming that 'the fall in death rate' was the 'likely' cause of the Palestinian Arabs' population increase, and then asserting that 'Medical and sanitary progress has made little headway among the Palestinian Arabs as yet, and cannot account for any considerable fall in the death-rate'.

If we consult the pages in *World Population* cited by Peters, however, we discover the following:

> Medical and sanitary progress, *so far as it affects the personal health and customs*, has made little headway among the Palestinian Arabs as yet, and cannot account for any considerable fall in the death-rate. But general administrative measures, in the region of quarantine, for example, have been designed in the light of modern knowledge and have been adequately carried out. Measures of this kind can be enforced almost overnight... Therefore we can find in these administrative changes, brought about by the British occupation of Palestine, what is in any case a tenable explanation of the natural increase of population among Arabs. (pp. 310-11; my emphasis)

Carr-Saunders does indeed state that 'medical and sanitary progress' couldn't explain the 'fall in death rate', but only insofar as such progress impinges on the 'personal health and customs' of the Palestinian Arabs. He then goes on to say that recently-implemented medical and sanitary administrative measures such as the quarantine could explain the decline in the mortality rate. The 'contradiction' evidently results, not from a lapse in Carr-

Saunders's reasoning, but from Peters's (unacknowledged) deletion of the crucial qualifying phrase in her citation from *World
Population*.

Next, Peters mentions the 'administrative measures' explanation only to dismiss it as a 'rather lame possibility'. She offers not
a single reason for this evaluation. Peters concludes her mini-
inquisition with the following summary of Carr-Saunders's position:

> In other words, the new 'phenomenal' rise in the Arab population of
> Palestine, which had remained sparse and static for two hundred years
> despite constant replenishing, was attributed to a sudden, hyped,
> natural increase of the 'existing' long-settled indigenes. That phen-
> omenon, or so went the rationalization, resulted from *new* conditions.
> Yet, it was *also* acknowledged that because of its recent timing, the
> introduction of those new conditions *could not in fact have been
> responsible* for the population increase in the period of time for which it
> was credited! (Peters's emphases)

Note that Carr-Saunders's finding is precisely the opposite of the
one Peters attributes to him: the new conditions – i.e., 'general
administrative measures' – offer a 'tenable explanation of the
natural increase of population among Arabs'.

Having thus mangled what she now qualifies as a 'self-
contradicting expert source', Peters swings her cleaver in the
direction of the 1938 *Palestine Partition Commission Report* which
she reproves for 'tr[ying] to reconcile contradictory "facts"'
(pp. 224-5). She cites, without comment, the following excerpt
from the *Report* to illustrate this supposed shortcoming:

> We thus have the Arab population reflecting simultaneously two widely
> different tendencies – a birth-rate characteristic of a peasant commun-
> ity in which the unrestricted family is normal, and a death-rate which
> could only be brought about under an enlightened modern administra-
> tion, with both the will and the necessary funds at its disposal to enable
> it to serve a population unable to help itself. It is indeed an ironic
> commentary on the working of the Mandate and perhaps on the
> science of government, that this result which so far from encouraging
> *has almost certainly hindered close settlement by Jews on the land*, could
> scarcely have been brought about except through the appropriation of
> tax-revenue contributed by the Jews. (Peters's emphasis)

Peters is apparently unaware that different tendencies often
coexist in the real world and that the observation of the Partition
Commission cited above is no more than a commonplace
illustration of this fact.

In this manner, Peters sets aside the conventional wisdom on the demographics of Palestine's Arab population during the Mandate years. She is now in a position to advance her own explanations of the Arab population's unusual growth – namely, massive 'hidden' immigration. That is, Peters avers that a significant part of the population of Palestine in 1947 was not indigenous.

Peters is reluctant to specify the exact percentage of Palestinian Arabs who were not indigenous. This is a curious omission on the part of an author who elsewhere pretends to achieve scientific precision in her calculations. The few hints that Peters does give about this crucial matter are remarkable for their inconsistency. This, too, is odd in a study that devotes so much space to alleged numerical discrepancies in refugee reports, population statistics, and other documents.

On two occasions, Peters suggests that the number of illegal Arab immigrants who had settled in the Jewish areas of Palestine was 'great enough to compare with [the] admittedly immigration-based increase of the Jews' (p. 275; see also p. 337). That would put total 'illegal' or 'unrecorded' Arab immigration at about 370,000. Elsewhere (p. 381), Peters seems to set her sights considerably lower – 'at least 200,000' through 1939, she reports. In a third place (p. 298), she implies that almost the entire Arab population of Palestine was immigrant and not indigenous.[3] That would put the total number of 'hidden' Arab immigrants and their descendents at roughly 1,300,000. In still a fourth place (p. 253), Peters muses whether Arab immigration into the Jewish-settled areas of Palestine between 1893 and 1947 may have been in the ten-to-one ratio to Jewish immigration she purports to establish for the first years of modern Zionist settlement.[4] By this calculation, Arab immigration into Palestine's Jewish-settled areas through 1947 would have been on the order of 3,700,000, that is, well over one thousand percent greater than the second of Peters's estimates quoted above. What is even more astonishing is that this figure is nearly three times the *total* Arab population in *all* of Palestine in 1947.[5]

For the sake of argument, let us assume that the figure Peters wishes to propose for illegal Arab immigration is somewhere between 200,000 and 400,000. Peters is thus alleging that non-indigenous Arabs constituted fully one-half of the Arab population residing in the region of Palestine that became Israel in 1949.

The first thing to be said about this thesis is that Peters's own data refute it. Peters's demographic study (see pp. 49–57 below) shows that Palestine's Arab population expanded 'naturally' by a factor of (at least) 2.7 between 1893 and 1947.[6] She puts Palestine's Arab population at 466,400 in 1893 (p. 255, Table G). Multiplying 2.7 by 466,400 we get 1,259,280. Palestine's total Arab population stood at 1,303,800 in 1947 (*ibid.*). Natural increase therefore accounts for all but (at most) 44,520 of the Arabs in Palestine in 1947. The thesis Peters intends to prove is thus, by her own reckoning, untenable. Was Peters unaware that the results of the demographic study demolished her thesis? Did she simply elect to ignore this unpleasant fact?

Citing 'British government records' (p. 427), Peters puts the official estimate of illegal Arab immigrants who had settled in Palestine at about 10,000 for *all* thirty years of the British Mandate. She herself contends, on the contrary, that on average for *each* of the thirty years of the Mandate, 10,000 Arabs had settled illegally in the Jewish areas of Palestine.

This thesis is, to say the least, audacious.[7] The burden of her case is to prove the plausibility of this extraordinary revisionist figure. To do so, she draws on what reviewers have claimed is prodigious original research. Even John C. Campbell, in one of the few lukewarm notices to date (*The New York Times Book Review*, 13 May 1984), acclaimed Peters's 'massive research ... [which] would have daunted Hercules'. In fact, nothing could be further from the truth. A close reading of Peters's voluminous footnotes reveals that she relies almost exclusively on the standard official documents of the period – the 1930 *Hope Simpson Report*, the 1937 *Peel Commission Report*, the 1945-6 Anglo-American *Survey of Palestine*, the annual British reports to the League of Nations, and so on. None of this evidence is new.[8]

This discovery raises an interesting question. Without exception these official, mostly British-authored reports concluded that – in the words of the *Survey of Palestine* – 'Arab immigration for the purposes of settlement [in Palestine] is insignificant'.[9] Yet, Peters manages to use these very same documents to 'prove' precisely the contrary. How does she manage this astonishing *volte face*?

In effect, Peters uses a three-pronged strategy to supply evidence where none exists: 1) multiple references; 2) a 'tip of the iceberg' theory; and 3) major surgery.

1) *Multiple references*. The fragments of evidence that Peters does offer the reader (almost all of which are, in any case, falsified) are repeated over and over again. Peters's wildly chaotic

presentation of the relevant material manages to conceal this fact to some extent.

2) *'Tip of the iceberg' theory*. Peters repeatedly implies that the scant evidence she does come up with is actually worth many times its apparent value. This is because the British purportedly turned a blind eye to all but the most flagrant cases of illegal Arab immigration into Palestine. It follows that for every *reported* Arab deported from Palestine, many other illegal Arab immigrants must have been allowed to stay behind. This argument hinges on the allegation that the British were indifferent to all but the most egregious instances of illegal Arab infiltration. Unfortunately for Peters, however, save for a relatively brief period during World War II (October 1942-October 1944), there isn't a particle of evidence to support this 'theory'.

But Peters doesn't let this obstacle deter her. She completely falsifies a section of the 1930 *Hope Simpson Report* to secure the crucial evidence and then repeatedly refers back to this same doctored material at each critical juncture in the text to clinch her argument. Peters construes the section in question to mean that the British only deported 'flagrant' illegal Arab immigrants, letting many others stay. This is sheer invention. The document says nothing of the sort. Rather, it makes the following recommendations for handling illegal immigration – Jewish, Arab, etc. – into Palestine:

> *Discouragement of illicit entry*. As to the treatment of such [illegal] immigrants, when they are discovered, it should be the rule that they are at once returned to the country whence they came. The rule may possibly work harshly in individual cases, but unless it is understood that detection is invariably followed by expulsion the practice will not cease. It is probable that it will cease entirely as soon as it is discovered that the rule is actually in force.
>
> The case of the 'pseudo-traveller' who comes in with permission for a limited time and continues in Palestine after the term of his permission has expired is more difficult. Where the case is flagrant, recourse should certainly be had to expulsion. In case of no special flagrancy, and where there is no special objection to the individual, it is probably sufficient to maintain the present practice, under which he is counted against the Labor Schedule, though this method does a certain injustice to the Jewish immigrant outside the country, whose place is taken by the traveller concerned.[10]

Before turning to Peters's rendering of these two paragraphs, the following points should be stressed: 1) the *Report* evidently urges that illegal immigrants be deported 'at once'; 2) a *single* exception is made in the case of the 'pseudo-traveller' of 'no special flagrancy' – he may be reclassified as a legal immigrant; 3) *Jews* were by far the main beneficiaries of the latter special provision;[11] 4) the British *included*, in the total figure for recorded Arab immigration,[12] *all* Arab 'travellers' reclassified as legal immigrants.[13] The special case of the reclassified 'pseudo-traveller' is thus, for the purposes of Peters's argument, completely irrelevant. Recall that Peters alleges, in addition to the officially registered Arab immigrants, some 300,000 *unrecorded* Arabs had entered and settled in Palestine. The only policy statement in the *Hope Simpson Report* pertinent to her thesis reads: illegal immigrants should 'at once [be] returned to the country whence they came'.

Peters makes nineteen – sometimes implicit, more often explicit – references to the section of the *Hope Simpson Report* cited above. She purports that it 'says' or 'admits' or 'acknowledges' or 'suggests' the force of her own thesis about 'illegal' Arab immigration into Mandatory Palestine (see pp. 229, 232-3, 296-7, 326, 375-9, 394, 402). As comparison with the full text of the cited section of the *Hope Simpson Report* shows, every one of these references to its content falsifies both the letter and the spirit of the document.

To sum up, Peters argues *ad nauseam* that, since the British responded to only the most flagrant instances of illegal Arab immigration, we should assume for every illegal Arab immigrant reported as deported during the Mandate years many times more illegal immigrants must have remained in Palestine. Without the falsification of the *Hope Simpson Report*, Peters couldn't have sustained this thesis, which is fundamental to the argument of her book.

3) *Major surgery.* Peters still needs the 'tip' to prove the 'iceberg'. She still needs a fact before she can make multiple references to it. Peters resolves this problem by embarking on a falsification spree that, in John Campbell's phrase cited earlier, 'would have daunted Hercules'.

Peters does not adduce one substantive, pertinent piece of evidence to document her thesis that is not in some way mangled. But though Peters is a gross falsifier, she is clever. For example, the quotations she distorts in the text are often accurately rendered somewhere in a note. I suspect that Peters will at some point argue that she couldn't possibly have intended to conceal anything since the full quotation is right there, buried in her one hundred and twenty pages of notes.

This is not the place to document all of Peters's crude and shameless distortions. In the space available, I will first sample and gloss Peters's characteristic methods. These are illustrated in Table 1 below.

The examples in Table 1 are typical of Peters's falsification technique. Here are some more inspired misrepresentations:

1) Peters writes: 'From [1920,] the preoccupation of Palestine's administration would be concentrated solely upon *limiting* the immigration of the *Jews*. As a British report attested, for "Arab immigration" a "different" set of rules applied' (p. 275; her emphases). But the context of the quotation in the *Survey of Palestine* is a discussion of how Arab housing differs from Jewish housing. The document continues: 'Although different considerations apply to Arab immigration, special consideration need not be given to the latter as, out of a total number of 360,822 immigrants who entered Palestine between 1920 and 1942, only 27,981 or 7.8% were Arabs. The number of room units to house Arab immigrants has, therefore, been calculated on the same basis as Jewish immigrants...' The phrase 'different considerations', which Peters finds so sinister and pregnant, refers, *not* to immigration policy, but to housing construction. Peters repeats this same falsification on pp. 250 and 514, note 31.

2) Peters asserts that, in 1893, some 60,000 Jews and 92,300 non-Jews inhabited the region of Palestine that became Israel after the 1948 war (pp. 250-1).[14] Since 38,000 of the non-Jews were Christians, Jews were 'perhaps' a 'marginal majority'. But, according to Peters's tables in the back of the book (pp. 424-5), not 92,300, but 218,000 Arabs resided, in 1893, in that slice of Palestine which became Israel. Peters manages this neat little trick by dividing the region of Palestine that became Israel into three areas and then 'forgetting' (in her text) the two areas of what became Israel in which there was virtually no Jewish, but significant Arab, settlement.[15]

3) To prove that the Mandatory authorities were more hostile to illegal Jewish than illegal Arab immigration, Peters cites (pp. 346 and 548, note 26) the 'self-contradicting' 1933 annual *Report to the League of Nations* which states on page 35 that '[t]here

Table 1

1. *Hope Simpson Report* (1930)	*From Time Immemorial*
'In Palestine, " . . . Egyptian labor is being employed in certain individual cases. . ."'	'[A]ccording to that *Report*, evidence of Arab immigration abounded: "Egyptian labor is being employed"' (p. 297)
Comments Peters doesn't even insert an ellipsis after 'employed' to indicate something – in this case, the crucial qualifier – was deleted. She corrects for her 'oversight' in the footnote where the quotation appears in full.	
'[A]rab unemployment is liable to be used as a political pawn. Arab politicians are sufficiently astute to realize at once what may appear an easy method of blocking that [Jewish] immigration to which they are radically averse, and attempts may and probably will be made to swell the list of Arabs unemployed with names which should not be there, or perhaps to ensure the registration of an unemployed man in the books of more than one exchange. It should not prove difficult to defeat this manoeuvre.'	The *Report* "had strongly indicated . . . that the condition of Arab 'unemployment' was being blown out of all semblance to reality by the Arab leaders who had indeed found 'the method of blocking that [Jewish] immigration to which they are radically averse,'"' (p. 298)
	The illicit Arab immigration from 'Syria and Trans-jordan' . . . had 'swollen unemployment lists' and was 'used as a political pawn' toward 'blocking immigration to which they are radically averse'. . . (p. 374)
Comments The entire paragraph is addressing a hypothetical situation, one which, in the *Report*'s words, 'It should not prove difficult to defeat'.	

2. Peel Commission Report (1937)

'A large proportion of Arab immigrants into Palestine come from the Hauran. These people go in considerable numbers to Haifa, where they work in the port. It is, however, important to realize that the extent of the yearly exodus from the Hauran depends mainly on the state of the crops there. *In a good year the amount of illegal immigration into Palestine is negligible* and confined to the younger members of large families whose presence is not required in the fields. Most persons *in this category* probably remain permanently in Palestine, wages there being considerably higher than in Syria. According to an authoritative estimate as many as ten or eleven thousand Hauranis go to Palestine temporarily in search of work in a really bad year. The Deputy Inspector-General of the Criminal Investigation Department has recently estimated that the number of Hauranis illegally in the country at the present time is roughly 2,500.' (my emphases)

From Time Immemorial

"'The 'Arab immigrants', particularly 'Hauranis' from Syria", the *Report* stated, "probably remain permanently in Palestine." But although the number of Hauranis who illegally immigrated was "authoritatively estimated" at 10,000-11,000 during a "bad" year in the Hauran, only the unrealistically, perhaps disingenuously low Government estimate of 2,500 were concluded to be "in the country at the present time." (p. 310)

Comments Recall that Peters must prove not only that massive numbers of Arabs had entered but also that they had settled in Palestine. In the original text, the Hauranis who 'remained permanently' explicitly refers, *not* to the '10,000-11,000 during a "bad" year', but rather to a 'negligible' sum who immigrate in a 'good' year. This particular falsification serves a triple purpose: (i) 'documenting' massive illegal Arab settlement in Palestine, (ii) illustrating the bad faith and untrustworthiness of the British reports ('unrealistically, perhaps disingenuously low Government estimate of 2,500') and (iii) pointing up the alleged 'contradictions' between the facts reported in the official documents and their conclusions. (The *Peel Commission Report*, like every other document of the period, concluded that 'Arab illegal immigration is mainly casual, temporary and seasonal.')

Table 1 continued

3. Anglo-American *Survey of Palestine* (1945-6)

'Arab illegal immigration is mainly ... casual, temporary and seasonal.' The *Survey* observes that, for example, immigration increases in 'boom' and emigration in 'bust' periods. To illustrate this particular pattern of temporary immigration, the following example is cited: '[T]he "boom" conditions in Palestine in the years 1934-6 led to an inward movement in Palestine particularly from Syria. The depression due to the state of public disorder during 1936-9 led to the return of these people and also a substantial outward movement of Palestinian Arabs who thought it prudent to live for a time in the Lebanon and Syria.'

From Time Immemorial

'Under the heading "Arab Illegal Immigration," a 1945-6 report noted that " ... the 'boom' conditions in Palestine in the years 1934-6 led to an inward movement into Palestine particularly from Syria." ' (p. 517, footnote 49)

Comments The quotation is used in Peters's section headed 'Hints of Substantial Unrecorded Immigration.' It points up one of Peters's favorite techniques for falsifying a document – wrenching an observation from its critical context.

The Survey divides Arab immigration into Palestine during World War II into two categories: first, the 3,800 Arabs who were brought in under 'official' arrangements and, second, the 'considerable numbers', of which 'no estimates are available', who were either recruited by private contractors or else 'entered individually'.

'What the official Anglo-American Survey of 1945-6 definitively disclosed ... is that ... tens of thousands of "Arab illegal immigrants" [were] *recorded* as having been "brought" into Palestine ... In addition, other *unestimated* "considerable" numbers immigrated "unofficially" or as "individuals" during the war, according to the report.' (p. 379; all emphases in Peters's text)

Comments The latter sentence in Peters's rendering refers unmistakably to the second category of Arab immigrant workers: note, for example, the quotation marks around 'considerable,' 'unofficially,' 'individuals,' and the italics in 'unestimated.' The 'tens of thousands' must then refer to the first category – those who entered 'under official arrangements'. Yet, the Survey records only 3,800 such immigrant workers.

'In one group of nearly ten thousand reported "foreign workers" – most of whom eventually "deserted" or "remained in Palestine illlegally" – the Survey states that the Arab "illegal immigrants [were] Egyptians, Syrians, Lebanese ... also small numbers from Trans-Jordan, Persia, India, Somaliland, Abyssinia and the Hejaz."' (p. 378)

Comments There is no such reference in the Survey. Peters fabricates it by splicing together two categories of immigrant workers listed in the document that she has already tallied. Peters's falsified presentation (pp. 378-9) of the – for her purposes – crucial section of the Survey from which this quotation is allegedly taken is, even by her exalted standards, in a class all its own.

was a considerable increase of *illicit* immigration, *mostly of Jews*, entering as transit travellers or tourists' (Peters's emphasis), yet

> on p. 180, separated from the 'immigration' material by 145 pages, was the report that 'The extent of illicit and unrecorded immigration into Palestine from or through Syria and Transjordan has been estimated at about 2,000 and Jewish as to fifty per cent.' From 'mostly Jews,' the estimate had dropped to fifty per cent.

This 'revelation' is simply untrue. The breakdown on p. 180 of the *Report* refers only to illicit immigration through contiguous territories. Peters 'forgets' that there was also infiltration directly through Palestine's ports, with would-be immigrants posing as 'transit travellers' and 'tourists'. There is no contradiction between the two statements in the report. I would add parenthetically that, in general, the British reports are models of precision, clarity and internal consistency. The 'contradictions' Peters purports to have 'uncovered' in them are all of her own making.

4) Peters tells us in her chapter on 'Official Disregard of Arab Immigration' that, contrary to popular belief, Jews were not dispossessing the indigenous Arab population but, rather, the landless Arab peasants in Palestine were 'mostly new Arab entrants' (p. 323). Her only documentation for this thesis is an article by Moshe Braver, an Israeli professor. Peters quotes Braver as follows (p. 546, note 76): 'landless peasants were new immigrants'. But Braver actually wrote, 'The immigrants were mostly landless laborers. . .' In other words, he does not say that all landless Arabs were immigrants. He says the immigrants were landless.

5) To document the British Mandatory Government's indifference to Arab infiltration of Palestine, Peters cites the 1935 annual *Report to the League of Nations* in which, she asserts, 'only "Jewish Immigration into Palestine" was catalogued; that was the only heading. . .' (p. 275). In fact, the British report in question meticulously and exhaustively tabulates every conceivable aspect of Arab immigration on *nine* consecutive pages. Peters could hardly have overlooked these tabulations since the comparable statistics for Jewish immigration appear *on the very same pages in parallel columns. Every* annual British report on Palestine – and Peters purports to have scrutinized *thirteen* of them – contains identical exhaustive tabulations of Arab immigration under the same chapter heading, 'Immigration and Emigration'.[16]

In this connection, another of Peters's falsifications merits special comment. Peters and her reviewers make much of the alleged remarks of an anonymous 'thirty-year archivist – a specialist in the Foreign Office and Colonial Office records on the Middle East for the Public Record Office' in London. He purportedly told her that Arab immigration into Palestine 'did not exist. There was no such thing. No one ever kept track of *that*' (p. 270; Peters's emphasis). Yet, every British annual report to the League of Nations and every major official British study of the period includes an exhaustive tabulation and detailed commentary on Arab immigration. If 'no one ever kept track of' Arab immigration, how were the tables composed? Where did the numbers come from?

Finally, let me turn to the central piece of evidence Peters brings to bear in support of her thesis. The item is tucked away in the minutes of the League of Nations Permanent Mandates Commission hearings on Britain's Palestine Mandate. The first – and last – reference to it in the Commission minutes comes during a June 1935 exchange prompted by the Jewish Agency's allegation of 'considerable immigration of labor from Egypt, Syria and Transjordan'. Assistant Chief Secretary of the Government of Palestine Moody, a British government representative at the hearings, denied the allegation, stating that, whereas Transjordanians and Syrians had indeed entered Palestine, the right to settle there had been given over almost exclusively to the Jews. I quote now the relevant minutes of the exchange in their entirety:

> Lord Lugard [a Mandates Commission member] said that *La Syrie* had published, on August 12th, 1934, an interview with Tewfik Bey El-Huriani, Governor of the Hauran, who said that in the last few months from 30,000 to 36,000 Hauranese had entered Palestine and settled there. The accredited representative would note the Governor's statement that these Hauranese had actually 'settled'.
>
> ... Mr Moody expressed the view that the statement of the Governor of the Hauran was a gross exaggeration.
>
> Mr Orts [also a Commission member] did not know how much value could be attached to the statement, but the statement itself was definite. The Governor even referred to the large sums remitted by these immigrants to their families, who remained in the Hauran.
>
> Mr Moody said he had read the article in question. As he had said, he thought that the figure must be grossly exaggerated, because the Palestine Government had taken special measures on the eastern and northeastern frontier with a view to keeping out undesirable people.

Peters cites the Mandates Commission reference to the report in *La Syrie* on seven different occasions (pp. 230, 231, 272, 275, 297, 319, 431). She classifies this reference in the Commission minutes as 'hard evidence' (p. 297) and lists this reported entry of 30,000-36,000 Hauranis into Palestine flat out as a fact in her chronology of significant events in the history of the British mandate (p. 319; see also p. 272, where the item is again presented, without qualification, as fact). Yet, Peters cites not a single cross-reference for a report which, in the view of the British government representative, was 'grossly exaggerated'. The representative's vigorous rejoinder, *also* cited in the Commission minutes, doesn't rate a single mention in Peters's book. Instead, citing these same June 1935 minutes, Peters falsely states that the Mandates Commission 'verified' (p. 231) and 'recognized' (p. 319) the influx, in the space of just a few months, of 30,000 to 36,000 Hauranis, and that the Commission 'took special "note" . . . that the Hauranese, not merely passing through, had indeed settled' (p. 230).[17]

To be sure, Hauranis did enter Palestine in fairly significant numbers in the mid-1930s, but they departed, in equal numbers, soon thereafter. The *Survey of Palestine* reported that 'the "boom" conditions in Palestine in the years 1934-6 led to an inward movement into Palestine particularly from Syria. The depression due to the state of public disorder during 1936-9 led to the return of these people. . .'[18] Peters herself devotes considerable space to documenting the 'hasty leavetaking' (p. 272) of the Hauranis in 1936.[19] She quotes one private British government memorandum to the effect that '128 Hauranis left today. Many more are expected to leave tomorrow . . .' According to a second memorandum, 'countrymen from Hauran' had 'applied urgently and pleadingly to be sent back to their homes for reason that there was no work . . . and they did not wish to be involved in more trouble'.

Peters seems not to be aware that the batch of memoranda she cites on the frantic exodus of Hauranis between 1936-39 renders her most significant find, her 'hard evidence' of massive illegal Arab immigration and settlement – namely, the (unverified) *La Syrie* report mentioned in the Mandates Commission hearings – worthless. Recall that Peters wishes to prove that fully fifty percent of the Arabs residing in the 'Jewish-settled' areas of Palestine in 1947 were really illegal Arab immigrants. But by 1947, the Hauranis had long since departed from Palestine.

The Strange Case of Area IV

Peters's highly touted demographic study is the centerpiece of *From Time Immemorial*. Yet, this study is marred by serious flaws: 1) several extremely significant calculations are wrong; and 2) numbers are used selectively to support otherwise baseless conclusions.

Peters claims to plot demographic growth and shifts *within* Palestine (i.e., the region bordered on the east by the Jordan River and on the west by the Mediterranean Sea) between the years 1893 and 1948. Her central thesis is that at least 170,000 of the 600,000 odd refugees in 1948 were and *had to be* recent migrants from the West Bank and Gaza Strip.

For the purposes of her study, Peters divides Palestine into five areas, three of which (I, II, and IV) correspond to the whole of pre-1967 Israel·and the remaining two (III and V) to the West Bank and Gaza. Area I was the main zone of Jewish settlement between the years 1893 and 1948. Peters provides the following geographic breakdown of Palestine's indigenous Arab population in 1893:

Area I:	92,300
Area II:	38,900
Area III:	14,300
Area IV:	87,400
Area V:	233,500

She next suggests that the indigenous Palestinian Arab population expanded by a factor of 2.7 between 1893 and 1947.[20] (Peters assumes for the Palestinian Arab population in the area of Jewish concentration the same rate of natural increase that she has calculated for the Palestinian Arab population in the non-Jewish areas between 1893 and 1947.) However, actual population figures for Palestinian-born Arabs in certain of the five areas differed markedly from the projected increase. Table 2 below, based on Peters's data (pp. 424-5, Appendix V), juxtaposes the actual number of indigenous Palestinian Arabs in each of the five areas in 1947 (column A) against what the figure would have been had the indigenous population in each area expanded by natural increase alone (column B).

Peters contends that the excessive number of indigenous Palestinian Arabs in Area I (center of Jewish settlement) and the

Table 2*

	A	B	C
	actual indigenous Palestinian Arab population (1947) in . . .	projected indigenous Palestinian Arab population (1947) in . . .	net in-migration (+)/ out-migration (−) in . . . [column A minus column B]
Area I	417,300	249,210	+168,090
Area II	110,900	105,030	+ 5,870
Area III	39,900	38,610	+ 1,290
Area IV	125,100	235,980	−110,880
Area V	507,200	630,450	−123,250

*Peters uses a uniform national rate of natural growth to project the 1947 indigenous Palestinian Arab population in each of the five areas from the 1893 census. From the data for Area I (1893 pop.: 92,300; projected 1947 pop.: 249,210), a rate of 2.7 is inferred (249,210/92,300).[22] Aside from the data for Area IV, to which I will return in a moment, my significant calculations differ only slightly from those of the author.

unnaturally sparse Palestinian Arab population in Area V (center of Arab settlement) can only be explained by Arab in-migration.[21] In other words, approximately 170,000 Palestinian Arabs forsook their native soil in the West Bank/Gaza region of Palestine and moved into the areas of Jewish settlement in order to take advantage of the new opportunities opened up by the thriving *Yishuv* economy. Peters further argues that these 170,000 Palestinian Arab in-migrants probably found themselves among the refugees in 1948 since their roots in the Jewish-settled part of Palestine were not very deep. But – and this is her crucial point – these Arabs weren't really refugees since they had *followed* the Jews into this corner of Palestine and thus were not indigenous to it; their real homes were in the West Bank and Gaza areas of Palestine. Peters thus concludes:

> From the evidence, then, among the estimated 430,000-650,000 Arab 'refugees' reported in 1948, well over 170,000 are apparently Arabs who were *returning* to 'Arab areas' in . . . Palestine (the West Bank or Gaza) from the land that became Israel – the Jewish-settled areas where those Arabs had recently arrived in search of better opportunities. (p. 258; Peters's emphasis)[23]

The first point to be made about this argument is that the case Peters mounts for massive illegal Arab immigration into Palestine contradicts it. Peters arrives at the figures in column A of Table 2 by deducting the *officially* tabulated number of nomads and legal and illegal immigrants for each area from the total Arab population for that area. For example, Peters puts the total Arab population in Area I at 462,900. From this sum she subtracts the 8,000 nomads, 27,300 legal immigrants and 8,500 illegal immigrants officially tallied for this region (p. 425), and thus obtains the figure of 417,300. Recall, however, that Peters puts the real number of illegal immigrants in Area I at about 300,000. (Peters assumes that the Arab immigrants illegally entering Palestine all settled in the main zone of Jewish colonization, Area I; see p. 425, Appendix V, 1947, column D.) In that case, column A in Table 2 should actually read 126,800 and column C (−122,410). But then nothing remains of Peters's central conclusion from her demographic study. Simply put, if Arabs immigrated in massive numbers to Area I, there could not have been any in-migration to this region. Further, even if Peters's argument is evaluated on its own terms, the demographic evidence in the study does not support the 170,000 figure cited repeatedly in the text. Her actual findings are, at best, trivial.

Let us look closely at Area IV (the western Galilee, etc.) in Table 2. This region is also 'short' by approximately 111,000 indigenous Palestinian Arabs. Couldn't these 111,000 souls have migrated to Area I? But recall that this region was incorporated into Israel in 1948, in which case, if they did indeed flee, these Arabs were genuine refugees. In other words, Arab 'indigenes' from the western Galilee region of what became Israel migrated to the *Yishuv* areas during the Mandate period and then fled (for whatever reason) in 1948 and became refugees. (It seems not to have occurred to Peters that 170,000 Arab in-migrants could not have *all* come from the West Bank and Gaza if, by her own reckoning, these areas were not 'short' by that many Arabs!) Peters offers not a single word to explain why these 111,000 migrants from Area IV (a part of Israel) should not be subtracted from the 170,000 migrants who were allegedly returning home in 1948.[24]

Not only does Peters completely ignore the significant demographic changes in Area IV when they threaten to render her findings trivial, she actually falsifies the relevant numbers. According to Peters's chart (p. 425, Appendix V), there were only 71,200 fewer indigenous Arabs in Area IV than the projection based on the 1893 census. The real number is closer to 111,000 (see Table 2 above).[25]

What is more, the data are arranged in what can only be described as a curiously confusing manner. For no apparent reason, the regions that eventually comprised Israel are labeled I, II and IV and the remainder of Palestine III and V (see key to map, p. 246). As a result, all but the most attentive readers can easily be misled. For example, in the chart on p. 425, Areas I, II and III are boxed off from Areas IV and V. It is very easy to forget that the first of the latter two regions (IV) – from which, as we have seen, there was very significant out-migration – became part of Israel. Why *did Peters section off Area III, and not Area IV, with Areas I and II?* Another example: in the legend to Peters's Appendix V (p. 424), Areas I, II and III are bracketed off and labeled 'contained most of Jewish population'; Areas IV and V are similarly bracketed off and labeled 'contained very little Jewish population'. But, according to Peters's map on p. 246, Area III contained *no* Jews. By grouping the five regions in this highly misleading and altogether erroneous fashion, the distinct impression is again left that the first three areas became Israel while the remaining two fell within the jurisdiction of the Arabs in 1948: *Area IV easily gets lost in the shuffle.*[26]

Had Peters properly grouped the five areas in her charts, it would have been obvious to any attentive reader that: 1) the demographic changes *within* what became Israel could have more or less cancelled each other out; therefore, 2) the amount of in-migration from the West Bank/Gaza region could have been relatively insignificant; and finally, 3) the number of West Bank/Gaza natives among the 1948 Arab refugees could also have been relatively insignificant.

Had Peters used Roman numerals I, II and III to designate the constituent areas of Israel and IV and V for the West Bank/Gaza, as common sense would recommend, the significance of the population changes *within* Israel would also have been highlighted. Why did Peters choose the far more clumsy method of labeling Israel I, II and IV, the West Bank/Gaza, III and V, and then section off the areas in such a way that the significant population shift within Israel is concealed? Why did Peters include 'intermediate' areas at all in her study? Why didn't she simply divide the map of Palestine into the region that became Israel and the region that fell outside its boundaries after the 1949 Armistice Agreements? What purpose do the 'intermediate' areas serve in Peter's study other than to conceal and obscure crucial data?

Figure 1 Simplified diagrammatic explanation

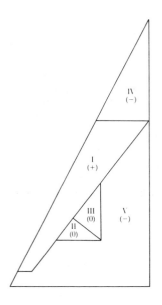

Demographic shifts in Palestine, 1893-1947

− 'too few' indigenous Arabs based on 1893 projection

+ 'too many' indigenous Arabs based on 1893 projection

0 1947 population more or less corresponds to 1893 projection

Area I:	Israel	+168,090
Area II:	Israel	0
Area III:	West Bank	0
Area IV:	Israel	−110,880
Area V:	West Bank/Gaza	−123,150

Peters's argument the 'missing' indigenous Arabs from Area V (West Bank/Gaza) must have in-migrated to Area I (Israel) during the Mandate years and then fled in 1948.

Peters's conclusion since they were indigenous in Area V (West Bank/Gaza), these refugees couldn't claim what became Israel as their homeland 'from time immemorial'.

The fraud the 'too many' indigenous Arabs in Area I (Israel) may *just as likely* have come from Area IV (Israel). But *these* Arabs, once having become refugees in 1948, could have justly claimed that Israel was their homeland 'from time immemorial'. Hence Peter's falsification and concealment of the population change in Area IV.

Table 3 The Transubstantiation of Categories

From Time Immemorial	*Comments*
p. 246 (printings 1-6)	
Area I: 'Main areas of Jewish settlement, 98% of Jewish population'	
Area II: 'Intermediate areas, mainly Arab, some Jews'	
Area III: 'Intermediate areas, no Jewish settlement'	
Area IV: 'Intermediate areas, no Jewish settlement'	
Area V: 'Main areas of Arab settlement, no Jewish settlement'	
p. 246 (printing 7)	
Area I: 'Main areas of Jewish settlement, 98% of Jewish population'	Areas III and IV now contain 'some Jewish settlement'.
Area II: 'Intermediate areas, mainly Arab, some Jews'	
Area III: 'Intermediate areas, some Jewish settlement'	
Area IV: 'Intermediate areas, some Jewish settlement'	
Area V: 'Main areas of Arab settlement, no Jewish settlement'	

p. 254 (all printings)

Peters states that she has divided Palestine 'into 1) those subdistricts that were heavily or mainly settled by Jews, [68] 2) those regions that had little Jewish development, [69] and 3) those areas from which Jews were being expelled [no note].'

Note 68 reads: 'Areas I and II'
Note 69 reads: 'Areas III, IV and V'

p. 255, Table G (all printings)

Area I: 'Main areas of Jewish settlement'
Area II: 'Some Jews, mainly Arab'
Area III: 'Intermediate'
Area IV: 'Intermediate'
Area V: 'Main areas of Arab settlement – no Jewish settlement'

p. 424 (all printings)

Area I: 'Main areas of Jewish settle-ment' ⎤
Area II: 'Intermediate areas'   ⎦ 'Contain most of Jewish population'
Area III: 'Intermediate areas'
Area IV: 'Intermediate areas'   ⎤
Area V: 'Main area of Arab settle-ment' ⎦ 'Contain very little Jewish population'

Area II is now 'mainly or heavily' Jewish. Area V now has a 'little Jewish development'. Areas III, IV and V are grouped together. The last category in this tripartite classification subsumes none of the five areas – why was it included?

Area II now contains only 'some Jews' and is 'mainly Arab'. Areas III and IV ('Intermediate') are now separated out from Area V ('no Jewish settlement'). Area V now has 'no Jewish settlement'.

Area II is now listed under the exact same rubric as Areas III and IV. The bracketing corresponds neither with the category divisions nor with the data presented on other pages in the book (see below).

Table 3 continued

From Time Immemorial

p. 425 (all printings)

According to Peters's geographic breakdown of Jewish settlement as presented in the charts on this page: 1) Areas II and III contained no Jews in any years for which the breakdown is available; 2) Area IV contained 6,000 Jews in 1944 and 5,300 Jews in 1947; 3) Area V contained 3,400 Jews in 1944 and more Jews than Area II, III or IV in 1947 (Area II: 0; Area III: 0; Area IV: 5,300; Area V: 6,500).

Comments

The actual geographic and numerical breakdown of Jewish settlement in Palestine contradicts all the category divisions of Areas II-V listed above.

The weight of the evidence suggests that Peters's demographic 'study' is a carefully contrived, premeditated hoax. How else to explain why, in reading off the data from the very same Appendix chart (p. 425) for the table she assembles on p. 257, Peters 'remembers' to add Area IV in all the columns (e.g., in the column for 'nomads', column B in the Appendix) but 'forgets' to add Area IV in the column for 'Arab in-migrants' (E in the Appendix)?[27]

Handling the 'mechanics of citation'

As is now clear, much of the 'prodigious' research praised by reviewers of Peters's book is an optical illusion. Much else is simply laughable.[28] Yet, it is difficult not to be impressed by, say, the obscure travelogues and other recondite sources Peters apparently plowed through to document the state of Palestine on the eve of Zionist colonization. But one's legitimate admiration for such diligence will surely vanish once it is recognized that she didn't read them.

That this is so becomes clear when one compares Peters's text (pp. 158-9) with Ernst Frankenstein's citations from the same source in his frankly partisan tract, *Justice for My People* (NY, 1944), pp. 122-4. Table 4 below aligns the relevant passages opposite each other:

Peters's only original contribution here – other than juggling the quotations – is to put the estimate of Syria's population in her footnote whereas Frankenstein has it in the body of the text.

When this remarkable 'coincidence' was brought to the attention of Aaron Asher at Harper and Row, he told *The Nation* magazine (13 October 1984) that this 'so-called plagiarism' was 'a teapot tempest'. Had he known about it he might, as her editor, have suggested that Peters handle the 'mechanics of citation' differently. Asher also stated that he has been assured Peters has copies of all the relevant citations in her files. This suggests that even if she did not acknowledge her debt to Frankenstein, she had examined his original sources.

Yet, elsewhere in her book (p. 197), Peters qotes another travelogue, W.F. Lynch's *Narrative of the United States Expedition to the River Jordan and the Dead Sea* (London, 1849), as follows: 'In 1844, "*the American expedition under Lynch*" recorded *fewer than* 8,000 "Turks" in Jaffa in a population of 13,000' (my emphases).

Table 4

Peters

Another writer, describing 'Syria' (and Palestine) some sixty years later in 1843, stated that, in Volney's day, 'the land had not fully reached its last prophetic degree of desolation and depopulation'.[1]

From place to place the reporters varied, but not the reports: J.S. Buckingham described his visit of 1816 to Jaffa, which 'has all the appearances of a poor village, and every part of it that we saw was of corresponding meanness.'[2] Buckingham described Ramle, 'where, as throughout the greater part of Palestine, the ruined portion seemed more extensive than that which was inhabited.'[3]

After a visit in 1917-8, travelers reported that there was not a 'single boat of any description on the lake [Tiberias].'[4] In a German encyclopedia published in 1827, Palestine was depicted as 'desolate and roamed through by Arab bands of robbers.'[5]

Frankenstein

Buckingham, who visited the country in 1816, states that Jaffa 'has all the appearances of a poor village, and every part of it that we saw was of corresponding meanness.'[1] He visited Ramleh, 'where, as throughout the greater part of Palestine, the ruined portion seemed more extensive than that which was inhabited.'[2] ...

Thereafter conditions deteriorated further. 'In his (Volney's) day,' writes Keith in 1843,[3] 'the land had not fully reached its last prophetic degree of desolation and depopulation. The population (viz., of the whole of Syria), rated by Volney at two million and a half, is now estimated at half that amount.'

This statement corresponds to the observations of other travellers, for instance Olin (1840) who is a specially valuable witness, since he admires the Palestinian ('Syrian') population ('a fine-spirited race of men') and ridicules the idea of Jewish colonization.[4] According to him 'the population is on the decline.'[5] In Hebron, 'many

Throughout the nineteenth century the abandonment and dismal state of the terrain was lamented. In 1840 an observer, who was traveling through, wrote of his admiration for the Syrian 'fine spirited race of men' whose 'population is on the decline.'[6] While scorning the idea of Jewish colonization, the writer observed that the once populous area between Hebron and Bethlehem was 'now abandoned and desolate' with 'dilapidated towns.'[7] Jerusalem consisted of 'a large number of houses .. in a dilapidated and ruinous state,' and 'the masses really seem to be without any regular employment.'

Notes

1. A. Keith, *The Land of Israel* (Edinburgh, 1843), p. 465. 'The population (viz., of the whole of Syria), rated by Volney at two million and a half, is now estimated at half that amount.'
2. J.S. Buckingham, *Travels in Palestine* (London, 1821), p. 146.
3. *Ibid.*, p. 162.
4. James Mangles and the Honorable C.L. Irby, *Travels in Egypt and Nubia* (London, 1823), p. 295.
5. Brockhaus, *Allg. deutsch Real-Encyklopaedie*, 7th ed. (Leipzig 1827), vol. viii, p. 206.
6. S. Olin, *Travels in Egypt, Arabia Petraea and the Holy Land* (New York, 1843), vol. 2, pp. 438-9.
7. *Ibid.*, pp. 77-8.

houses are in a dilapidated state and uninhabited'; the once populated region between Hebron and Bethlehem is 'now abandoned and desolate' and has 'dilapidated towns.'[6] In Jerusalem 'a large number of houses are in a dilapidated and ruinous state'; 'the masses really seem to be without any regular employment.'[7] ...

A German Encyclopedia published in 1827 calls Palestine 'desolate and roamed through by Arab bands of robbers.'[8] Irby, who visited the country in 1817-8, found 'not a single boat of any description on the lake (of Tiberias),'[9] ...

Notes

1. J.S. Buckingham, *Travels in Palestine*, London, 1821, p. 146.
2. *Ibid.*, p. 162.
3. A. Keith, *The Land of Israel*, Edinburgh, 1843, p. 465.
4. S. Olin, *Travels in Egypt, Arab Petraea and the Holy Land*, New York, 1843, vol. ii, p. 438.
5. *Ibid.*, p. 439.
6. *Ibid.*, pp. 77, 88.
7. *Ibid.*, pp. 135, 138.
8. Brockhaus, *Allg. deutsch Real-Encyklopaedie*, 7. Aufl. Leipzig, 1827. vol. viii, p. 206.
9. James Mangles and Hon. C.L. Irby, *Travels in Egypt and Nubia*, London, 1823, p. 295.

Frankenstein also refers to this source (pp. 127-8): 'In 1844 the American expedition under Lynch found *fewer than* eight thousand "Turks" in Jaffa among a population of thirteen thousand' (my emphasis). Turning to Lynch's work, we read the following: 'The population of Jaffa is now about 13,000, viz.: Turks, 8,000; Greeks, 2,000...' If Peters read through Frankenstein's sources, why are her quotation marks around a phrase ('the American expedition under Lynch') that appears, not in Lynch, but in Frankenstein? How also to explain her repetition of Frankenstein's little error on the number of Turks (*fewer than 8,000*) in Jaffa?[29]

Readers who can't help being impressed by Peters's virtuoso performance when it comes to numbers and statistics should consider the following. On pp. 244-5, Peters claims to have calculated '[a]ccording to projection of statistics of Vital Cuinet for 1895, and ... *Murray's Handbook for Travellers in Syria and Palestine*, which was reprinted in the *Encyclopedia Britannica*, 8th edition, 1860, vol. xx, p. 905' (p. 523, notes 40, 41), the 'settled' Muslim population in Palestine for 1882 (the eve of modern Jewish colonization) and 1895. This is no mean accomplishment since, among many other things, Palestine did not yet exist as a single national entity; numerous partial statistics thus have to be collated. Peters compares the two figures (1882: 141,000; 1895: 252,000) and concludes:

> Even if we assume a high rate of natural increase of 1.5 percent per annum for that thirteen-year period, the population would not have increased to more than 170,000 or so... The only plausible answer is that ... [Arab immigration] coincided exactly with the time Jewish development commenced. (pp. 244-5)

Peters's statistical *tour de force* has thus apparently produced a highly original conclusion.[30]

But Peters need not have gone to all the trouble. Ernst Frankenstein used the exact same sources (even the same edition of *Murray's Handbook*!), did the exact same calculations, and derived identical figures. His conclusion reads almost word for word like Peters's:

> Even if we admit the possibility of a natural increase of 20-25 percent during these thirteen years [Frankenstein converts the 20-25 percent to the 1.5 per annum percentage used in Peters's text in his next paragraph] ... the 141,000 settled Moslems of 1882 cannot possibly, by natural increase, have exceeded the figure of 170,000 to 175,000.

Here, therefore, we are confronted ... with a large immigration of Arabic-speaking people which coincides with the development of the Jewish settlements. (p. 128).[31]

In her fulsome blurb for *From Time Immemorial*, Nazi holocaust scholar Lucy Dawidowicz congratulates Peters for having 'dug beneath a half-century's accumulation of propaganda and brought into the light the historical truth about the Middle East'. What Peters actually did was dig beneath a half-century's accumulation of pro-Zionist propaganda tracts and unearth a particularly ludicrous one, from which she proceeded to plagiarize generously.[32]

Postscript

By the end of 1984, *From Time Immemorial* had gone through eight printings (cloth) and received some two hundred notices, ranging from ecstasy to awe, in the US. The only 'false' notes in this chorus of praise were the *Journal of Palestine Studies*, which ran a highly critical review by Bill Farrell; the small Chicago-based newsweekly, *In These Times*, which published a condensed version of my findings, and Alexander Cockburn, who devoted a splendid series of columns in *The Nation* to exposing the fraud. Otherwise, it proved impossible to open any discussion of the book. Joan Peters, via her publisher, peremptorily dismissed my findings as 'without merit', and Harper and Row defended Peters's right not to reply to 'published attacks on her work, regardless of their nature or provenance'. The periodicals in which *From Time Immemorial* had already been favorably reviewed refused to run any critical correspondence (e.g., *The New Republic, Atlantic, Commentary*). Periodicals which had yet to review the book rejected my manuscript as of little or no consequence (e.g., *The Village Voice, Dissent, The New York Review of Books*). Within four months *From Time Immemorial* would be honored with the prestigious National Jewish Book Award. Not a single national newspaper or columnist contacted found newsworthy that a best-selling, award-winning, effusively-praised 'study' of the Middle East conflict was a threadbare hoax.

Yet, in early 1985, the disinformation effort began to unravel as Peters's book went into a British edition. The reviews in England were devastating. Oxford's great orientalist, Albert Hourani, dismissed *From Time Immemorial* in *The Observer* as 'ludicrous and worthless'. Ian and David Gilmour, in the *London Review of Books*, concluded an exhaustive 8,000-word dissection of the book by calling it 'preposterous'. The *Spectator* of London likened it to the Clifford Irving 'autobiography' of Howard Hughes. The Israelis also got into the act, and a Hebrew edition of the book had not yet even appeared. The Labor Party daily, *Davar*, compared *From Time Immemorial* to Israel's more lamentable past propaganda exercises; the liberal weekly, *Koteret Rashit*, published a detailed exposé of the cover-up by the US media; and the chair of the philosophy department at the Hebrew University, Avishai Margalit, denounced Peters's 'web of deceit'.

Back in the US, the Peters affair was fast becoming a singular embarrassment as word began to circulate that a major literary-political scandal was being suppressed. In February 1985, *The New York Review of Books* finally commissioned and in early March received a lengthy piece on *From Time Immemorial* by the noted Israeli scholar, Yehoshua Porath. Published some nine months later, the Porath review discounted out-of-hand Peters's 'theses', yet scrupulously avoided any mention of her fraudulent scholarship; every effort to raise this obviously crucial issue in the *Review*'s correspondence columns proved unavailing. In October, Professor Edward Said delivered a stinging and eloquent riposte to Peters and her acolytes in the pages of *The Nation*. In November, after more than a year of foot-dragging, *The New York Times* finally ran a story on the 'controversy' – in the Thanksgiving Day (non-)issue, on the theater page, without even a listing in the index. Porath was quoted to the effect that *From Time Immemorial* 'is a sheer forgery', and that 'In Israel, at least, the book was almost universally dismissed as sheer rubbish, except maybe as a propaganda weapon', while historian Barbara Tuchman continued to insist the Palestinian people were 'a fairy tale'. Martin Peretz, editor-in-chief of *The New Republic*, alleged that the attack on Peters was part of a calculated leftist plot. Peters herself refused, for the nth time, to be interviewed. In January 1986, Anthony Lewis of *The New York Times* devoted a full column to the hoax, entitled, appropriately enough, 'There Were No Indians'. In the June and October numbers of *Commentary*, some thirty pages were given over to defending Peters against the mounting onslaught on her book. But, alas, by this point there was little that could be salvaged from the wreckage. The 15 June 1986 issue of *Haaretz* (Israel) reported that, at an international conference on Palestinian demography at Haifa University, virtually all the participants ridiculed Peters's demographic 'theses', and the most authoritative scholar in attendance, Professor Yehoshua Ben-Arieh of Hebrew University, condemned the Peters enterprise for discrediting the 'Zionist cause'.

Among Peters's original endorsers, to date (December 1986) only Daniel Pipes and Ronald Sanders have publicly distanced themselves from Peters's scholarship, if not from her 'theses'.

Notes

1. The following essay was completed and widely circulated in December 1984. The only substantive criticism of its content I am aware of appeared in the June and October 1986 numbers of *Commentary*. I have used this opportunity to reply to the latter critique. Otherwise, the text is unchanged. I would like to thank Cyrus Veeser, Israel Shahak and the Public Affairs Division staff of the New York City Public Library for their assistance and encouragement. My special thanks to Noam Chomsky who has assisted me in ways too numerous to enumerate.

2. The findings of a number of these authorities are cited by Peters on pp. 223-5 and 513, note 19. For a recent restatement of the conventional view, see Dov Friedlander and Calvin Goldscheider, *The Population of Israel* (NY, 1979), where the authors write that Arab population growth during the British mandate period 'was almost entirely the result of high natural increase – high fertility and low, declining mortality' (p. 17). Friedlander is associate professor in the departments of demography and statistics and director of the Levi Eshkol Institute for Economic, Social and Political Research at the Hebrew University. Goldscheider is chair of the department of demography at the Hebrew University.

3. Peters attributes this view to John Hope Simpson, but there is nothing in the report he authored that even remotely suggests such a conclusion. On p. 170, Peters claims there is a 'profusion of evidence' that Palestine was 'uninhabited' on the eve of modern Zionist colonization.

4. Peters speculates (pp. 252-4) that, even as early as 1878-93, literally thousands of Arab immigrants and in-migrants may have been flocking to the Jewish settlements in Palestine because of their 'economic attractions'. Further, to judge by the base figures in her demographic study (p. 255, Table G), the Zionist colonies attracted, not thousands, but nearly a *half million* Arab immigrants during these years. Yet, according to Walter Laqueur, the impoverished first *aliya* settlements established in 1881 and thereabouts didn't even become 'going concerns' until the first decade of the twentieth century (*A History of Zionism* [NY, 1976], p. 79). Neville Mandel, in his authoritative study of the period, writes that 'only a limited number of Arab villagers and a few passing Bedouin could have directly felt the presence of the Jewish settlers during the years before 1908' (*The Arabs and Zionism Before World War I* [Berkeley, 1976], p. 34).

5. Peters's handling of numbers throughout does not inspire great confidence. I will have more to say about this topic further on, but allow me one example here. Peters quotes five different 'authoritative' figures (pp. 223, 242, 244, 245 and 523, note 38), ranging from under 150,000 to 600,000, for the Palestinian Arab population on the eve of modern Zionist settlement, yet she hardly seems aware of the wide discrepancy among them. For instance, the one significant calculation Peters – or, rather, Ernst Frankenstein (see pp. 57–60) – makes for this early period (Chapter 12, pp. 244-5) is based on one of the untenably low estimates. Had

Peters used any of the higher figures cited, she could not have sustained her argument in Chapter 12 (which, in any case, is contradicted by the findings of every historian of the period).

6. Peters assumes that the rate of natural increase for the Arab population in the region of Jewish settlement was no higher than the one she calculated for the predominantly Arab areas in Palestine.

7. But not terribly original. Had Peters's reviewers spent less time enthusing about the magnitude of her research and devoted a little time to investigating her sources, they would have discovered that Peters relies heavily on – and plagiarizes extensively from – Ernst Frankenstein, who tried to prove the exact point more than forty years ago. In a 1975 Jerusalem symposium, the Israeli orentalist Yehoshua Porath ridiculed this stale theme of massive Arab immigration as a 'pointless legend' (cited in Noam Chomsky, *Towards a New Cold War* [NY, 1982], p. 440, note 74).

8. The few scraps of 'original' archival material Peters does cite to substantiate her thesis are worthless. Consider the following examples:

1) To document the 'prevalence of illicit Arab immigration into Palestine', Peters reproduces (p. 270) a batch of the Mandatory's inter-office memoranda. For instance, she quotes the following 'urgent' order sent in 1925 to the 'Northern District Commissioner' from the 'Controller of Permits':

> Subject: Refugees from Syria
> . . . to the officer in charge at Ras-El-Nakurah. . . Will you be so good as to . . . furnish him as speedily as possible with a mimeographed supply of the blank passes'. (all ellipses in Peters's text)

This 'evidence' is presented by Peters without any context or comment.

2) In her chapter, 'A Hidden Movement: Illegal Arab Immigration', Peters devotes eighteen pages (278-95) to the correspondence between various British officials on how to curb the influx of Arab 'provocateurs' during the 1936-39 Arab revolt. Readers who wade through these tedious pages will finally discover that the exchanges have nothing whatever to do with the thesis Peters is supposedly trying to prove: there isn't a jot of evidence in the memoranda pointing to the conclusion that these 'outside agitators' either intended to or actually did *settle* in Palestine.

9. Peters acknowledges this crucial point, but in her own fashion: 'According to all reports of the period, Arab "recorded" immigration to Palestine was minimal, casual and unquantifiable' (p. 226). She has evidently 'erred' in two respects:

1) the British assessments were *explicitly not limited* to 'recorded' immigration; and

2) no report ever stated that 'recorded' immigration was 'unquantifiable'.

Peters should have taken full credit for this remarkable contribution to demographic science.

10. The Mandatory government pegged the Jewish immigration quota (a.k.a. the 'Labor Schedule') to Palestine's capacity for absorbing new permanent workers. The 'present practice' refers to the British policy of deducting a certain number of immigration certificates from the Labor Schedule in anticipation of illegal immigration.

11. **Table 5** Number of 'Travellers' Reclassified as Legal Immigrants in Selected Years[a]

	Jews	*Muslims*	*Christians*[b]
1926	611	149	300
1927	705	85	430
1928*	1287	143	436
1932**	3730	109	719
1933**	2465	63	344

	Jews	*Non-Jews (Muslims, Christians, etc.)*
1934	4114	752
1935	3804	625
1936	1817	467
1937	681	431
1938	1427	421

*totals include 'travellers and others who received permission to stay'
**totals include 'persons who had entered Palestine as travellers or without permission'

   [a] *Source*: annual British reports to the League of Nations cited in Peters's bibliography.
   [b] In Peters's special universe, 'Christian'-Arab is a contradiction in terms, an 'Arab propaganda claim' (p. 250). In any case, the provenance of roughly 2/3 of the Christian immigrants to Palestine in any given year was the non-Arab world.

12. According to Peters (p. 425), the British put the number of legally registered Arab immigrants at 27,300.

13. See p. 431 of Peters's text for a reproduction of the relevant British document. Note line three: 'Including persons who entered as travellers and subsequently registered as immigrants.'

14. On these (and other) pages in her text, Peters employs the vaguer expression 'Jewish-settled areas' to designate the region of Palestine that became Israel after the 1949 Armistice Agreements. She explicitly clarifies this peculiar usage elsewhere in her text (cf. p. 264 – 'what is now Israel, i.e., Jewish-settled areas').

15. Peters's apologists seem not to understand that, if in fact she were referring only to Area I, her 'revelation' is a meaningless tautology. The only germane demographic comparisons are between the Arab and Jewish populations in all of Palestine and, arguably, between the Arab and Jewish populations in the region of Palestine that later became Israel. Even if Peters's numbers were accurate (which they aren't) and even if she were referring only to Area I (which she isn't), all she would have 'proven' is the Jews were a majority where they were a majority.

16. Before 1930, these tabulations are collected under the chapter heading, 'Immigration and Labor' or 'Immigration and Travel' in the annual British reports.

17. It is not without interest to compare Peters's treatment of this material with

the manner in which it is handled by another, equally partisan, author. In his openly apologetic tract, *Justice for My People* (1944), Ernst Frankenstein observed only that, 'The Mandates Commission *discussed* in 1935 a declaration of the governor of the (Syrian) Hauran district that in 1934, in a few months, 30,000 Hauranese had entered Palestine and settled there' (pp. 128-9; my emphasis). Even in a book devoid of any scholarly pretensions, the documentary record is not mangled in so scandalous a fashion as in Peters's work. Virtually all the reviewers who acclaimed Peters's 'prodigious research' and 'brilliant detective work' highlighted her citation from the Mandates Commission hearing on the massive influx of Hauranis. It appears that Peters's find was neither especially original nor quite so difficult to track down. On Peters's intimate knowledge of Frankenstein's work, see pp. 57–60.

18. See also the 1937 *Peel Commission Report* which states: 'The deputy Inspector-General of the Criminal Investigation Department has recently estimated that the number of Hauranis in the country at the present time is roughly 2,500'.

19. She asserts that a 'smaller number' of the Hauranis exited Palestine than had earlier entered but offers not a scatch of evidence to substantiate this claim. Cf. *The Survey of Palestine* observations already cited.

20. On pp. 253-4, Peters argues that the 1893 figure for Area I may itself include as many as 11,000 Arab immigrants and migrants (from other parts of Palestine) who settled in this region between 1870 and 1893, in which case 'anywhere from 45,000 to 350,000' of the Arabs counted as indigenous to Area I in 1947 may also have been relatively recent immigrants and migrants and their offspring. Yet, 2.7 times 11,000 equals 29,700. Peters offers no explanation for her bizarre projection of 45,000 to 350,000. On Arab immigration and migration to Area I before the turn of the century, see note 4.

21. Peters reserves the term 'in-migration' for the movement of indigenous Palestinian Arabs from any other part of Palestine into the Jewish-settled area. Her handling of this – not terribly complex – concept is remarkably inept. See, *inter alia*, p. 245 (the same page on which her definition appears!), where Peters attributes the (alleged) aberrant growth in Palestine's *overall* Arab population between 1882 and 1895 to Arab immigration and *in-migration*; p. 376, where she condemns Britain's supposedly 'cynical policy' in Palestine, by which 'illegal Arab immigrants entered unheeded *along with Arab in-migrants*, and all were counted as "natives" unless they were "flagrant" '; and p. 157, where she surmises that, given the 'acute decline' Palestine's population suffered before modern Jewish settlement, '[a]n enormous swell of Arab population could only have resulted from immigration and *in-migration*' (my emphases).

22. In an appendix (pp. 427-8), Philip Hauser, the 'population expert' thanked by Peters for 'correcting, checking, and re-checking' (p. ix) the demographic study, certifies all her data for Area I. (Hauser is former director of the United States Census and director emeritus of the Population Research Center at the University of Chicago.) In a recent *Commentary* article (October 1986), Erich and Rael Jean Isaac claim I have used the wrong factor of natural increase. They allege the correct multiple is 2.795. Yet, in Peters's text, 2.795 refers not to the factor of *natural* increase between 1893 and 1947 but to the factor by which the *total* Palestinian Arab population increased between 1893 and 1948, including, for example, the Arabs who immigrated into Palestine during those years:

$$\frac{1,303,800 \quad \text{(total Arab pop. 1947)}}{466,400 \quad \text{(total Arab pop. 1893)}} = 2.795$$

23. In a footnote some 250 pages earlier (p. 16), we learn that the 430,000 figure Peters repeatedly uses as her low estimate includes only 'genuine refugees', i.e., those who were in need of relief after 1948. The source from which she took this figure put the total number of refugees in 1948 at 539,000.

24. In the *Commentary* article (see note 22), the Isaacs offer an ingenious rationale for this omission: Peters need not have taken Area IV into account since historical evidence points to the conclusion that 'it is most unlikely' Arabs out-migrated from that region. But, alas, if we are to believe Peters's demographic study, that is exactly what they did do. Either 1) the Isaacs's historical deductions are correct, in which case Peters's study is fraudulent or else 2) Peters's projection for Area IV is correct, in which case her conclusion is fraudulent. There is no third possibility.

25. In the *Commentary* article, the Isaacs claim I have miscalculated and that Peters's figure is correct. Yet, Peters's method (p. 256) yields the following results for Area IV:

87,400.0	(1893 pop.)
× 2.7	(factor of natural increase)
235,980.0	(projected 1947 pop.)
125,100.0	(actual 1947 pop. minus immigrants and nomads)
−110,880.0	(net out-migration from Area IV)

There can be no question about the manner of calculation since, for Area I, it yields the exact figure certified by Philip Hauser in Appendix IV, p. 428:

92,300.0	(1893 pop.)
× 2.7	(factor of natural increase)
249,210.0	(projected 1947 pop.)
417,300.0	(actual 1947 pop. minus immigrants and nomads)
+168,090.0	(net in-migration to Area I)

26. Peters received a copy of my findings on her demographic study in June 1984. In September 1984, Harper and Row issued the seventh printing of *From Time Immemorial*, which contained several 'minor corrections' in the demographic study (in the words of Aaron Asher, Peters's editor at Harper and Row). Specifically, Peters has emended the legend to the map on p. 246. Where she originally claimed there was 'no Jewish settlement' in Areas III and IV, she has since discovered that there was 'some Jewish settlement' in those two areas. The legend for the map on p. 246 now technically corresponds to the bracketing in the legend on p. 424 *but*:

1) this 'correction' still doesn't explain why Areas I, II and III are bracketed off from Areas IV and V; and

2) the legend to the map on p. 246 *contradicts* the data collected in the tables on p. 425. Area V, which is listed on p. 246 as having 'no Jewish settlement' still contained 6,500 Jews in 1947 according to the tables; Areas II and III, which are listed as having 'some Jewish settlement' on p. 246, contained no Jews in any years for which there is a breakdown in the tables. To conceal the data in Area IV, Peters evidently sacrificed internal consistency. Areas II-V of Peters's demographic study undergo a remarkable series of metamorphoses in the pages of *From Time Immemorial*.

27. By excluding from her calculations the 'out'-migrants from Area IV, Peters comes up with a figure for the 1948 indigenous Arab population within what became Israel that is some 110,000 short of the real number. From this figure, a second incorrect sum is derived (see column headed 'Arab settled population' in Table H, p. 257). These falsified numbers are then repeated elsewhere in the text (see, e.g., p. 262). For the correct figure, see my Table 2, column B: (Area I) 249,210 + (Area II) 105,030 + (Area IV) 235,980 = 590,220. Peters's falsified base figure is 483,000 (from which a second falsified figure is derived).

28. A full discussion of *From Time Immemorial*'s 'scholarly apparatus' would take us well beyond the scope of this essay. I will therefore limit myself to a few brief remarks.

1) *From Time Immemorial* has all the earmarks of a 'cut-and-paste' job, but with the additional shortcoming that quotations are repeatedly 'cut' from irrelevant sources. The result is a succession of arguments that are massively 'documented' yet completely unsubstantiated.

2) For all her alleged research, Peters is apparently ignorant of even watershed developments in the political history of Israel, e.g., the 'Lavon Affair' (see pp. 49 and 458, note 125). .

3) Peters makes sixty explicit references to Jacob de Haas's 19*34* popular 'history' of Palestine, eight to an entry in the 19*11* edition of the *Encyclopedia Britannica*, nine to Ernst Frankenstein's 1942 tract, *Justice for My People*, eight to the 'works' of the former chair of the American Christian Palestine Committee (Carl Hermann Voss), twenty-one to Samuel Katz's *Battleground: Fact and Fantasy in Palestine*, etc. These 'sources' have the combined scholarly weight of a classic comic book.

4) Yehoshua Porath's standard two-volume work on the origins of Palestinian nationalism receives no mention in a book that devotes more than a few pages to this theme. Peters makes no reference to Erskine Childers's classic research on the 1948 Palestinian Arab exodus from Israel in her treatment of this topic. The findings of both authors completely contradict Peters's conclusions – conclusions that, in actuality, are nothing more than a rehash of the oldest and most tired Zionist apologetics without a shred of new evidence to support them.

5) In a blurb for *From Time Immemorial*, Arthur Goldberg makes his little contribution to the myth of Peters's 'monumental' research: '*From Time Immemorial* is, to my knowledge, the first book in the English language which tells the story of the expulsion of Jews from Arab countries. . .' Had Goldberg bothered to consult Peters's notes, he would have discovered that her entire discussion of this topic is based on a book by Joseph Schechtman and two pamphlets, and that all three of these references are in English.

29. For a more comical example of Peters's going awry because of hewing too closely to Frankenstein's line, see Alexander Cockburn's column in the 13 October 1984 *Nation*, where he observes that:

Peters does acknowledge Frankenstein elsewhere, but not always in a manner that enhances either her credibility or that of her guide. On page 169 she writes: 'Kurds, Turcomans, Naim [sic] and other colonists arrived in Palestine around the same time as the Jewish immigration waves began. Eighteen thousand "tents" of Tartars,[207] the "armies of Turks and Kurds", whole villages settled in the nineteenth century of Bosnians and Moors and "Circassians" and "Algerians" and Egyptians, etc. – all were continually brought in to people the land called Palestine.' Footnote 207 reads: 'Makrizi, *Histoire des Sultans Mamlouks*, II, pp. 29-30, cited in Frankenstein, *Justice*, p. 122.' If we turn to R.A. Nicholson's *A Literary History of the Arabs*, we discover that Makrizi was born in 1364 and died in 1442. He is thus a dubious authority on matters of nineteenth-century population movement, though his work on the migration of Tartar hordes in the Middle Ages is no doubt beyond reproach. In view of Peters's assertion about material she has cited, we must assume that both she and Frankenstein made entirely coincidental blunders about the date and utility of Makrizi's work.

30. Though one which contradicts every serious historical and demographic study of the period. Cf. notes 4 and 5 above.

31. Peters is simply repeating Frankenstein when she observes that, even if an unusually high rate of natural increase is assumed, the point still stands. Yet, in her one oblique reference to Frankenstein (pp. 245 and 523, note 42), Peters has the audacity to write that: 1) it is *Frankenstein* who assumes an unusually high rate of natural increase for the period; and 2) even if *his* 'unlikely' assumption is credited, the argument *she* has worked out on Arab immigration between 1882 and 1895 is still valid!

32. For further evidence of plagiarism, compare pp. 17-19 of Peters's text with Joseph Schechtman, *The Refugee in the World* (NY, 1963), pp. 200-8, 248-9.

PART TWO

Myths Old and New

3

Broadcasts

Christopher Hitchens

It is probably safe to say that nobody interested enough in the Middle East to have even *overheard* an argument about it can be a stranger to the story of 'the broadcasts'. Confronted with the charge that the Palestinian Arabs were forcibly dispossessed in 1948, Israeli propaganda resorts routinely to the claim that the Palestinians did indeed run away, but that they were induced or incited to do so by their own leadership. For example, the official Israeli government pamphlet on the refugee question, first published in 1953, states plainly that the Palestinian exodus followed 'express instructions broadcast by the president of the Arab Higher Executive (the Mufti)'. The same claim has been repeated before the United Nations, by countless Israeli diplomats in numerous countries, by overseas Zionist organizations, by pro-Israeli academics and journalists and by hundreds of thousands of honest partisans of the Israeli cause who in all probability sincerely believe it.

Considered from almost any level of moral elevation, the question of whether the Palestinians ran away 'under orders' or 'under pressure' is a secondary one. Whatever may have prompted their flight, they had a right to expect to return home after the end of hostilities. Nobody has so far been so bold as to deny that that right was stripped from them. But alas the argument about the Palestinian refugees has not been carried on in any elevated manner. Thus the simple question, did they flee or were they driven out, assumes an importance of its own. To put it no higher, an awful lot of moral capital has been sunk into the argument. The

73

claim that 'broadcasts' were transmitted urging flight has become virtually totemic. It is clung to with an almost neurotic zeal. What is the evidence for it?

In January 1986, the Israeli historian Dr Benny Morris published an article of extraordinary importance in *Middle Eastern Studies*. Dr Morris had obtained a copy of a report by the intelligence branch of the Israeli Defense Forces, entitled *The Emigration of the Arabs of Palestine in the Period 1/12/1947 – 1/6/1948*. These months saw almost half of the refugees leave their homes, and thus may be taken as 'typical'. The IDF intelligence made a meticulous study of the departure of these 391,000 people, and listed three major causes in their assigned order of importance:

1) Direct, hostile Jewish operations against Arab settlements.

2) The effect of our hostile operations on nearby settlements . . . especially the fall of large neighboring centers.

3) Operations of the dissidents.

I should explain that when the report says 'our' or 'Jewish' it is explicit in identifying the Israeli army or the Ben-Gurionist Haganah. By 'dissidents' it no less explicitly means the Irgun and the Stern Gang: unofficial Zionist military formations who provide the political ancestry of Messrs Begin and Shamir. The report divides reponsibility for the flight by saying that, 'at least 55 per cent of the total of the exodus was caused by our operations and their influence', while the Irgun and Stern groups 'directly caused some 15 per cent . . . of the emigration'. Among other causes of Palestinian flight, according to the report, were 'Jewish whispering operations aimed at frightening away Arab inhabitants' and 'ultimate expulsion orders' by the army and the Haganah. These last are said to account for some 2 per cent apiece, a total which Dr Morris considers 'somewhat low' and ascribes to 'a perhaps understandable tendency to minimise the role direct expulsion orders played in bringing about part of the Palestinian exodus'. However apprehensive the authors of the report may have been on this score, their own evidence shows that fully 72 per cent of the Palestinian refugees in this crucial period were expelled by Israeli military force. This admission by the IDF deserves, perhaps, more publicity than it has yet received.

So does that section of the report which deals with 'the broadcasts'. As Dr Morris writes, 'the report goes out of its way to stress that the exodus was contrary to the political-strategic desires of both the Arab Higher Committee and the governments of the neighbouring Arab states'. IDF intelligence found that 'the Arab institutions attempted to struggle against the phenomenon of flight and evacuation, and to curb the waves of emigration.' There *were* some broadcasts, but as Dr Morris shows with the help of the report, 'the Arab Higher Committee decided to impose restrictions and issued threats, punishments and propaganda in the radio and press to curb emigration . . . the report makes no mention of any blanket order issued over Arab radio stations or through other means to Palestinians to evacuate their homes and villages. Had such an order been issued, it would without doubt have been mentioned or cited in this document; the Haganah intelligence service and the IDF intelligence branch closely monitored Arab radio transmissions and the Arabic press.'

Given this evidence, Dr Morris's conclusion is almost otiose. The IDF intelligence report, as he puts it, 'thoroughly undermines the traditional official Israeli "explanation" of a mass flight ordered or "incited" by the Arab leadership for political-strategic reasons.'

This confirmation, by an Israeli historian using the most scrupulous and authentic Zionist sources, at last allows one to write *finis* to a debate which has been going on for a quarter of a century. I am not speaking here of the debate over the 1948 refugees, which of course began from the first day of the Palestinian diaspora. I am referring to the long and little-known exchange between Erskine B. Childers and Jon Kimche. Erskine Childers is an Irish diplomat and journalist, grandson of the author of *The Riddle of the Sands* and son of the President of the Irish Republic, both of whom bore the same name. Jon Kimche is a distinguished Israeli journalist and historian who was at this period the editor of the London *Jewish Observer*.

In an article in the London *Spectator* published on 12 May 1961, Dr Childers explained his bafflement about the best-known Israeli propaganda claim: *viz*, that Arab Palestinians had been urged to flee by their own leadership:

> Examining every official Israeli statement about the Arab exodus, I was struck by the fact that no primary evidence of evacuation orders was ever produced. The charge, Israel claimed, was 'documented', but where were the documents? There had allegedly been Arab radio broadcasts ordering the evacuation; but no dates, names of stations, or texts of messages were ever cited. In Israel in 1958, as a guest of the Foreign Office and therefore doubly hopeful of serious assistance, I

asked to be shown the proofs. I was assured they existed, and was promised them. None had been offered when I left, but I was again assured. I asked to have the material sent on to me. I am still waiting.

While in Israel, however, I met Dr Leo Kohn, professor of political science at Hebrew University and an ambassador-rank advisor to the Israeli Foreign Office. He had written one of the first official pamphlets on the Arab refugees. I asked him for concrete evidence of the Arab evacuation orders. Agitatedly, Dr Kohn replied: 'Evidence? Evidence? What more could you want than this?' and he took up his own pamphlet. 'Look at this *Economist* report,' and he pointed to a quotation. 'You will surely not suggest that the *Economist* is a Zionist journal?'

The quotation is one of about five that appear in every Israeli speech and pamphlet, and are in turn used by every sympathetic analysis. It seemed very impressive: it referred to the exodus from Haifa, and to an Arab broadcast order as one major reason for that exodus.

Dr Childers was sufficiently intrigued to turn up the original *Economist* article, which had appeared on 2 October 1948. His first suspicion was aroused by the use of the bland euphemism 'incident' to describe the notorious massacre of the Arab villagers of Deir Yassin. Further checking showed that the report in the *Economist*, which made a vague reference to 'announcements made over the air' by the Arab Higher Committee, had been written from Cyprus by a correspondent who used an uncorroborated Israeli source. It hardly counted as evidence, let alone first-hand testimony.

Further misgivings were aroused by the claim, also made in official Israeli publications, that the Greek-Catholic Archbishop of Galilee had reported exhortations to his flock to leave. 'I wrote to His Grace,' said Childers. 'I hold signed letters from him, with permission to publish, in which he categorically denied ever alleging Arab evacuation orders; he states that no such orders were ever given. He says that his name has been abused for years and that the Arabs fled because of panic and forcible eviction.' Yet Abba Eban told the United Nations Special Political Committee that the same Archbishop had 'fully confirmed that Arabs were urged to flee by their own leaders'.

Childers decided that the only scholarly recourse was to test the undocumented charge which, as he said, could fortunately be done thoroughly because the BBC monitored all Middle East broadcasts throughout 1948. The transcripts, together with corroborative ones from an American monitoring unit, were available at the

British Museum. Childers went through the lot. Let me quote his conclusion:

> There was not a single order, or appeal, or suggestion about evacuation from Palestine from any Arab radio station, inside or outside Palestine, in 1948. There is repeated monitored record of Arab appeals, even flat orders, to the civilians of Palestine *to stay put*.

As a small embellishment to this historic finding (which has never been challenged, let alone rebutted) Dr Childers mentioned that Israeli broadcasts in Hebrew, and many Jewish newspapers, reported those very same Arab appeals to stay put.

On 2 June 1961, Jon Kimche joined battle. 'Unlike Mr Childers,' he wrote, 'I was present at most of the decisive phases of the "Exodus" of the Palestinian Arabs and I have spent some years since then checking and rejecting not only the evidence but also the so-called sources of the evidence.' He went on to make three points. The first of these was more in the nature of an innuendo:

> It would be interesting to know how Mr Childers checked all the Middle East broadcasts, who monitored them and where, and whether there were really no gaps at all in these monitorings of *all* Middle East broadcasts in 1948.

Secondly, Mr Kimche departed a little from the official Israeli script:

> The suggestion that the Israeli case rested on the evidence of a *broadcast* order from the Arab leaders to the Palestinians is a myth invented and exploited by Professor Walid Khalidi, on whose researches Mr Childers seems to have based himself. But Professor Khalidi had told us earlier (in the December 1959 issue of the *Middle East Forum*) that contact between the Arab leaders and the National Committee in Haifa was maintained, not by broadcasts, but 'through messengers and telephone conversations', which I presume Mr Childers has not been able to check. In fact, I came to the conclusion some time ago that this is not something which can be established by a written piece of paper.

Third, there came a reference to a written piece of paper:

> There is now a mountain of independent evidence to show that the initiative for the Arab exodus came from the Arab side and not from the Jews. For example, the files of the British CID headquarters in

Haifa have a whole series of reports on the situation between 26 April and the end of the month. Let me conclude with a sentence from the report of 28 April 1948 (AAIGCID). 'The Jews,' it says, 'are still making every effort to persuade the Arab population to remain and settle down to their normal lives in the town. . .' It is signed, 'A.J. Bidmead for the Superintendent of Police'. But the Arab leaders insisted that the Arab population be evacuated and that the British military authorities should provide them with the necessary transport.

It was perhaps odd that Mr Kimche should have cited the case of Haifa, since the situation there had been dealt with by Childers in his original article. Childers had written, apropos of the Jewish appeal to Arabs to stay:

> There is one recorded instance of such an appeal. It is beyond dispute, even by Arabs, that in Haifa the late, gentle Mayor, Shabetai Levi, with the tears streaming down his face, implored the city's Arabs to stay. But elsewhere in Haifa, other Zionists were terrorising Arabs. Arthur Koestler wrote in his book that Haganah loudspeaker vans and the Haganah radio promised that city's Arabs escort to 'Arab territory' and 'hinted at terrible consequences if their warnings were disregarded'.

Kimche chose not to take up this evidence from Koestler, one of Zionism's most militant witnesses, even though Koestler's evidence would supply a motive for Arab requests for a British 'escort' (the term which is significantly used in both accounts). Perhaps they did not fancy being 'escorted' by the Haganah? Neither Kimche nor Childers asked why, if the Israelis were so keen on the Arabs staying, the Arabs would have asked for an 'escort' at all.

Childers sent a rejoinder to the *Spectator*, which was published on 9 June 1961. He took the points more or less in the order in which they were made:

> He questions whether the BBC monitors may not have missed some 1948 Arab broadcasts, since I found their record contained no broadcast Arab evacuation orders to the Palestinians. His concern about this might be more convincing, had he not refrained from mentioning the other vital fact I reported; that this monitor record shows repeated Arab broadcasts ordering and appealing to the Palestinians *not* to evacuate and announcing many measures to prevent and stem the exodus. Are we really to believe that the monitors fabricated this record? I can cite to him *Zionist* newspapers and

broadcasts in Palestine in 1948 reporting these Arab anti-evacuation measures.

But Mr Kimche judiciously covers himself by next claiming that in any case the Israeli version of the exodus has never rested on the 'existence of a *broadcast* order from the Arab leaders' – a myth, he says, invented by Dr Khalidi. Doubtless Dr Khalidi will be writing from Princeton for himself. I will therefore simply refer Mr Kimche to only one example of Israel very definitely resting her case on this radio story: her 1953 official pamphlet on the Arab refugees alleged that the exodus followed 'express instructions broadcast by the President of the Arab Higher Executive'.

What next? Mr Kimche next covers himself by saying that he has concluded that the cause of the exodus 'is not something that can be established by a written piece of paper'. Good: we may then take it that Mr Kimche, Zionist editor and author of a book endorsed by Mr Ben-Gurion, refutes all Israeli claims of 'documentary evidence' of the alleged Arab evacuation orders.

Childers went on to dispute other allegations and counter-allegations made by Kimche about why the Arabs actually *did* leave, which are not material to this essay. Towards the end of his reply he asked, rather scornfully:

And what else from Mr Kimche's 'mountain'? How was his alleged 'Arab initiative' implemented? He exploits a reference by Dr Khalidi to Haifa contact with Arab leaders by telephone and messenger. From this we are supposed to credit that 650,000 civilians, rooted to their homes, obediently fled out of Palestine on orders from Arab leaders that were *not broadcast* and *not written*, but allegedly sent by messenger and phone all over the country: and that these 650,000 civilians so fled despite the fact that the same Arab leaders *were* broadcasting to them *not* to leave!

On 16 June 1961, Professor Leo Kohn joined the fray (the same Leo Kohn cited by Childers in his first article). His contribution was printed posthumously because he died between writing it and the day of publication. It sought to re-state the case for an Arab-sponsored exodus, or rather for considering the exodus as Arab-sponsored. A core quotation was adduced:

There is also a wealth of evidence [wrote Kohn, descending somewhat from Kimche's 'mountain'] from Arab sources to show that the Arab League at an early stage of the campaign adopted a policy of evacuating the Arab population to the neighbouring countries, being convinced that their absence would be of short duration and would facilitate the impending military operations: 'This wholesale exodus was partly due to the belief of the Arabs, encouraged by the boasting of an unrealistic Arab press and the irresponsible utterances of some of the Arab leaders, that it could only be a matter of some weeks before the Jews were defeated.'

From *The Arabs* by Edward Atiyah, formerly Secretary of the Arab League Office in London, Penguin Books 1955, p. 183

To this Childers replied, in a companion article printed the same week:

I think I must explain why I comment without inhibition on the late Dr Kohn's article. It was written, not on his own behalf, but Israel's, and not in personal testimony, but by use of published material. And it concerns the fate of 650,000 human beings. I could not, honestly, treat the above version of their fate differently, notwithstanding the news of Dr Kohn's death.

I stated in my article that Israel had failed over ten years to produce anything remotely resembling proof of the Arab evacuation orders she has always alleged. Dr Kohn had available the entire resources of the Government of Israel, yet his reply contains *no* evidence *whatsoever*. It repeats the assertion that there is 'a wealth of evidence' of an Arab League evacuation policy. It does not – and we may therefore presume that Israel *cannot* – say when the decision was taken or how this alleged policy was implemented.

On 23 June 1961, the same Edward Atiyah cited by Professor Kohn wrote to offer a gloss on the quotation that had been attributed to him. His main point was as follows:

It leaves out my very next sentence which reads: 'But it was also, and in many parts of the country, largely due to a policy of deliberate terrorism and eviction followed by the Jewish commanders in the areas they occupied, and reaching its peak of brutality in the massacre of Deir Yassin.

My second comment is that there is no suggestion whatever in what I wrote that the exodus of the Arab refugees was a result of a *policy* of evacuating the Arab population. What I said is something quite different from the Zionist allegation that the Arab refugees were *ordered* or ever *told* by their leaders to evacuate, which is the main point in the whole controversy.

In the same week Jon Kimche defended himself once more. His letter descended yet further down the 'mountain of evidence' with which he had opened the bidding. He now wrote:

The Arab Exodus [no more quotation marks for exodus as in earlier letters] was a complicated and confused affair. Its origins cannot be settled by rhetorical but meaningless questions such as 'were there Arab broadcast orders or were there not?' I have never said that there were.

In the same letter Kimche averred that:

> There is, in fact, no slick explanation of the Arab exodus from Palestine. During this initial phase, the responsibility was partly that of the British Administration and largely that of the Arab leadership – those who should have set an example were the first to go. Later the responsibility was in part that of the invading Arab armies and the Israelis who 'encouraged' and in some cases forced the Arabs to leave. But, in general, it was the initial propaganda pattern set by the Arab leaders that created panic whenever the Israelis appeared, and led to indiscriminate flight. In truth – as distinct from propaganda – it is a very mixed-up story and not easy to unravel.

Having conceded much (putting the word 'encouraged' in inverted commas obviously cost him something) Kimche made a final stand on the issue which began the controversy:

> And as for the broadcast reports which Professor Khalidi and Mr Childers have so carefully checked in the British Museum: may I suggest they forget all about them. They are so ludicrously incomplete that they cannot be considered as evidence. They do not cover even ten per cent of the broadcasts. They prove nothing.

Mr Kimche did not say whether he had checked the broadcast reports, or had had them checked. He may also have been embarrassed, in his dual rule as a historian of the period and editor of a pro-Zionist newspaper in London, by a speech made by David Ben-Gurion during the course of this exchange of letters. On 18 May 1961, the London *Times* reported Mr Ben-Gurion as having 'denied in the Knesset yesterday that a single Arab resident had been expelled by the Government since the establishment of the State of Israel and he said the pre-State Jewish undergound had announced that any Arab could remain where he was. He said the fugitives had fled under the orders of Arab leaders.'

In the final round of the correspondence, Childers noted that Kimche had 'conceded the whole broadcasts issue'. He also pointed out that the idea of an exodus ordered by telephones and messengers appeared to have gone into eclipse. For good measure, he emphasized that the CIA monitoring records for Middle East broadcasting in 1948, which were open to inspection at Princeton University, bore out the same pattern as those of the BBC.

Jon Kimche had the last word in a very brief letter published on 4 August 1961. He summed up his own view rather surprisingly in the words of a leading Arabist: 'What matters is what Sir John Glubb said: what is to happen to the refugees? What is now going to be done for them?'

A good question. I wrote earlier that it would not matter how or why the refugees had left if they had been allowed to return. Even Kimche admits, in his 23 June letter, that Israel did indeed expel many Arabs after the fighting, though he remains reluctant to admit they expelled any *before* it. What we have here, I suspect, is *prima facie* evidence of a very bad conscience which shifts jerkily from angry claims about 'mountains of evidence' for Arab-ordered flight, to sentimental invocations of Sir John Glubb. One is compelled to believe that some kind of denial is at work here. In Kimche's own history of 1948, we read how Moshe Dayan and his column on 11 July 1948,

> drove at full speed into Lydda, shooting up the town and creating confusion and a degree of terror among the population ... its Arab population of 30,000 either fled or were herded on the road to Ramallah. The next day Ramle also surrendered and its Arab population suffered the same fate. Both towns were sacked by the victorious Israelis.

Mr Kimche cannot overlook that and many similar 'incidents'. But he cannot bear to attribute generalized Palestinian flight to this kind of conduct. So it becomes necessary (even if impossible on the basis of the evidence) for him to construct an imaginary Arab higher command, which mysteriously (and quite variously) orders the Palestinians to dematerialize and reassemble elsewhere.

In spite of the fact that it has been ridiculed and confuted so many times, the 'broadcast' excuse continues to appear in print. This may be because it has been repeated so many times that it cannot be disowned without embarrassment. It may be because, like many lies, it takes no time to tell and much time to expose. It may be, as I suggest above, that it meets some psychological need to displace responsibility. No doubt there are elements of all three. The fact remains that as late as October 1986, David Gilmour was able to catch out an Israeli propagandist in the pages of *Middle East International*. This propagandist had written, in 1981, that 'the

Arab Higher Committee had ordered the Arabs in Haifa to leave the town'. Gilmour pointed out that an earlier account by the same author had accused the Arab *League* – a very different and distinct entity – of issuing the orders. The name of the propagandist was Jon Kimche.

Gilmour also waded through a book called *Battleground* by Samuel Katz, which had been recommended by the Israeli lobby to all British Members of Parliament as 'a very valuable source of reference', providing 'a most informed understanding of the situation in the Middle East'. Katz's book states calmly that 'the Arab refugees were not driven from Palestine by anyone. The vast majority left, whether of their own free will or at the orders or exhortations of their leaders.' Even as I was finishing this chapter, I noticed a lavish full-page advertisement in *The New Republic* from a body calling itself CAMERA: The Committee for Accuracy in Middle East Reporting in America. Entitled 'Mid-East Refugees: Who Are They, What is The Story?' the advertisement commenced by saying:

> In 1948, on the day of the proclamation of the State of Israel, five Arab armies invaded the new country from all sides. In frightful radio broadcasts, they urged the Arabs living there to leave, so that the invading armies could operate without interference. . .

I wrote to CAMERA on 20 February 1987, asking for an authenticated case of such a broadcast, whether 'frightful' or otherwise. By late August I had received no evidence.

Even though nobody has ever testified to having heard them, and even though no record of their transmission has ever been found, we shall hear of these orders and broadcasts again and again.

4

Truth Whereby Nations Live

Peretz Kidron

My debut as a 'ghost' was quite fortuitous. In 1974, shortly after taking up writing as a profession – principally in journalism and translation – a mutual friend introduced me to Ben Dunkelman, a Canadian Jew then on a visit to Israel where he sought help in writing his memoirs. A wealthy businessman now in retirement, Dunkelman in his younger days had made a name for himself as a combat officer with the Canadian expeditionary force which fought in France during World War Two. Later, he volunteered for the Israeli army during the 1948 war which coincided with the proclamation of Israel's independence. With an eventful life behind him, Dunkelman obviously had an interesting story to tell, and in spite of claiming no experience as a 'ghost', I willingly undertook the assignment.

In the autumn of the same year, I went to stay at the Dunkelman home outside Toronto, where I lived and worked in close proximity with my 'subject'. It was an extremely convenient arrangement. Having almost no written material to go on, my work rested upon lengthy sessions with Ben – we were soon on first-name terms – in which he launched into rambling but colorful reminiscences about the highlights of his career. After getting the gist of a particular story or episode, I would immediately retire to my basement study and write it up to the best of my ability, endeavouring as far as I could to remain faithful in style and substance to what I had so recently heard 'from the horse's mouth'. When I completed a draft chapter more or less to my satisfaction, I would submit it to Ben for his comments and corrections. Helped by the immediacy of the situation, I must have done quite an acceptable job because Dunkelman generally pronounced himself satisfied with my rendering of his account. The changes he made were few and, for the most part, minor. When the chapter received his final okay, it would be passed to Ben's Israel-born wife Yael who retyped it. (The manuscript was later published in somewhat condensed form by Macmillan under the title 'Dual Loyalty'; it was also translated into Hebrew and issued by Schocken.)

Dunkelman proved to be an excellent raconteur, and I was fascinated by his yarns. But I naturally found the greatest interest in his stories about the 1948 war, this being a subject with which I was familiar from extensive reading, and from personal accounts I had heard from participants. Having myself settled in Israel only three years after the war, I felt I was close to home ground. It was while Ben was relating this part of his memoirs that he made a startling revelation.

To summarize his account: reaching Israel at a time when the Israeli army was desperately short of officers with combat experience such as he had acquired in Europe, Dunkelman soon found himself appointed to the relatively senior post of brigade commander, charged with the task of dislodging the Arab forces which maintained a powerful foothold in central and upper Galilee. After some preliminary skirmishes, Dunkelman decided to lunge for Nazareth, the largest Arab town in Galilee and a key strategic objective. He led his own Seventh Brigade and support units in a pincer thrust along an undefended rear road into Nazareth; after little more than token resistance, the town capitulated. The surrender was enshrined in a formal document whereby the town's dignitaries undertook to cease hostilities, in return for which the Israeli officers headed by Dunkelman solemnly pledged that no harm would befall the civilian population.

As to what happened next, it is best presented in my own version as recorded within hours of hearing the story from Dunkelman:

Two days after the second truce came into effect, the Seventh Brigade was ordered to withdraw from Nazareth. Avraham Yaffe, who had commanded the 13th battalion in the assault on the city, now reported to me with orders from Moshe Carmel to take over from me as its military governor. I complied with the order, but only after Avraham had given me his word of honour that he would do nothing to harm or displace the Arab population. My demand may sound strange, but I had good reason to feel concerned on this subject.

Only a few hours previously, Haim Laskov had come to me with astounding orders: Nazareth's civilian population was to be evacuated! I was shocked and horrified. I told him I would do nothing of the sort – in view of our promises to safeguard the city's people, such a move would be both superfluous and harmful. I reminded him that scarcely a day earlier, he and I, as representatives of the Israeli army, had signed the surrender document, in which we solemnly pledged to do nothing to harm the city or its population. When Haim saw that I refused to obey the order, he left.

A scarce twelve hours later, Avraham Yaffe came to tell me that his battalion was relieving my brigade; I felt sure that this order had been given because of my defiance of the evacuation order. But although I was withdrawn from Nazareth, it seems that my disobedience did have some effect. It seems to have given the high command time for second thoughts, which led them to the conclusion that it would, indeed, be wrong to expel the inhabitants of Nazareth. To the best of my knowledge, there was never any more talk of the evacuation plan, and the city's Arab citizens have lived there ever since.

I included this episode in the draft chapter describing the Seventh Brigade's Galilee campaign, which I handed to Ben for his study and comments. The next day, he gave it back to me. To the best of my recollection, he said nothing, but as I glanced through the text, I came to the above episode, where I was surprised to find the following comment pencilled in the margin: 'I WISH TO CONSIDER WEATHER [sic!] I SHOULD INCLUDE THIS OR NOT.'

Ben's second thoughts came as a disappointment to me. I took the matter up with him at our next session, attempting to persuade him that, as an important piece of historical testimony, the episode should be placed on record. Uncharacteristically for a man of his vigorous convictions, Ben made no effort to explain his back-tracking – making me suspect that the idea was not his own, and that Yael had exerted her very considerable influence. Be that as it may, when I saw that his mind was in fact set against including the passage, I abandoned my attempt; after all, I told myself, this being his story, it was his prerogative to decide what to tell – and what to omit. (In passing, I should mention that, with the exception of one innocently scurrilous incident involving a Canadian officer friend, this was the sole instance I can recall of Ben having second thoughts about a story he had related for inclusion in the manuscript.)

*

While bowing to Dunkelman's wishes with regard to deletion of the offensive passage, I found myself in a grave dilemma. I was convinced of the importance of publishing the incident, which touched upon one of the most sensitive and explosive issues in the Arab-Israeli conflict.

It will be recalled that the 1948 war uprooted hundreds of thousands of Palestinian Arabs from their homes. When the fighting ended, the refugees – temporarily lodged in makeshift camps – expected permission to return to their homes, which now lay in Israeli territory. But the Israeli authorities resolutely refused to sanction their return, resisting diplomatic pressure and ignoring UN resolutions for repatriation. The motives behind this policy have been discussed at length, and I will not consider that aspect of the issue. But it is significant that the Israeli authorities defended their refusal in part by charging that the refugee problem was of the Arabs' own making, claiming that the civilians had abandoned their homes at the behest of their leaders who allegedly urged them to 'leave the way clear for the Arab armies to throw the Jews into the sea'. Refugee spokesmen charged that the Israeli forces had followed a deliberate policy of mass expulsions employing violence and threats to induce a forced exodus – the Israeli authorities indignantly and consistently denied the allegations. The Israeli version, presented with considerable vigor and skill, came to be accepted not only within Israel and in Jewish public opinion in the Diaspora, but also among circles claiming familiarity with the Mid-eastern conflict.

Hence the importance of Dunkelman's account. If his story was accurate, he had received explicit orders from his superiors to drive out unarmed civilians who had formally surrendered and thrown themselves upon the mercy of the Israeli forces. (It is of course entirely to Dunkelman's credit that, true to his solemn undertaking, he resisted the order; thanks to him, Nazareth remains an Arab city.) To the best of my knowledge, this was the first testimony concerning such an order to come firsthand from someone who had held a senior position in the Israeli command. The significance of the incident was more than purely local: it stood to reason that if such an order had been issued with regard to Nazareth, similar directives may have been given concerning other Arab population centers whose inhabitants allegedly 'fled'. That was why I considered it so important that Dunkelman's testimony be made public; if he declined to do it, it was surely up to me.

In spite of that conviction, however, I was painfully aware of various constraints. For one thing, Dunkelman's senior rank notwithstanding, his account was unsupported, resting entirely upon his own personal recollection of events which had taken place nearly a quarter of a century earlier. Could his testimony stand up against the unanimous protestations of Israel's military and political leadership, which had consistently denied acting in the manner indicated by Dunkelman's account?

There were also personal and professional inhibitions. Although my relationship with Ben was hardly that of a doctor or lawyer, I had nevertheless been made privy to his story in a professional capacity: would it be ethical for me to disclose an episode he had explicitly requested to have suppressed? The problem transcended professional formality. Ben had treated me throughout with great consideration and generosity. Would it not be base ingratitude to violate his confidence? Another consideration was anxiety for my own career: should I acquire a reputation for indiscretion, might I not find myself shunned by potential clients?

Faced with a dilemma that pitted political commitment against personal and professional ethics, as well as private interest, I found no unequivocal solution. Consequently, I settled for a compromise to keep my options open. When I finished my work – it took me just six weeks to complete the manuscript – I cleared out my desk, throwing away heaps of papers, semi-completed drafts and notes. But I took the page with the Nazareth episode – authenticated by Ben's pencilled comment, which implicitly endorsed its authenticity – and carefully packed it with my personal effects. I sensed some pangs of conscience over my underhand behavior towards Ben, though I could argue that, in view of the desperate plight of hundreds of thousands of homeless refugees whose cause might be helped by publication of his testimony, my personal misconduct had some moral justification.

*

Returning to Israel late in December 1974, I reverted to my routine activities, which included involvement with the radical left. It was the doldrum period after the Yom Kippur war. In spite of hopes among many of my friends that the 1973 upheaval would open Israeli eyes and produce a swing towards the dovish options advocated by the left – particularly with regard to an understanding with the Palestinians – in fact, we witnessed the groundswell which culminated two years later in the electoral triumph of the right wing Likud under Menachem Begin. But in 1975 power was still in the hands of the Labour establishment which had ruled Israel right from the start. After nearly a decade of occupation of the West Bank and the Gaza Strip, the Israeli authorities' sole mode of dealing with the Palestinians was by continued repression.

The Israeli left was deeply divided and confused. Regularly attending meetings and rallies, I found no group with which I could actively identify. Increasingly, I found myself in the role of observer, though I occasionally joined in the interminable arguments about the rights and wrongs of the Arab-Israeli conflict. When right-wingers trotted out their stock arguments – which included the inevitable claim that the refugee problem had been created by the Arabs themselves – I had the advantage of being able to draw upon my little nugget of personal information culled from Ben Dunkelman. However, as is normal in ideological confrontation, the facts made little impact on firmly entrenched conviction. As for publication of Dunkelman's account, I was dubious about its efficacy in the absence of a political organization which could take the matter up.

During this period, I made my living as a Hebrew-English translator; with growing proficiency in a field where demand exceeded supply, I soon found myself inundated with work. Most of my assignments were translations into English of Hebrew books of topical or political interest – 'Operation Susanna' about an Israeli spy ring in Egypt, Michael Bar Zohar's biography of David Ben-Gurion and other works. One of these was Ezer Weizmann's first book of memoirs, which he wrote with the assistance of journalist Dov Goldstein. It was through Goldstein that I was approached subsequently to translate the memoirs of Yitzhak Rabin (which Goldstein likewise 'ghosted').

It was now late 1978 or early 1979. Rabin, recently unseated as prime minister, had ample time to compose his book. He also had plenty of material to draw upon. A brigade commander in 1948, his military career culminated in the mid-sixties with his appointment as commander-in-chief, in which capacity he led the Israeli forces to their stunning 1967 victory. Subsequently, he served some years as ambassador to Washington; after the 1973 war which so gravely discredited the Labour old guard, he was recalled from the US and soon found himself prime minister, until his downfall in 1977.

When I commenced work on the Rabin manuscript, I was alerted to a minor difficulty: the material delivered to me for translation was not yet final, for although cleared by military censorship, it required additional vetting by a special ministerial committee (under Israeli law, such supplementary censorship is mandatory for persons who have held senior military or political posts). I was accordingly instructed to proceed with the translation; any changes or deletions ordered by the ministerial committee would be conveyed to me in due course.

I had progressed some way into the manuscript (which I found painfully lengthy and dry) when I got a call from Goldstein. The ministerial committee had finally pronounced its verdict, he told me, and proceeded to dictate a series of page numbers and paragraphs to specify deletions.

No sooner had I put down the phone than, feeling highly intrigued, I hastened to scan the manuscript, to find out what the ministers in their wisdom deemed unfit for publication over the signature of an ex-prime minister. It was a most instructive list. Even though the military censor had approved the manuscript – thereby indicating that it contained nothing prejudicial to national security – the ministerial committee insisted on deleting significant passages. For example, they struck out Rabin's account of the Israeli attack on the US spy ship 'Liberty' during the early hours of the Six-Day war in 1967, even though Rabin's version staunchly upheld the Israeli claim that the strike was a genuine mistake, with no ulterior motive. With equal firmness, the ministerial committee deleted any reference, however remote, to Israel's nuclear development program, with which Rabin had sporadic encounters in his successive posts as commander-in-chief, ambassador and prime minister. (This blanket of secrecy is currently of added interest in view of Mordechai Vanounu's sensational disclosures about Israel's nuclear arsenal.)

As I scanned the list of erasures, I came across one which sent my pulse racing. It was in the section of the manuscript describing the 1948 war, when Rabin commanded the Harel brigade. Having taken an active part in the fighting in and around Jerusalem, Harel was transferred to the central front, where it participated in 'Operation Larlar' (so named after the initials of its objectives: the Arab towns of Lydda, Ramleh, Latrun and Ramallah). The operation's successful first phase led the Israeli forces to occupy Lydda (now Lod) and Ramleh. Subsequent events are depicted in the Rabin manuscript (in the rather rough translation I made at the time and never polished):

> While the fighting was still in progress, we had to grapple with a troublesome problem: the fate of the populations of Lod and Ramleh, numbering some fifty thousand civilians. Not even Ben-Gurion could offer any solution, and during the discussions at operational head-quarters, he remained silent, as was his habit in such situations.

Clearly, we could not leave Lod's hostile and armed populace in our rear, where it could endanger the supply route to Yiftach, which was advancing eastwards.

We walked outside, Ben-Gurion accompanying us. Alon repeated his question: 'What is to be done with the population?' BG waved his hand in a gesture which said: Drive them out! Alon and I held a consultation. I agreed that it was essential to drive the inhabitants out. We took them on foot towards the Bet Horon road, assuming that the Legion would be obliged to look after them, thereby shouldering logistic difficulties which would burden its fighting capacity, making things easier for us.

'Driving out' is a term with a harsh ring. Psychologically, this was one of the most difficult actions we undertook. The population of Lod (Lydda) did not leave willingly. There was no way of avoiding the use of force and warning shots in order to make the inhabitants march the 10–15 miles to the point where they met up with the Legion.

The inhabitants of Ramleh watched, and learned the lesson: their leaders agreed to be evacuated voluntarily, on condition that the evacuation was carried out by vehicles. Buses took them to Latrun, and from there they were evacuated by the Legion. Great suffering was inflicted upon the men taking part in the eviction action. Soldiers of the Yiftach brigade included youth movement graduates, who had been inculcated with values such as international fraternity and humaneness. The eviction action went beyond the concepts they were used to. There were some fellows who refused to take part in the expulsion action. Prolonged propaganda activities were required after the action, to remove the bitterness of these youth movement groups, and explain why we were obliged to undertake such a harsh and cruel action.

Today, in hindsight, I think the action was essential. The removal of those fifty thousand Arabs was an important contribution to Israel's security, in one of the most sensitive of regions, linking the coastal plain with Jerusalem. After the War of Independence, some of the inhabitants were permitted to return to their home towns.

This episode naturally brought to mind Ben Dunkelman's account of the order to depopulate Nazareth. Delving into my files, I found the precious page I had brought back from Toronto and hastened to compare the two texts. The points of similarity were striking. The two incidents occurred within days of one another. In both cases, the advancing Israeli forces had occupied large Arab population centers. In both cases, orders had been issued for the forcible eviction of the civilians. In both cases, the order was given personally, without any written record being kept. Ben-Gurion's behavior as depicted by Rabin – the mute wave of the hand – bears out Dunkelman's verbal account (I did not include it in the draft, but I recall it clearly) that when he demanded written authorization from Ben-Gurion, the expulsion order was not followed through. In brief, the two descriptions, particularly when taken together, proved beyond any shadow of doubt that there were high-level directives for mass expulsions of the Arab population, and that the decision-makers, evidently aware of the discreditable and unlawful nature of such a policy, were careful to leave no incriminating evidence about their personal and political responsibility.

*

I now found myself in possession of two pieces of original – and unquestionably reliable – testimony about the origins of the Palestinian refugee tragedy. My doubts about Dunkelman's unsupported account were utterly dispelled by Rabin's story.

My doubts had been resolved, but not so my dilemma. On the contrary: my complex heartsearchings about publication of Dunkelman's account were now compounded by the awareness that Rabin's testimony was being suppressed by a legally-empowered ministerial committee. Were I to publish the deleted passage, I would run the risk of prosecution for flagrant violation of censorship. Nevertheless, while wrestling with the problem, I took the precaution of xeroxing the relevant passage in the Rabin manuscript. When I completed the translation and returned the Hebrew original, I stored away the copy I had made.

Not having kept a chronicle of events at that time, I have no precise recollection as to how long I agonized over my dilemma, but the period probably extended into months rather than weeks. Finally, in September or October 1979, concluding that any other course would be abject cowardice and an evasion of my personal and political responsibility, I made up my mind to 'publish and be damned'. With some trepidation, I called the *New York Times*'s Jerusalem correspondent, David Shippler. When we met, I gave him copies of the two suppressed passages, and provided a full and candid account of how they came into my possession. Foreseeing that the Rabin disclosure would be the more explosive of the two – and would consequently evoke attempts by Israeli officials to dismiss it as a fabrication – I authorized Shippler to use my name in connection with the revelation. Since it was common knowledge that I was the translator, my name would bear out its authenticity, thereby perhaps precluding pointless wrangling on that point, and clearing the way for candid discussion of the substance of the account.

The die having been cast, I sat back to await the consequences. But days passed, and nothing happened. I sensed a blend of disappointment and anti-climax. Obviously I had exaggerated the explosive nature of the material. If Shippler or his editors found it unworthy of publication, my prolonged heartsearching struck me as having been a futile exercise in irrelevance. Disappointed at my bombshell turning out to be a damp squib, and with time on my hands, I left for a visit to England.

I was staying at a boarding house in London several weeks later when I got an agitated phone call from Israel. 'The shit has hit the fan!' It had indeed. The *New York Times* of 23 October 1979 had published the story ('Israel Bars Rabin from Relating '48 Eviction of Arabs'), which was promptly reprinted under banner headlines by the Israeli press (under Israeli law, the local media are at liberty to print any item which has been published abroad, even if it was previously banned by the Israeli censors).

As I was to learn later, the publication sparked off a major sensation in Israel, with extensive media comment, and some feeble denials from establishment figures. (Yigal Alon, cited by Rabin as being present when Ben-Gurion gave the expulsion order, flatly contradicted Rabin's account.) As was natural under the circumstances, I came in for extensive abuse for my indiscretion, and Rabin confessed to having neglected 'field security' when he entrusted his manuscript to a person of my views.

However, as is equally customary in such cases, the excitement soon died down, and other issues grabbed the headlines. Because the *New York Times* had focussed exclusively upon Rabin's revelations about Lydda and Ramleh, with no mention of Dunkelman's account about the abortive attempt to depopulate Nazareth, I later provided that story to the Israeli weekly *Ha'olam Hazeh*, which published it in July 1980. At the same time, I approached Communist Knesset member Tuffik Zayyad, then as now mayor of Nazareth. I urged Zayyad to seize upon the impending publication of the story to table a question in the Knesset and demand official explanations about the order to make his city 'Araber-rein'. But here again, the matter failed to gain more than fleeting public attention.

This account would be incomplete without a mention of subsequent developments, which display a strong streak of irony. To some extent, the disclosures did have some lasting effect. Since the *New York Times* publication, Israeli propaganda has largely relinquished the claim that the Palestinian exodus of 1948 was 'self-inspired'. Official circles implicitly concede that the Arab population fled as a result of Israeli action – whether directly, as in the case of Lydda and Ramleh, or indirectly, due to the panic that and similar actions (the Der Yassin massacre) inspired in Arab population centers throughout Palestine. However, even though the historical record has been grudgingly set straight, the Israeli establishment still refuses to accept moral or political responsibility for the refugee problem it – or its predecessors – actively generated.

The broader political effect was equally disappointing. I had hoped that an acquaintance with the facts would induce Israeli public opinion to rethink its attitude towards the Palestinians – the 1948 refugees in particular – and, by recognizing Israel's culpability in that tragedy, adopt a more enlightened view towards Palestinian resentments and claims. Those hopes, far from being fulfilled, actually backfired. Whether in public debate or private conversation, it is difficult to detect remorse over Israel's treatment of the Palestinians in 1948. On the contrary: right-wingers frequently incline towards a kind of reverse morality; conceding that Israel engineered the 1948 exodus, they consequently imply – or declare outright – that there can be no moral constraints against expelling much or all of the Arab population remaining in Israel or the occupied territories.

Just as my political hopes were shown to have been naively optimistic, my own personal expectations turned out to have been needlessly pessimistic. Before returning to Israel from London in 1980, I contacted the well-known attorney Amnon Zichroni, seeking his advice on my line of defense when charged with violating censorship (in relation to the Rabin manuscript). To my surprise, Zichroni wrote back that I had nothing to fear, since I had broken no law! The material I had published had been cleared by military censorship, the only legal constraint to which I was subject. The ministerial committee's deletions were binding upon Rabin alone; as an ordinary citizen, I did not come under the committee's jurisdiction and I could therefore not be prosecuted.

While relieved by Zichroni's reassurances, I remained anxious about my professional career. Since it was generally known that I had leaked confidential material received in the course of my work, I expected to be shunned by potential clients wary of my disregard of professional ethics. How would I make a living?

What I failed to take into account is that media leaks are a standard feature of Israeli public life. Cabinet ministers vie with generals and senior officials in disclosing information of the most confidential nature, whenever it suits their personal or political purposes. A leak is an everyday political device, employed with few inhibitions. Contrary to my glum predictions, I encountered no one who thought the worse of me for my breach of confidentiality. Of course, I have no way of knowing if my reputation for political indiscretion has deterred some potential client from employing me. But to the best of my knowledge, I have suffered no material harm. I continue to work in my profession. I am sought after to translate works of all kinds, including books by prominent figures of the political or journalistic establishment, not excluding some from the far right! In short, the whole affair was far less earth-shattering or portentous – whether in political impact or personal fall-out – than I had foreseen.

Accordingly, my personal advice to anyone in possession of confidential information he or she feels conscience-bound to place in the public domain, is best expressed in the immortal line uttered by the late Zero Mostel in *The Producers*: sighting an expensively-dressed blond getting out of a fancy limousine, he leans out of the window and yells at the top of his voice: 'That's right baby – if you've got it, flaunt it!'

But to avoid excessive hopes that such revelations will alter the course of world history, it is wise to recall what Thoreau wrote: 'It takes two to speak the truth – one to speak, another to hear.'

5

Middle East Terrorism and the American Ideological System

Noam Chomsky

On 17 October 1985, President Reagan met in Washington with Israeli Prime Minister Shimon Peres, who told him that Israel was prepared to take 'bold steps' in the Middle East and extend 'the hand of peace' to Jordan. 'Mr Peres's visit comes at a moment of unusual American-Israeli harmony,' David Shipler commented in the *New York Times*, quoting a State Department official who described US relations with Israel as 'extraordinarily close and strong'. And indeed, Peres was warmly welcomed by the American media as a man of peace, and commended for his forthright commitment to 'bear the cost of peace in preference to the price of war', in his words. The President said that he and Mr Peres discussed 'the evil scourge of terrorism, which has claimed so many Israeli, American and Arab victims and brought tragedy to many others', adding that 'We agreed that terrorism must not blunt our efforts to achieve peace in the Middle East.'[1]

It would require the talents of a Jonathan Swift to do justice to this exchange between two of the world's leading terrorist commanders, whose shared conception of 'peace', furthermore, excludes entirely one of the two groups that claim the right of national self-determination in the former Palestine: the indigenous population. So extreme is Reagan-Peres rejectionism that the Palestinians are not even to be permitted to select their own representatives in eventual negotiations – just as they are denied municipal elections or other democratic forms under the Israeli military occupation. The concept that they might have rights comparable to those of the settlers who largely displaced them is

97

excluded a priori, with the full support of articulate opinion in the United States. The Jordan Valley is 'an inseparable part of the State of Israel', Shimon Peres, the man of peace, declared while touring Israeli settlements there in 1985, consistent with his unwavering stand that 'The past is immutable and the Bible is the decisive document in determining the fate of our land' and that a Palestinian state would 'threaten Israel's very existence'.[2] His conception of a Jewish state, much lauded in the US for its moderation, does not *threaten*, but rather *eliminates* the existence of the Palestinian people. But this consequence is considered of little moment, at worst a minor defect in an imperfect world.

Neither Peres nor any other Israeli leader has moved an inch from the position of current President Chaim Herzog in 1972 that the Palestinians can never be 'partners in any way in a land that has been holy to our people for thousands of years', though the 'doves' prefer to exclude West Bank areas of heavy Arab population from the Jewish State to avoid what they euphemistically term 'the demographic problem'. Former Chief of Israeli intelligence Shlomo Gazit, a senior official of the military administration from 1967 to 1973, observes that its basic principle was 'that it is necessary to prevent the inhabitants of the [occupied] territories from participating in shaping the political future of the territory and they must not be seen as a partner for dealings with Israel'; hence 'the absolute prohibition of any political organization, for it was clearly understood by everyone that if political activism and organization were permitted, its leaders would become potential participants in political affairs'. The same considerations require 'the destruction of all initiative and every effort on the part of the inhabitants of the territories to serve as a pipeline for negotiations, to be a channel to the Palestinian Arab leadership outside of the territories'. Israeli policy is a 'success story', Gazit concludes, because these goals, which persist until today, have been achieved. Israel's position, with US support, remains that of Prime Minister (now Defense Minister) Yitzhak Rabin, when the PLO and the Arab states submitted a proposal for a peaceful two-state settlement to the United Nations in January 1976: Israel will reject any negotiations with the PLO even if it recognizes Israel and renounces terrorism, and will not enter into 'political negotiations with Palestinians', PLO or not.[3] Neither Peres nor Reagan has been willing even to consider the explicit proposals by the PLO – which both know has overwhelming support among the Palestinians and as much legitimacy as did the Zionist organization in 1947 – for negotiations leading to mutual recognition in a two-state settlement in accord with the broad international consensus that has been blocked at every turn by the US and Israel for many years.[4]

These crucial political realities provide the necessary framework for any discussion of 'the evil scourge of terrorism', which, in the racist terms of American discourse, refers to terrorist acts by Arabs, but not by Jews, just as 'peace' means a settlement that honors the right of national self-determination of Jews, but not of Palestinians.

Peres arrived in Washington to discourse on peace and terrorism with his partner in crime directly after having sent his bombers to attack Tunis, where they killed twenty Tunisians and fifty-five Palestinians, Israeli journalist Amnon Kapeliouk reported from the scene. The target was undefended, 'a vacation resort with several dozen homes, vacation cottages and PLO offices side by side and intermingled in such a way that even from close by it is difficult to distinguish' among them. The weapons were more sophisticated than those used in Beirut, 'smart bombs' apparently, which crushed their targets to dust. 'The people who were in the bombed buildings were mangled beyond recognition. They showed me a series of pictures of the dead. "You may take them", I was told. I left the pictures in the office. No newspaper in the world would publish terror photos such as these. I was told that a Tunisian boy who sold sandwiches near the headquarters was torn to pieces. His father identified the body by a scar on his ankle. "Some of the wounded were brought out from under the rubble, apparently healthy and unhurt," my guide told me. "Half an hour later they collapsed in contortions and died. Apparently their internal organs had been destroyed from the power of the blast." '[5]

Tunisia had accepted the Palestinians at Reagan's behest after they had been expelled from Beirut in a US-supported invasion that left some twenty thousand killed and much of the country destroyed. 'You used a hammer against a fly,' military correspondent Ze'ev Schiff was informed by 'a leading Pentagon figure, a general who is familiar with the Israeli military (IDF) and several other armies of the region'. 'You struck many civilians without need. We were astounded by your attitude to the Lebanese civilians,' a feeling shared by Israeli soldiers and senior officers who were appalled at the savagery of the attack and the treatment of civilians and prisoners[6] – though support in Israel for the aggression and for the Begin-Sharon team increased in parallel to the atrocities, reaching its peak after the terror bombing of Beirut in August. Shimon Peres, the man of peace and respected figure in the Socialist International, kept his silence until the costs to Israel began to mount with the postwar Sabra-Shatila massacres and the toll taken by the Lebanese resistance, which undermined Israel's plan of establishing a 'New Order' in Lebanon with Israel in control of large areas of the south and the remnants ruled by Israel's Phalangist allies and selected Muslim elites.

There can be no doubt, Kapeliouk observes, that Arafat was the target of the Tunis attack. In the PLO office to which he was taken, a picture of Arafat stands amidst the ruins with the caption: 'They wanted to kill me instead of negotiating with me'. 'The PLO wishes negotiations,' Kapeliouk was told, 'but Israel rejects any discussion' – a simple statement of fact, effectively concealed by the US media, or worse, dismissed as irrelevant given the guiding racist premises.

There can also be no serious doubt of US complicity in the Tunis attack. The US did not even warn the victims – close American allies – that the killers were on the way. One who credits the American pretense that the Sixth Fleet and the extensive US surveillance system in the region were incapable of detecting the Israeli planes refueled en route over the Mediterranean should be calling for a congressional investigation of the utter incompetence of the American military, which surely leaves us and our allies wide open to enemy attack. 'News reports now quote government sources as saying the US Sixth Fleet was undoubtedly aware of the coming raid but decided not to inform Tunisian officials,' *The Los Angeles Times* reported, citing wire services. But 'that very significant statement was not reported in the two major east coast papers, *The New York Times* and *The Washington Post*, nor in the other US papers, nor was it used in the overseas service' of AP and UPI, London *Economist* Mideast correspondent Godfrey Jansen reported, adding that 'US passive collusion was absolutely certain'.[7]

One of the victims of the Tunis bombing was Mahmoud el-Mughrabi, born in Jerusalem in 1960, under detention twelve times by the age of 16, one of the informants for the London *Sunday Times* exposé of torture in Israel (19 June 1977), who 'managed to escape to Jordan after years of increasingly marginal existence under steadily deteriorating conditions of the military occupation', according to a memorial notice by Israeli Jewish friends that was repeatedly denied publication in Arab newspapers in East Jerusalem by Israeli military censorship.[8] These facts would, of course, be meaningless in the United States, if only because the *Sunday Times* study was largely excluded from the press, though it was noted in the liberal *New Republic*, along with an explicit defense of torture of Arabs that elicited no public reaction.[9]

The United States officially welcomed the Israeli bombing of Tunis as 'a legitimate response' to 'terrorist attacks'. Secretary of State Shultz confirmed this judgment in a telephone call to Israeli Foreign Minister Yitzhak Shamir, informing him that the President and others 'had considerable sympathy for the Israeli action', the press reported.[10] The US drew back from such open support after an adverse global reaction, but it abstained from the UN condemnation of this 'act of armed aggression' in 'flagrant violation of the Charter of the United Nations, international law and norms of conduct' – alone as usual. The intellectual and cultural climate in the US is reflected by the fact that the abstention was bitterly condemned as yet another instance of a 'pro-PLO' and 'anti-Israel' stance, and a refusal to strike hard at – carefully selected – terrorists.

One might argue that the Israeli bombing does not fall under the rubric of international terrorism because it is an instance of the far more serious crime of 'aggression', as the UN Security Council maintained. Or one might hold that it is unfair to apply to Israel the definition of 'international terrorism' designed by others. To counter the latter complaint, we may consider its own doctrine, as formulated by Ambassador Benjamin Netanyahu at an International Conference on Terrorism. The distinguishing factor in terrorism, he explained, is 'deliberate and systematic murder and maiming [of civilians] designed to inspire fear'.[11] Clearly the Tunis attack and other Israeli atrocities over the years fall under this definition, though most acts of international terrorism do not, including the most outrageous terrorist attacks against Israelis (Ma'alot, the Munich massacre, the coastal road atrocity of 1978 that provided the pretext for invading Lebanon, etc.), or even airplane hijacking or taking of hostages quite generally, the very topic of the conference he was attending.

The attack on Arafat's PLO headquarters was allegedly in retaliation for the murder of three Israelis in Larnaca, Cyprus, by assailants who were captured and face trial for their crime. 'Western diplomatic experts on the PLO' doubt that Arafat was aware of the planned mission, and 'The Israelis, too, have dropped their original contention that Mr Arafat had been involved.'[12] Apologists for Israeli terrorism here, who assure us that 'Israel's Tunisian raid precisely targeted people responsible for terrorist activities', are unimpressed, explaining that whatever the facts, 'the larger moral responsibility for atrocities ... is *all* Yasir Arafat's' because 'he was, and remains, the founding father of contemporary Palestinian violence'. In an address to the Israeli lobbying group AIPAC, Attorney-General Edwin Meese stated that the US will hold Arafat 'accountable for acts of international terrorism' quite generally, facts apparently being irrelevant.[13] Therefore any act 'against the PLO' – a very broad category, as the historical record demonstrates – is legitimate.

The Tunis attack was consistent with Israeli practice since the earliest days of the state: retaliation is directed against those who are vulnerable, not the perpetrators of atrocities. A standard condemnation of the PLO is that 'Instead of directly attacking security-minded foes like Israel, for example, Palestinians have attacked softer Israeli targets in Italy, Austria and elsewhere,'[14] another sign of their vile and cowardly nature. The similar Israeli practice, initiated long before and vastly greater in scale, escapes notice in the midst of the general praise for Israeli heroism and military efficiency. The concept of 'retaliation' also raises more than a few questions, a matter to which we turn directly.

As 1985 came to an end, the press reviewed the record of 'a year of bloody international terrorism', including the murders in Larnaca on 25 September and the Achille Lauro hijacking and murder of an American tourist on 7 October. Israel's 1 October attack was not included in the list. In its lengthy year-end review of terrorism, the *New York Times* briefly notes the Tunis bombing as an example of retaliation, not terrorism, describing it as 'an act of desperation that had little effect on Palestinian violence and provoked an outcry by other nations'. Harvard Law Professor Alan Dershowitz, condemning Italy for complicity in international terrorism by releasing the man 'who allegedly masterminded the hijacking', observed that the US 'would certainly extradite any Israeli terrorist who had done violence to citizens of another country' – Ariel Sharon, Yitzhak Shamir or Menachem Begin, for example. This statement appeared on the very day that Shimon Peres was being feted in Washington immediately after the Tunis bombing and lauded for his commitment to peace. It is considered entirely natural in the reigning cultural climate.[15]

Reagan's pronouncements on terrorism are reported and discussed with apparent seriousness in the mainstream, but occasional critics have remarked upon the hypocrisy of those who fulminate about international terrorism while sending their client armies to murder, mutilate, torture and destroy in Nicaragua and – less commonly noted, since these acts are considered a grand success – to massacre tens of thousands in El Salvador. Shortly after the Reagan-Peres discourse on peace and terror, a group of 120 doctors, nurses and other health professionals returned from an investigation in Nicaragua endorsed by the American Public Health Association and the World Health Organization, reporting the destruction of clinics and hospitals, murder of health professionals, looting of rural pharmacies leading to critical shortage of medicines, and successful disruption of a polio vaccination program, one small part of a campaign of violence organized in the centers of international terrorism in Washington and Miami.[16] *New York Times* reporters in Nicaragua match their *Pravda* colleagues in Afghanistan in their zeal to unearth or check the massive evidence of *Contra* atrocities, and this report, like many others, was ignored in the 'Newspaper of Record'.

The raid near Tunis yields a measure of the hypocrisy, which is not always easy to grasp. Suppose that Nicaragua were to carry out bombings in Washington aimed at Reagan, Shultz and other gangsters, killing some one hundred thousand people 'by accident'. This would be entirely justified retaliation by American standards, if indeed a ratio of twenty-five to one is acceptable, as in the Larnaca-Tunis exchange, though we might add for accuracy that in this case at least the perpetrators would be targeted and there is no question about who initiated the terror, and perhaps the appropriate number of deaths should be multiplied by some factor in consideration of the relative population sizes. 'Terrorists, and those who support them, must, and will, be held to account,' President Reagan has declaimed,[17] thus providing the moral basis for any such act of retaliation, with his harshest critics in the mainstream press in full accord.

Peres had already distinguished himself as a 'man of peace' in Lebanon.[18] After he became Prime Minister, Israel's 'counter-terror' programs against civilians in occupied southern Lebanon intensified, reaching their peak of savagery with the Iron Fist operations of early 1985, which had 'the earmarks of Latin American death squads', Curtis Wilkie commented, affirming reports of other journalists on the scene. In the village of Zrariya, for example, the IDF, pursuing its vocation of 'purity of arms', carried out an operation well to the north of its then-current frontline. After several hours of heavy shelling of Zrariya and three nearby villages, the IDF carted off the entire male population, killing 35-40 villagers, some in cars crushed by Israeli tanks; other villagers were beaten or simply murdered, a tank shell was fired at Red Cross workers who were warned to stay away, and Israeli troops miraculously escaped without casualties from what was officially described as a gun battle with heavily-armed guerrillas. The day before, twelve Israeli soldiers had been killed in a suicide attack near the border, but Israel denied that the attack on Zrariya was retaliation. The Israeli claim is dutifully presented as fact by apologists here, who explain that 'intelligence had established that the town had become a base for terrorists... No less than 34 Shi'ite guerrillas were killed in the gun battle and more than 100 men were taken away for questioning – from one small village' (Eric Breindel), which indicates the scale of the Shi'ite terror network. Unaware of the party line, Israeli soldiers painted the slogan 'Revenge of the Israeli Defense Forces' in Arabic on walls of the town, reporters on the scene observed.[19]

Elsewhere, Israeli gunners shot at hospitals and schools and took 'suspects', including patients in hospital beds and operating rooms, for 'interrogation' (prisoners are sometimes shot 'while trying to escape', in the familiar fashion) or to Israeli concentration camps, among numerous other atrocities that a Western diplomat who often travels in the area described as reaching new depths of 'calculated brutality and arbitrary murder'.[20]

The head of the IDF liaison unit in Lebanon, General Shlomo Ilya, 'said the only weapon against terrorism is terrorism and that Israel has options beyond those already used for "speaking the language the terrorists understand" '. The concept is not a novel one. Thus, Gestapo operations in occupied Europe also 'were justified in the name of combating "terrorism" ', and one of Klaus Barbie's victims was found murdered with a note pinned to his chest reading 'Terror against Terror'. This latter is the name adopted by an Israeli terrorist group, and provided the heading for the cover story in *Der Spiegel* on the US terror bombing of Libya in April 1986. A UN Security Council resolution calling for condemnation of 'Israeli practices and measures against the civilian population in southern Lebanon' was vetoed by the United States on the grounds that it 'applies double standards': 'We don't believe an unbalanced resolution will end the agony of Lebanon', Jeane Kirkpatrick explained.[21]

Israel's terror operations continued as its forces were compelled to withdraw by the resistance. To mention only one case, Israeli troops and their South Lebanon Army (SLA mercenaries) brought the 'year of bloody international terrorism' to an end on 31 December 1985, as they 'stormed a Shi'ite Moslem village [Kunin] in southern Lebanon and forced its entire population of about 2,000 to leave,' blowing up houses and setting others on fire and rounding up thirty-two young men; old men, women and children from the village were reported to be streaming into a town outside the Israeli 'security zone', where the UN force has a command post.[22]

This report, compiled from accounts by witnesses quoted by the Lebanese police, a journalist from the conservative Beirut journal *An Nahar*, and the Shi'ite Amal movement, is filed from Beirut. From Jerusalem, Joel Greenberg provides a different version, not on the basis of any identified sources, but as simple fact: 'villagers fearful of an SLA reprisal fled the Shi'ite village of Kunin after two SLA soldiers were slain in the village'.[23]

The difference in the two accounts, which is quite typical, is instructive. Israeli propaganda benefits greatly from the fact that the media rely overwhelmingly on Israel-based correspondents. This yields two crucial advantages: first, the 'news' is presented to the American audience through official Israeli eyes; second, on the rare occasions when US correspondents write something critical instead of simply relying on their genial hosts, the Israeli propaganda system and its numerous US affiliates can complain bitterly that Arab crimes are ignored while Israel is subjected to detailed scrutiny for any minor imperfection, given the density of reporting.

Inability to manage the news in this fashion sometimes creates problems, for example, during the 1982 Lebanon war, when Israel had no way to control the eyewitness reports by Lebanon-based journalists. This evoked a huge protest over alleged atrocity-mongering and fabrication in a 'broad-scale mass psychological war' waged against pitiful little Israel, another sign of the inveterate anti-Semitism of world opinion; Israel became the victim, not the aggressor. It is easily demonstrated that the charges are false, often merely comical, and that the media predictably bent over backwards to see things from the Israeli point of view – not an easy matter for journalists attempting to survive Israeli terror bombings. In fact, testimony from Israeli sources was often far harsher than what was reported in the US press, and what appeared in US journals was often a considerably watered-down version of what journalists actually perceived.[24] But the charges are taken very seriously despite their manifest absurdity, while accurate critique of the media for its subordination to the US-Israeli perspective and suppression of unacceptable fact is, as usual, entirely ignored. Typically, a study of 'Published Analyses of Media Coverage of the 1982 War in Lebanon' includes numerous denunciations of the press for an alleged anti-Israel stance and a few defenses of the media against these charges, but not even a reference to the fact that there were extensive, and quite accurate, critical analyses of exactly the opposite phenom-enon.[25] Within the narrow constraints of the highly ideological US intellectual climate, only the former criticism can even be heard.

The Iron Fist operations, which the Israeli command is happy to describe as 'terrorism', had two main purposes. The first, John Kifner observes (from Lebanon), was 'to turn the population against the guerrillas by making the cost of supporting them too high'; in short, to hold the population hostage to terrorist attack, unless they accept the arrangements Israel intends to impose by force. The second purpose was to exacerbate internal conflicts in Lebanon and to implement a general population exchange after intercommunal strife, much of which appears to have been incited by the occupier since 1982, in the classic manner. 'There is a great deal of evidence,' Lebanon-based correspondent Jim Muir observes, 'that the Israelis helped fuel and encourage the Christian-Druze conflict' in the Chouf region. In the south, a senior international aid official said: 'Their dirty tricks department did everything it could to stir up trouble, but it just didn't work. Their behaviour was wicked', a view 'shared by the international relief community as a whole'. 'Local eyewitnesses reported that Israeli soldiers frequently shot into the Palestinian camps from nearby Christian areas in an effort to incite the Palestinians against the Christians,' while residents in the Christian villages reported that Israeli patrols forced Christians and Muslims at gunpoint to punch one another among other forms of 'bizarre humiliation'. The techniques finally worked. Israel's Christian allies attacked Muslims near Sidon in a manner guaranteed to elicit a response from considerably more powerful forces, initiating a bloody cycle of violence that ultimately led to the flight of tens of thousands of Christians, many to the Israeli-dominated regions in the south, while tens of thousands of Shi'ites were driven north by the Iron Fist operations.[26]

The pretense in the United States was that Israel was always planning to withdraw and that the Shi'ite terrorists were simply indulging in the usual Arab pleasure in violence for its own sake, delaying the planned withdrawal. But as Jim Muir correctly observes, 'it is a historical fact beyond serious dispute that the Israelis would not be withdrawing now were it not for the attacks and the casualties they have caused'. The extent of the withdrawal would be determined by the intensity of the resistance.[27]

The Israeli high command explained that the victims of the

Iron Fist operations were 'terrorist villagers'; it was thus understandable that thirteen of them were massacred by SLA militiamen in the incident that elicited this observation. Yossi Olmert of the Shiloah Institute, Israel's Institute of Strategic Studies, observed that 'these terrorists operate with the support of most of the local population'. An Israeli commander complained that 'the terrorist . . . has many eyes here, because he lives here', while the military correspondent of the *Jerusalem Post* described the problems faced in combating the 'terrorist mercenary', 'fanatics, all of whom are sufficiently dedicated to their causes to go on running the risk of being killed while operating against the IDF', which must 'maintain order and security' despite 'the price the inhabitants will have to pay', arousing his 'admiration for the way in which they were doing their job'. Leon Wieseltier explained the difference between 'Shi'ite terrorism' against the occupying army and Palestinian terrorism, each a manifestation of the evil Arab nature: 'The Palestinians had murderers who wished to kill. The Shiites have murderers who wish to die', conducting actions 'inspired by a chiliastic demand of the world for which there can be no merely political or diplomatic satisfaction' – nothing so simple as removing the occupying army from their land. Rather, their 'secret army' Amal has been 'consecrated' to 'the destruction of Israel' since its founding in 1975 – perfect nonsense, needless to say, which goes well beyond the tales concocted by his mentors.[28]

The same concept of terrorism is widely used by US officials and commentators. Thus the press reports, without comment, that Secretary of State Shultz's concern over 'international terrorism' became 'his passion' after the suicide bombing of US Marines in Lebanon in October 1983, troops that much of the population saw, quite naturally, as a foreign military force sent to impose the 'New Order' established by the Israeli aggression. Barry Rubin writes that 'The most important use of Syrian-sponsored terrorism within Lebanon was to force the withdrawal of Israeli troops and US Marines', while both Iran and Syria have supported 'terrorist activity' by 'Shi'ite extremist groups' in southern Lebanon, such as attacks on 'the Israeli-backed South Lebanese army'. In the view of the apologist for state terror, resistance to an occupying army or its local mercenaries is terrorism, meriting harsh reprisal. The *New York Times* Israel correspondent Thomas Friedman routinely describes attacks in southern Lebanon directed against Israeli forces as 'terrorist bombings' or 'suicide terrorism', which, he assures us, is the product of 'psychological weaknesses or religious fervor'. He reports further that residents of Israel's 'security zone' who violate the rules established by the occupiers are 'shot on the spot, with questions asked later. Some of those shot have been innocent bystanders.' But this practice is not state terrorism. He also notes that Israel 'has taken great pains to limit the flow of news out of the area'; 'No reporters have been allowed to cover the aftermaths of suicide attacks, and virtually no information is released about them.' This fact does not prevent him from reporting with much confidence about the background and motives of those designated 'terrorists' by the occupiers.[29]

As Reagan and Peres were congratulating one another on their principled stand against 'the evil of terrorism' before their admiring audience, the press reported yet another terrorist act in southern Lebanon: 'Terrorists Kill 6, Demolish US-Owned Christian Radio Station in S. Lebanon', the headlines read on the same day.[30] Why should Lebanese terrorists destroy 'the Voice of Hope', run by American Christian missionaries? The question was barely raised, but let us look into it, in the interest of clarifying the concepts of terrorism and retaliation.

One reason is that the station 'speaks for the South Lebanon Army',[31] the mercenary force established by Israel in southern Lebanon to terrorize the population in its 'security zone'. The location of the station, near the village of Khiam, is also worthy of note. Khiam has a history, unknown here. Ze'ev Schiff alluded to this history in the midst of Peres's Iron Fist operations. He observed that when Israel invaded Lebanon in 1982, the village of Khiam was 'empty of inhabitants', though now it has ten thousand, and that the Lebanese town of Nabatiya had only five thousand inhabitants, today fifty thousand. 'These and others will once again be forced to abandon their homes if they permit extremists in their community or Palestinians to attack Israeli settlements,' Schiff explained.[32] That will be their fate if they mimic the IDF, which was then attacking Lebanese villages, randomly murdering civilians and destroying property in defense against the 'terrorism [that] has not disappeared' as 'Israeli soldiers are harassed daily in southern Lebanon'.[33]

For the Lebanese to whom the warning was addressed, and for at least some better-informed elements of his Israeli audience, Schiff did not have to explain why the population of Nabatiya had been reduced to five thousand and Khiam emptied by 1982. The population had been driven out, with hundreds killed, by Israeli terror bombardment from the early 1970s, and the handful who remained in Khiam were slaughtered during the 1978 invasion of

Lebanon, under the eyes of the elite Golani brigade, by Israel's Haddad militia, which 'succeeded in establishing relative peace in the region and preventing the return of PLO terrorists', the man of peace explained.[34] Khiam is also the site of a 'secret jail' maintained by 'Israel and its local militia allies in south Lebanon . . . where detainees are held in appalling conditions and subjected to beatings and electric-shock torture, according to former inmates and international relief officials in the area'. The Red Cross reported that 'Israelis were running the center' and that it had been refused entry by the IDF.[35]

There might have been more to say, then, about the terrorist attack by 'fanatics' at Khiam on 17 October 1985, were matters such as these considered fit to become part of historical memory alongside other acts of terror of greater ideological serviceability.

Nabatiya, too, has further stories to tell. The flight of 80 per cent of its population 'mostly because of fear of the [Israeli] shelling' was reported by two *Jerusalem Post* correspondents who were touring southern Lebanon in an effort to unearth evidence of PLO terror and atrocities, finding little, though there was ample evidence of Israeli terror and its effects.[36] One such bombardment was on 4 November 1977, when Nabatiya 'came under heavy artillery fire from [Israeli-supported] Lebanese Maronite positions and also from Israeli batteries on both sides of the frontier – including some of the six Israeli strongpoints inside Lebanon'. The attacks continued the next day, with three women killed among other casualties. On 6 November two rockets fired by Fatah guerrillas killed two Israelis in Nahariya, setting off an artillery battle and a second rocket attack that killed one Israeli. 'Then came the Israeli air raids in which some 70 people, nearly all Lebanese, were killed.'[37] This Israeli-initiated exchange, which threatened to lead to a major war, was cited by Egyptian President Sadat as a reason for his offer to visit Jerusalem a few days later.[38]

These events have entered historical memory in a different form, however, not only in journalism but also in scholarship: 'in an effort to disrupt the movement towards a peace conference,' Edward Haley writes on the basis of no evidence, 'the PLO fired Katyusha rockets into the northern Israeli village of Nahariya, on 6 and 8 November, killing three', and eliciting 'the inevitable Israeli reprisal' on 9 November, with over 100 killed in attacks 'in and around Tyre and two small towns to the south'.[39] As is the rule in properly sanitized history, Palestinians carry out terrorism, Israelis then retaliate, perhaps too harshly. In the real world, the truth is often rather different. It is this rather messier truth which must be confronted before we can fully comprehend terrorism in the Middle East.

The torment of Nabatiya was rarely noted by the Western press, though there are a few exceptions. One of the Israeli attacks was on 2 December 1975, when the Israeli air force bombed the town killing many Lebanese and Palestinian civilians, using antipersonnel weapons, bombs and rockets.[40] This raid, unusual in that it was reported, aroused no interest or concern in civilized circles, perhaps because it was apparently a 'retaliation': namely, retaliation against the UN Security Council, which had just agreed to devote a session to a peace offer by Syria, Jordan and Egypt – supported by the PLO and even 'prepared' by the PLO according to Israel's then UN representative Chaim Herzog – calling for a two-state settlement on the internationally recognized borders. The US predictably vetoed the resolution.[41] All of this has largely been eliminated from history, both in journalism and scholarship.[42]

The story continues today, with little change. In early 1986, while the eyes of the world were focused in horror on the terrorists in the Arab world, the press reported that Israeli tank cannon poured fire into the village of Sreifa in southern Lebanon, aiming at thirty houses from which the IDF claimed they had been fired upon by 'armed terrorists' resisting their military actions in the course of what they described as a search for two Israeli soldiers who had been 'kidnapped' in the Israeli 'security zone' in Lebanon. Largely kept from the American press was the report by the UN peace-keeping forces that Israeli troops 'went really crazy' in these operations, locking up entire villages, preventing the UN troops from sending in water, milk and oranges to the villagers, subjected to 'interrogation' – meaning brutal torture of men and women by Israeli forces and their local mercenaries. The IDF then departed, taking away many villagers including pregnant women, some brought to Israel in further violation of international law, levelling houses and looting and wrecking others, while Shimon Peres said that Israel's search 'expresses our attitude towards the value of human life and dignity'.[43]

A month later, on 24 March, Lebanese radio reported that Israeli forces, either IDF or SLA mercenaries, shelled Nabatiya killing three civilians and wounding twenty-two as 'shells slammed into the marketplace in the center of town at daybreak as crowds gathered for trading', allegedly in retaliation for an attack on Israel's mercenary forces in southern Lebanon. A leader of the Shi'ite Amal vowed that 'Israeli settlements and installations will not be beyond the blows of the resistance'. On 27 March, a

Katyusha rocket struck a schoolyard in northern Israel, injuring five people, and eliciting an Israeli attack on Palestinian refugee camps near Sidon, killing ten people and wounding twenty-two, while Israel's northern commander stated over Israeli army radio that the IDF had not determined whether the rocket had been fired by Shi'ite or Palestinian guerrillas. On 7 April, Israeli planes bombed the same camps and a neighboring village, killing two and wounding twenty, claiming that terrorists had set out from there with the intent of killing Israeli citizens.[44]

Of all these events, only the rocket attack on northern Israel merited anguished TV coverage and general outrage at 'the evil scourge of terrorism', though this was somewhat muted because of the mass hysteria then being orchestrated over a Nicaraguan 'invasion' of Honduras, as the Nicaraguan army exercised its legal right of hot pursuit in driving out of its territory terrorist gangs dispatched by their US directors in a show of force just prior to the Senate vote on Contra aid; recall that the only serious issue under debate in the terrorist state is whether the Contras can succeed in their aims. Israel, of course, was not exercising a legal right of hot pursuit in shelling and bombing towns and refugee camps, nor have its acts of wholesale terrorism and outright aggression in Lebanon ever fallen under this concept. But as a client state, Israel inherits from its master the 'right' of terrorism, torture and aggression. Nicaragua, as an enemy, plainly lacks the right to defend its territory from US international terrorism, though one might argue that US actions there reach the level of aggression, a war crime of the category for which people were hanged at Nuremberg and Tokyo. Consequently, it is natural that Israel's actions should be ignored, or dismissed as legitimate 'retaliation', while Congress, across the narrow spectrum, denounced the 'Nicaraguan Marxists' for this renewed demonstration of the threat they pose to regional peace and stability.

The Israeli invasion of Lebanon in June 1982 is also regularly presented in properly sanitized form. Shimon Peres writes that the 'Peace for Galilee' operation was fought 'in order to ensure that the Galilee will no longer be shelled by Katyusha rockets'. Eric Breindel explains that 'of course, the principal aim of the Israeli invasion in 1982' was 'to protect the Galilee region ... from Katyusha-rocket attacks and other shelling from Lebanon'. The news pages of the *New York Times* inform us that the invasion began 'after attacks by Palestine Liberation Organization guerrillas on Israel's northern settlements', and (without comment) that Israeli leaders 'said they wanted to end the rocket and shelling attacks on Israel's northern border', which 'has been accomplished for the three years the Israeli Army has spent in Lebanon'. Henry Kamm adds that 'for nearly three years, the people of Qiryat Shemona have not slept in their bomb shelters, and parents have not worried when their children went out to school or to play. The Soviet-made Katyusha rockets, which for many years struck this town near the Lebanese border at random intervals, have not fallen since Israel invaded Lebanon in June 1982.' And Thomas Friedman observes that 'If rockets again rain down on Israel's northern border after all that has been expended on Lebanon, the Israeli public will be outraged'; 'right now there are no rockets landing in northern Israel . . . and if large-scale attacks begin afresh on Israel's northern border that minority [that favors keeping the army in Lebanon] could grow into a majority again.' 'Operation Peace for Galilee – the Israeli invasion of Lebanon – was originally undertaken' to protect the civilian population from Palestinian gunners, Friedman reports in one of the numerous human interest stories on the travail of the suffering Israelis. Political figures regularly expound the same doctrine. Zbigniew Brzezinski writes that 'the increased Syrian military presence and the use of Lebanon by the Palestine Liberation Organization for incursions against Israel precipitated the Israeli invasion last year'. Ronald Reagan, in a typical display of moral cowardice, asks us to 'remember that when this [the invasion] all started, Israel, because of the violations of its own northern border by the Palestinians, the PLO, had gone all the way to Beirut', where it was '10,000 Palestinians [!] who had been bringing ruin down on Beirut', not the mad bombers whom he was joyously supporting.[45] These and innumerable other accounts, many with heartrending descriptions of the torment of the people of the Galilee subjected to random Katyusha bombardment, help create the approved picture of Soviet-armed Palestinian fanatics, the central component of the Russian-based international terror network, who compel Israel to invade and strike Palestinian refugee camps and other targets, as any state would do, to defend its people from merciless terrorist attack.

The real world, of course, is rather different. David Shipler writes that 'In the four years between the previous Israeli invasion of southern Lebanon in 1978, and the invasion of 6 June 1982, a total of 29 people were killed in northern Israel in all forms of attacks from Lebanon, including shelling and border crossings by terrorists,' but that for a year before the 1982 invasion, 'the border was quiet'.[46] This report has the merit of approaching at least half-truth. While the PLO refrained from cross-border actions for a year prior to the Israeli invasion, the border was far from quiet, since Israeli terror continued, killing many civilians; the border was 'quiet' only in the racist terms of US discourse. Nor do Shipler and his associates recall that while twenty-nine people were killed in northern Israel from 1978, thousands were killed by Israeli bombardments in Lebanon, barely noted here, and in no sense 'retaliatory'.

The bombardments from 1978 were a central element of the Camp David 'peace process', which, quite predictably, freed Israel to extend its takeover and repression in the occupied territories while attacking its northern neighbor, with the main Arab deterrent (Egypt) now removed from the conflict and US military support rapidly increasing.[47] The PLO observed the US-arranged cease-fire of July 1981, despite repeated Israeli efforts to evoke some action that could be used as a pretext for the planned invasion, including bombardment in late April 1982 killing two dozen people, sinking of fishing boats, etc. The only exceptions were a light retaliation in May after Israeli bombardment, and the response to heavy Israeli bombing and ground attacks in Lebanon in June that caused many civilian casualties. The Israeli attacks were in 'retaliation' for the attempted assassination of the Israeli ambassador in London by Abu Nidal, a sworn enemy of the PLO who did not even have an office in Lebanon – again, the familiar story of 'retaliation'. It was this assassination attempt that was used as the pretext for the long-planned invasion.

The *New Republic* tells us that the successes of UN negotiator Brian Urquhart 'have been minor, somehow forgettable: his negotiations of a PLO cease-fire [sic] in southern Lebanon in 1981, for instance'.[48] That strict 'party line' journals should prefer to 'forget' the facts is not surprising, but the prevalence of such convenient lapses of memory is noteworthy.

Furthermore, a look at what happened in July 1981 reveals the same pattern. On 28 May, Ze'ev Schiff and Ehud Ya'ari write, Prime Minister Menachem Begin and Chief-of-Staff Rafael Eitan 'took another step that would bring their country appreciably closer to a war in Lebanon with an action that was essentially calculated towards that end': they broke the cease-fire with bombing of 'PLO concentrations' (a term of newspeak, referring to any target Israel chooses to hit) in southern Lebanon. The attacks continued from air and sea until 2 June, Schiff and Ya'ari continue, while 'the Palestinians responded gingerly for fear that a vigorous reaction would only provoke a crushing Israeli ground operation'. A cease-fire was again established, broken again by Israel on 10 July with renewed bombardments. This time there was a Palestinian reaction, with rocket attacks that caused panic in the northern Galilee followed by heavy Israeli bombing of Beirut and other civilian targets. By the time a cease-fire was declared on 24 July, some 450 Arabs – nearly all Lebanese civilians – and six Israelis were killed.[49]

Of this story, all that is remembered is the torment of the northern Galilee, subjected to random Katyusha bombing by PLO terrorists that finally provoked Israel to retaliate in its June 1982 invasion of Lebanon. This is true even of serious journalists who do not simply provide a pipeline for official propaganda. Edward Walsh writes that 'the repeated rocket attacks in 1981 had put [Qiryat Shemona] once again under siege', describing the 'distraught parents' and the terror caused by 'the pounding of artillery and rocket barrages from the nearby Palestinian bases' in 1981, with no further word on what was happening. Curtis Wilkie, one of the more skeptical and perceptive of American journalists in the Middle East, writes that Qiryat Shemona 'came under withering fire from Palestinian Liberation Organization forces in 1981; the rain of Soviet-made Katyusha rockets was so intense at one point that those residents who had not fled were forced to spend eight consecutive days and nights in bomb shelters', again, with no further word on the reasons for this 'withering fire' or on the mood in Beirut and other civilian areas where hundreds were killed in the murderous Israeli bombardment. Nor were these matters raised elsewhere.[50] The example gives some further insight into the concept of 'terrorism' and 'retaliation', as conceived within the US ideological system, and into the racist assumptions which, as a matter of course, exclude the suffering of the primary victims, who are Arab and hence less than human.

The official story that 'the rocket and shelling attacks on Israel's northern border' were ended thanks to the 'Peace for Galilee' (as the NYT version has it) is doubly false. First, the border was quiet for a year prior to the invasion apart from Israeli terror attacks and provocations, and the major rocket attacks, in July 1981, were a response to Israeli terror which exacted a toll almost a hundred times greater than the PLO response in this incident alone. Second, in sharp contrast to the preceding period, rocket attacks began shortly after the invasion ended, from early 1983, and have continued since. A group of dissident Israeli journalists report that in two weeks of September 1985, fourteen Katyusha rockets were fired at the Galilee. Furthermore, 'terrorist attacks' increased by 50% in the West Bank in the months following the war, and by the end of 1983 had increased by 70% since the war in Lebanon, becoming a severe threat by 1985 – not a surprising outcome in view of the savage atrocities and the destruction of the civil society and political system of the Palestinians.[51]

The real reason for the 1982 invasion was not the threat to the northern Galilee, as the sanitized history would have it, but rather the opposite, as was plausibly explained by Israel's leading specialist on the Palestinians, Hebrew University Professor Yehoshua Porath (a 'moderate' in Israeli parlance, who supports the Labor Party's 'Jordanian solution' for the Palestinians), shortly after the invasion was launched. The decision to invade, he suggests, 'flowed from the very fact that the cease-fire had been observed'. This was a 'veritable catastrophe' for the Israeli government, because it threatened the policy of evading a political settlement. 'The government's hope,' he continued, 'is that the stricken PLO, lacking a logistic and territorial base, will return to its earlier terrorism; it will carry out bombings throughout the world, hijack airplanes, and murder many Israelis,' and thus 'will lose part of the political legitimacy it has gained' and 'undercut the danger' of negotiations with representative Palestinians, which would threaten the policy – shared by both major political groupings – of keeping effective control over the occupied territories.[52] The plausible assumption of the Israeli leadership was that those who shape public opinion in the United States – the only country that counts, now that Israel has chosen to become a mercenary state serving the interests of its provider – could be counted on to obliterate the actual history and portray the terrorist acts resulting from Israeli aggression and atrocities as random acts of violence ascribable to defects in Arab character and culture, if not racial deficiencies. Subsequent US commentary on terrorism fulfills these natural expectations with absolute precision, thus securing the propaganda objectives for state terrorists in Jerusalem and Washington.

The basic points are understood well enough in Israel. Prime Minister Yitzhak Shamir observed on Israeli television that Israel went to war because there was 'a terrible danger. . . Not so much a military one as a political one,' prompting the fine Israeli satirist B. Michael to write that 'the lame excuse of a military danger or a danger to the Galilee is dead', we 'have removed the political danger' by striking first, in time; now, 'Thank God, there is no one to talk to.' Columnist Aaron Bachar comments that 'it is easy to understand the mood of the Israeli leadership. Arafat has been accused of steadily moving towards some kind of political accommodation with Israel' and 'in the eyes of the Israeli Administration, this is the worst possible threat' – including Labor as well as Likud. Benny Morris observes that 'the PLO held its fire along the northern border for a whole year, on a number of occasions omitting completely to react to Israeli actions (designed specifically to draw PLO fire on the North)', commenting further that for the senior IDF officers, 'the war's inevitability rests on the PLO as a political threat to Israel and to Israel's hold on the occupied territories', since 'Palestinian hopes inside and outside the occupied territories for the maturation of nationalist aspirations rested on and revolved about the PLO.' Like every sane commentator, he ridicules the hysterical talk about captured weapons and the PLO military threat, and predicts that 'the Shi'ites of West Beirut, many of them refugees from previous Israeli bombardments of Southern Lebanon in the 1970s, will probably remember the IDF siege of June–August [1982] for a long time', with long-term repercussions in 'Shi'ite terrorism against Israeli targets'.[53]

On the right wing, Likud Knesset member Ehud Olmert commented that 'the danger posed by the PLO to Israel did not lie in its extremism, but in the fictitious moderation Arafat managed to display without ever losing sight of his ultimate aim, which is the destruction of Israel' (arguably true, in the sense in which David Ben-Gurion, while in power, never lost sight of his ultimate aim of expanding to 'the limits of Zionist aspirations', including much of the surrounding countries and on some occasions, the 'biblical borders' from the Nile to Iraq, while the native population would somehow be transferred). Former West Bank administrator Professor Menachem Milson states that 'it is a mistake to think that the threat to Israel represented by the PLO is essentially a military one; rather, it is a political and ideological one'. Defense Minister Ariel Sharon explained just before the invasion that 'quiet on the West Bank' requires 'the destruction of the PLO in Lebanon'. His ultra-right cohort, Chief of Staff Rafael Eitan, commented afterwards that the war was a success, because it severely weakened 'the political status' of the PLO and 'the struggle of the PLO for a Palestinian state' while enforcing Israel's capacity 'to block any such purpose'. Commenting on these statements, Israeli military historian Uri Milshtein (a supporter of Labor's 'Jordanian solution') observes that among the goals of the invasion in the Sharon-Eitan conception were 'to establish a New Order in Lebanon and the Middle East', 'to advance the process of

Sadatization in several Arab states', 'to guarantee the annexation of Judea and Samaria [the West Bank] to the state of Israel', and 'perhaps a solution of the Palestinian problem'. At the other end of the political spectrum, Knesset Member Amnon Rubinstein, much admired in the US for his liberal and dovish stance, writes that even though the cease-fire had been observed 'more or less', nevertheless the invasion of Lebanon was 'justified' because of a potential, not actual military threat: the arms and ammunition in southern Lebanon were intended for eventual use against Israel. Consider the implications of this astonishing argument in other contexts, even if we were to take seriously the claims about a potential PLO military threat to Israel.[54]

Note that Rubinstein anticipated the interesting doctrine enunciated by the Reagan Administration in justifying its April 1986 bombing of Libya in 'self-defense against future attack', a right that not even Hitler claimed, but that the US government had the gall to describe as in accord with the UN Charter, to much applause from left-liberal critics for this new departure in international lawlessness.[55]

American apologists for Israeli atrocities occasionally acknowledge the same truths. Just before the invasion, *New Republic* editor Martin Peretz, echoing Sharon and Eitan, urged that Israel should administer to the PLO a 'lasting military defeat' in Lebanon that 'will clarify to the Palestinians in the West Bank that their struggle for an independent state has suffered a setback of many years', so that 'the Palestinians will be turned into just another crushed nation, like the Kurds or the Afghans'. And Democratic Socialist Michael Walzer, who sees the solution for Palestinian Arabs – within Israel as well – in transfer of those 'marginal to the nation' (essentially, the position of the racist Rabbi Kahane), explained in the *New Republic* after the war that 'I certainly welcome the political *defeat* of the PLO, and I believe that the limited military operation required to inflict that defeat can be defended under the theory of just war'.[56]

In short, the goals of the war were political, the occupied territories being one prime target, the 'New Order' in Lebanon (and perhaps beyond) another. The tale about protecting the border from terrorism is Agitprop, eagerly swallowed by the docile US media. If Palestinian terrorism can be revived, so much the better. And if we can't pin the blame on Arafat, he can at least be stigmatized as 'the founding father of contemporary Palestinian violence', so that his efforts at political settlement can be evaded.

The problem of evading a political settlement did not end with the destruction of the political base for the PLO, as had been hoped, so the US media must remain vigilant to combat the threat and defend the doctrinal truth that the US and Israel seek peace but are blocked by Arab rejectionism. Thus, in April-May 1984, Arafat made a series of statements in Europe and Asia calling for negotiations with Israel leading to mutual recognition. The offer was immediately rejected by Israel. A UPI story on Arafat's proposals was featured in the *San Francisco Examiner*, and the facts were reported without prominence in the local quality press. The national press suppressed the story outright, apart from a bare mention in the *Washington Post* some weeks later. The *New York Times* refused to publish a word and even banned letters on the topic, while continuing (along with the media in general) to denounce Arafat for his unwillingness to pursue a diplomatic course. In general, the more significant the journal, the more it was determined to suppress the facts.[57]

In a suitably anguished article on 'extremism' and its successes in the Middle East, the *New York Times* Israel correspondent Thomas Friedman writes that 'Extremists have always been much better at exploiting the media'. He is quite right; Israel and the US have shown unparalleled mastery of this art, as his own articles and news reports indicate – leading some to wonder whether he should not be called 'Israel's *Times* correspondent'.[58] Under the term 'extremist' he does not include those who are responsible for the large majority of terrorist operations and who reject negotiations leading to mutual recognition and a political settlement in accord with the international consensus. Rather, those who advocate such a political settlement are the 'extremists' who stand in the way of peace, while the US and its Israeli ally, with their extreme rejectionism, are by definition the 'moderates'. In adopting this conceptual framework so as to exclude any possible comprehension of the facts and issues, the *New York Times* follows closely its Israeli mentors, for example, Yitzhak Rabin, a leading Israeli 'moderate' in *NYT* parlance, who explains that the aim of 'the Palestinian extremists (basically the PLO) is to create a sovereign Palestinian state in the West Bank and the Gaza Strip'. Naturally, then, when Friedman reviews 'Two Decades of Seeking Peace in the Mideast', the major Arab proposals rejected by the US and Israel are omitted, as inappropriate for the historical record. Meanwhile the Israeli leaders are praised for their 'healthy pragmatism' while the PLO is denounced for standing in the way of peace.[59]

Knowledgeable Israelis are of course aware of Arafat's stand.

Former chief of military intelligence Yehoshaphat Harkabi, an Arabist and well-known hawk for many years, notes that 'the PLO wishes a political settlement because it knows that the alternative is terrible and will lead to total destruction'. 'Arafat, like Hussein and the Arabs of the West Bank, is afraid that if there will not be a settlement, Israel will explode, and with it all its neighbors, including the Palestinians.' Therefore 'Arafat adopts relatively moderate positions with regard to Israel'.[60]

These observations underscore several points: 1) there is a crucial political context in which terrorism must be understood, if we are to be serious about it; 2) it is the other fellow's crimes, not our own comparable or worse ones, that constitute 'terrorism' – in this case, Palestinian but not Israeli or American crimes; 3) the concepts of 'terrorism' and 'retaliation' are used as terms of propaganda, not description. Crucially, the hysteria evoked over carefully selected acts of terrorism – those by Arabs, whether Palestinians, Lebanese Shi'ites, Libyans, Syrians, or even Iranians, who can count as Arabs for this purpose – is designed to achieve certain specific political goals. A further inquiry reinforces these conclusions.

Consider again the matter of retaliation. The first rocket attack by Shi'ites against Qiryat Shemona itself was in December 1985, after over three years of a military occupation of extreme brutality, which reached its peak during the Iron Fist operations under Shimon Peres in early 1985. But the occasionally reported savagery of the occupiers fails to convey anything like the full story, since it ignores the day-to-day reality; the same is true of the occasional reporting of Israeli atrocities in the occupied territories, which fails to convey the true picture of brutal degradation, repression, exploitation of cheap (including child) labor, harsh control over political and cultural life and curtailment of economic development. A more instructive picture is given by Julie Flint, recounting 'the story of life, and death, in one southern Lebanese village' of Shi'ites a month before the rocket attack. Kfar Roummane had been 'a prosperous agricultural town of 8,000 people' near Nabatiya during the period when, according to the official history, southern Lebanon was subjected to PLO terror. After what the *New York Times* called its 'liberation' from PLO rule, it was surrounded by 'two huge fortifications built by the Israelis and their Lebanese proxy, the South Lebanon Army', from which there is constant sniping and shelling, 'sometimes from dawn to dusk, sometimes only for a few hours', with many casualties, leading to the flight of six thousand people and leaving three-fourths of the town uninhabitable in this 'dying village' where there is no sign of resistance activities, and little likelihood of it among the apolitical farmers on a bare expanse of flat hillside.[61] Was the shelling of Qiryat Shemona 'terrorism' or 'retaliation', even putting aside the murderous atrocities of the Peres-Rabin Iron Fist operations?

A look at the lives of the terrorists is also instructive. One was interviewed by the *Washington Post* in a five-part series on terrorism. Serving an eighteen-year sentence in an Israeli jail, he was chosen as 'in many ways typical of terrorists now in jail from London to Kuwait'. 'In his life, a personal tragedy (the death of his father in a bomb blast in Jerusalem in 1947) combined with the discovery of a system of belief (Marxism) to plunge him into a world of cold-blooded political murder.' 'The bomb that killed his father and more than 90 other persons was set by the Irgun Zionist underground group, led by Menachem Begin, at British military headquarters in what is now the King David Hotel' – as it was then.[62] He 'was introduced to Marxism, he said, by the "reality" of conditions in Palestinian camps' in the occupied West Bank. The 'reality' of the occupied territories, not only in the camps, is bitter and cruel, contrary to what is reported in editorial pages of the nation's press, where we can learn that the occupation was 'a model of future cooperation' and an 'experiment in Arab-Israeli coexistence'.[63] To explain is not to justify, but plainly some questions arise about the easy use of such terms as 'retaliation.'

Or consider Suleiman Khater, the Egyptian soldier who murdered seven Israeli tourists on a Sinai beach on 5 October 1985. The Egyptian press reported that his mother said she was 'happy that these Jews had died', and a doctor in his village of Baher al-Bakr described the shootings as a warning against the 'illusory peace' between Egypt and Israel. Why this shocking reaction to an unspeakable crime? The Tunis bombing a few days earlier might be one reason, but there are others. In 1970, Israeli warplanes bombed Baher al-Bakr, killing forty-seven school-children, during the 'war of attrition', when extensive Israeli bombing, some deep inside Egypt, drove a million and a half civilians from the Suez Canal area, threatening general war when Soviet-piloted MIGs defending inner Egypt were shot down by newly-acquired Phantom jets over Egyptian territory.[64] Something is missing, then, when the *New York Times* Israel correspondent blandly reports that Khater 'acted out of motives that were nationalist and anti-Israel'[65] – something that would surely not have been ignored had the situation been reversed.

The PLO claimed that the three Israelis murdered on the yacht in Larnaca had been involved in Israeli hijacking of ships travelling from Cyprus to Lebanon; Israeli journalist David Shaham, however, identifies them as Israeli doves, known for their pro-Arab sympathies.[66]

Let us assume Shaham to be correct.[67] There is, however, no doubt that Israel has been carrying out hijacking operations and kidnapping at sea for many years, with little notice and no concern in the US over this crime, which arouses great passion and anger when the perpetrators are Arabs. In 1976, according to Knesset member (General, retired) Mattityahu Peled, the Israeli Navy began to capture boats belonging to Lebanese Moslems, turning them over to Israel's Lebanese Christian allies (who typically killed the crews) in an effort to abort attempts at conciliation between the PLO and Israel. Prime Minister Rabin conceded the facts but said that the boats were captured prior to these arrangements, while Defense Minister Shimon Peres refused to comment. After a prisoner exchange in November 1983, a front-page story in the *New York Times* mentioned in its eighteenth paragraph that thirty-seven of the Arab prisoners, who had been held at the notorious Ansar prison camp, 'had been seized recently by the Israeli Navy as they tried to make their way from Cyprus to Tripoli', north of Beirut, an observation that merited no comment there or elsewhere.[68]

In June 1984, Israel hijacked a ferryboat operating between Cyprus and Lebanon five miles off the Lebanese coast and forced it to Haifa, where nine people were removed and held, eight Lebanese and the ninth Syrian. Five were freed after interrogation and four held, including one woman and a schoolboy returning from England for a holiday in Beirut; two were released two weeks later, while the fate of the others remains unreported. The matter was considered so insignificant that one has to search for tiny items in the back pages even to learn this much about the fate of the kidnapped passengers. The London *Observer* suggested a 'political motive': to compel passengers to use the ferry operating from the Maronite port of Jounieh instead of Moslem West Beirut or to signal to the Lebanese that they are 'powerless' and must come to terms with Israel. Lebanon denounced this 'act of piracy', which Godfrey Jansen described as 'another item' in Israel's 'long list of international thuggery'. 'To maintain the maritime terrorist fiction,' he adds, 'the Israelis then bombed and bombarded a small island off Tripoli which was said to be a base for PLO seaborne operations,' a claim that he dismisses as 'absurd'. The Lebanese police reported that fifteen were killed, twenty wounded and twenty missing, all Lebanese, fishermen and children at a Sunni boy scout camp which was the 'worst hit' target.[69]

In its report on the Israeli 'interception' of the ferryboat, the *New York Times* observes that prior to the 1982 war, 'the Israeli Navy regularly intercepted ships bound for or leaving the ports of Tyre and Sidon in the south and searched them for guerrillas', as usual accepting Israeli claims at face value; PLO 'interception' of civilian Israeli ships on a similar pretext might be regarded a bit differently. Similarly, Israel's hijacking of a Libyan civilian jet on 4 February 1986 was accepted with equanimity, criticized, if at all, as an error based on faulty intelligence.[70] On 25 April 1985, several Palestinians were kidnapped from civilian boats operating between Lebanon and Cyprus and sent to secret destinations in Israel, a fact that became public knowledge (in Israel) when one was interviewed on Israeli television, leading to an appeal to the High Court of Justice for information; presumably there are others, unknown.[71]

None of these cases, most of them known only through incidental comment, arouses any interest or concern, any more than when it is reported in passing that Arab 'security prisoners' released in an exchange with Syria were in fact 'Druze residents of villages in the Israeli-annexed portion of the strategic Golan Heights'.[72] It is considered Israel's prerogative to carry out hijacking of ships and kidnappings, at will, as well as bombardment of what it will call 'terrorist targets' with the approval of articulate opinion in the United States, whatever the facts may be.

We might tarry a moment over the Israeli attack on the island off Tripoli north of Beirut, in which Lebanese fishermen and boy scouts at a camp were killed. This received scant notice, but that is the norm in the case of such regular Israeli terrorist atrocities, of which this is far from the most serious. Palestinian attacks fare differently. None is remembered with more horror than the atrocity at Ma'alot in 1974, where twenty-two members of a paramilitary youth group were killed in an exchange of fire after Moshe Dayan had refused, over the objections of General Mordechai Gur, to consider negotiations on the terrorists' demands for the release of Palestinian prisoners.[73] One might ask why the murder of Lebanese boy scouts is a lesser atrocity – or rather, no atrocity at all, since it was perpetuated by 'a country that cares for human life' (*Washington Post*), whose 'high moral purpose' (*Time*) is the object of never-ending awe and acclaim, a country which, according to its American propaganda chorus, 'is held to a higher law, as interpreted for it by journalists' (Walter Goodman).[74]

Two days before the Ma'alot attack, Israeli jets had bombed the Lebanese village of El-Kfeir, killing four civilians. According to Edward Said, the Ma'alot attack was 'preceded by weeks of sustained Israeli napalm bombing of Palestinian refugee camps in southern Lebanon' with over two hundred killed. At the time, Israel was engaged in large-scale scorched earth operations in southern Lebanon with air, artillery and gunboat attacks and commando operations using shells, bombs, antipersonnel weapons and napalm, with probably thousands killed (the West could not be troubled, so no accurate figures are available here) and hundreds of thousands driven north to slums around Beirut.[75] Interest was slight and reporting scanty. None of this is recorded in the annals of terrorism; nor did it even happen, as far as sanitized history is concerned, though the murderous Palestinian terrorist attacks of the early 1970s were (rightly of course) bitterly condemned, and still stand as proof that the Palestinians cannot be a partner to negotiations over their fate. Meanwhile the media are regularly condemned as overly critical of Israel and even 'pro-PLO', a propaganda coup of quite monumental proportions; the fact that these charges can be voiced without ridicule in itself reveals the extraordinary commitment of the American intellectual establishment to US-Israeli rejectionism and violence.

We might note the interpretation of these events offered by Israeli leaders honoured here as 'moderates', for example Yitzhak Rabin, who was Ambassador to Washington and then Prime Minister during the period of the worst Israeli atrocities in Lebanon, pre-Camp David: 'We could not ignore the plight of the civil population in southern Lebanon. . . It was our humanitarian duty to aid the population of the area and prevent it from being wiped out by the hostile terrorists'.[76] Reviewers of Rabin's memoirs, where these words appear, found nothing amiss in them, so effectively has an ideologically serviceable history been constructed, and so profound is anti-Arab racism in the West.

Israel is not alone in enjoying the right of piracy and hijacking. A Tass report condemning the *Achille Lauro* hijacking in October 1985 accused the United States of hypocrisy because two men who hijacked a Soviet airliner, killing a stewardess and wounding other crew members, were given refuge in the US, which refused extradition.[77] The case is not exactly well-known, and the charge of hypocrisy might appear to have a certain merit. One might also mention the first airplane hijacking in the Middle East, which is also not familiar fare. It was carried out by Israel in December 1954, when a Syrian Airways civilian jet was intercepted by Israeli fighters and forced to land at Lydda airport. Chief of Staff Moshe Dayan's intent was 'to get hostages in order to obtain the release of our prisoners in Damascus', Prime Minister Moshe Sharett wrote in his personal diary. The prisoners in question were Israeli soldiers who had been captured on a spy mission inside Syria; it was Dayan, we recall, who, twenty years later, ordered the rescue attempt that led to the death of Israeli teenagers in Ma'alot who had been taken hostage in an effort to obtain the release of Palestinian prisoners in Israel. Sharett wrote privately that 'we had no justification whatsoever to seize the plane' and that he had 'no reason to doubt the truth of the factual affirmation of the US State Department that our action was without precedent in the history of international practice'. But the incident has since disappeared from history, so that Israeli UN Ambassador Benjamin Netanyahu may appear on national television and accuse the PLO of 'inventing' the hijacking of airplanes and even the killing of diplomats, with no fear of contradiction.[78]

As for the killing of diplomats, we might only recall the assassination of UN mediator Folke Bernadotte in 1948 by a terrorist group commanded by Netanyahu's immediate superior, Foreign Minister Yitzhak Shamir, who was one of the three commanders who gave the orders for the assassination (a second, now dead, was a respected commentator in the Israeli press for many years, as is the third). A close friend of David Ben-Gurion's privately confessed that he was one of the assassins, but Ben-Gurion kept it secret, and the Israeli government arranged for the escape from prison and departure from the country of those responsible. In his eyewitness account, Zionist historian Jon Kimche writes that 'there was no nation-wide outcry or determination to catch the perpetrators' and 'not much moral indignation'. 'The attitude of the majority was that another enemy of the Jews had fallen by the wayside.' The assassination 'was condemned, regretted and deplored because it would cast reflections on Israel, and make the work of her diplomats more difficult; not because it was wrong in itself to resort to assassination'.[79]

In our usefully selective memory, only Arab actions remain as 'the evil scourge of terrorism'. After the hijacking of the *Achille Lauro* in retaliation for the Tunis bombing, the issue of ship hijacking became a major Western concern. A study by Reuters news agency concluded that 'there have been just a handful of ship hijackings since 1961', giving a few examples by Moslems; the Israeli hijackings were plainly not on the list.[80]

Hijacking is not the only form of terrorism that escapes this category when it is carried out by our friends. Jeane Kirkpatrick explained that the blowing up of the Greenpeace anti-nuclear protest ship by French agents with one man murdered was not terrorism: 'I'd like to say that the French clearly did not intend to attack civilians and bystanders and maim, torture or kill', an appeal that other terrorists could offer with ease. In its lead editorial, under the title 'Mitterrand's Finest Hour', the *Asian Wall St Journal* wrote that 'The Greenpeace campaign is fundamentally violent and dangerous... That the French government was prepared to use force against the *Rainbow Warrior* ... suggests that the government had its priorities straight.'[81] .

George Shultz may well deserve the prize for hypocrisy on this score. While urging an 'active' drive on terrorism, he described as 'insidious' the claim that 'one man's terrorist is another man's freedom fighter': 'Freedom fighters or revolutionaries don't blow up buses containing non-combatants. Terrorist murderers do. Freedom fighters don't assassinate innocent businessmen or hijack innocent men, women and children. Terrorist murderers do... The resistance fighters in Afghanistan do not destroy villages or kill the helpless. The Contras in Nicaragua do not blow up school buses or hold mass executions of civilians.' In fact, the terrorists Shultz commands in Nicaragua, as he knows, specialize precisely in murderous attacks on civilians, with torture, rape, mutilation; their odious record of terror is well-documented, though ignored and quickly forgotten, even denied by terrorist apologists. The resistance fighters in Afghanistan have also carried out brutal atrocities of a sort that would evoke fevered denunciations in the West if the attacking forces (who would then be called 'liberators' acting in 'self-defense') were American or Israeli.

As for Shultz's UNITA friends in Angola, only a few months before he spoke they were boasting of having shot down civilian airliners with 266 people killed and had released twenty-six hostages who had been held as long as nine months, including twenty-one Portuguese, and Spanish and Latin American missionaries; they had also announced 'a new campaign of urban terror', AP reported, noting a bombing in Luanda in which thirty people were killed and more than seventy injured when a jeep loaded with dynamite exploded in the city. They had also captured European teachers, doctors, and others, some 140 foreigners the press reported, including sixteen British technicians 'taken hostage', Jonas Savimbi stated, and not to 'be released until Prime Minister Thatcher offered his organization some kind of recognition'. Such actions continue regularly, e.g., the blowing up of an hotel in April 1986 with seventeen foreign civilians killed and many wounded. Savimbi 'is one of the few authentic heroes of our times', Jeane Kirkpatrick declaimed at a Conservative Political Action convention where Savimbi 'received enthusiastic applause after vowing to attack American oil installations in his country', a plan to kill Americans that did not invoke the doctrine of 'self-defense against future attack' employed to justify the bombing of 'mad dog' Qaddafi, just as there was no bombing of Johannesburg when South African mercenaries were captured in May 1985 in northern Angola on a mission to destroy these facilities and kill Americans. A terrorist state must exercise subtle judgments. In the real world, Savimbi qualifies as a freedom fighter for Shultz, Kirkpatrick and other leading terrorist commanders and advocates primarily because 'UNITA is the most extensively backed of South Africa's client groups used to destabilize the neighbouring states', as Barry Munslow and Phil O'Keefe observe.[82]

As for Shultz's Contra armies, their prime task is to hold the entire civilian population of Nicaragua hostage under the threat of sadistic terror to compel the government to abandon any commitment to the needs of the poor majority, in preference to the 'moderate' and 'democratic' policy of addressing the transcendent needs of US business and its local associates as in more properly behaved states under the US aegis. But in the corrupt and depraved cultural climate in which these terrorist commanders and apologists thrive, Shultz's statements and others like them pass with barely a raised eyebrow.

Taking of hostages plainly falls under the rubric of terrorism. There is no doubt, then, that Israel was guilty of a serious act of international terrorism when it removed some 1200 prisoners, mainly Lebanese Shi'ites, to Israel in violation of international law in the course of its retreat from Lebanon, explaining that they would be released 'on an unspecified schedule to be determined by the security situation in southern Lebanon' – that is, making it quite clear that they were to be held as hostages, pending a demonstration of 'good behavior' on the part of the local population kept under guard by Israeli forces and their mercenaries in the 'security zone' in southern Lebanon and in surrounding areas. As Mary McGrory observed in a rare departure from the general conformity, the prisoners were 'hostages in Israeli jails'; 'They are not criminals; they were scooped up as insurance against attack when the Israelis were finally quitting Lebanon' – in fact, there was no intention to quit southern Lebanon, where Israel retains its 'security zone', and even the partial withdrawal was the achievement of the Lebanese resistance. A hundred and forty prisoners had been secretly removed to Israel in November 1983 in violation of an agreement with the Red Cross to release them in a prisoner exchange, after the closing (temporary, as it turned out) of the Ansar prison camp, the scene of brutal atrocities; they were refused even Red Cross visits until July 1984. Israeli Defense Ministry spokesman Nachman Shai stated that four hundred of the 766 still in custody in June 1985 had been arrested for 'terrorist activities' – meaning resistance to the Israeli military occupation – while 'the rest were arrested for less violent forms of political activism or organizing activities designed to undermine the Israeli Army presence in Lebanon, Mr Shai indicated'.[83]

Israel had promised to release 340 of the hostages on 10 June, 'but canceled the release at the last minute for security reasons that were never fully explained'.[84] Four days later, Lebanese Shi'ites, reported to be friends and relatives of the Israeli-held hostages,[85] hijacked TWA flight 847, taking hostages in an attempt to free those held by Israel, provoking another bout of well-orchestrated and hypocritical hysteria in the United States, with overtly racist undertones and numerous attacks on the media for allowing the hijackers an occasional opportunity to explain their position, thus interfering with the totalitarian discipline deemed appropriate within the propaganda system. The Israeli kidnappers needed no access to the US media, which were delighted to deliver their message for them, often as 'news'.

The press dismissed the hijackers' statements that they wished to secure the release of the Israeli-held hostages – who were, of course, not hostages in US parlance, since they were held by 'our side'. The 'absurdity' of the Shi'ite pretense was easily exposed. Flora Lewis explained that 'it is out of character for militant Shi'ites, who extol martyrdom and show little reluctance to take the lives of others, to be so concerned with the timing of the prisoners' return', another version of the useful concept that the lower orders feel no pain. The *New York Times* editors offered the pathetic argument that 'Israel had planned to appease the resentful Shi'ites last week [that is, a few days prior to the TWA hijacking], but was delayed by the kidnapping of some Finnish UN troops in Lebanon'; in a 90-word news item, the *NYT* had noted the charge by Finland that during this entirely unrelated event, 'Israeli officers had watched Lebanese militiamen beat up kidnapped Finnish soldiers serving with the United Nations in Lebanon, but had done nothing to help them' while they 'were beaten with iron bars, water hoses and rifles by members of the South Lebanon Army'. 'There are crimes aplenty here', the *New York Times* thundered, denouncing the TWA hijackers, the Greek authorities (for their laxity), and even the United States – for 'having failed to punish Iran for sheltering the killers of two Americans in a hijacking last year'. But the Israeli hostage-taking was not one of these crimes.[86]

Bernard Lewis, his scholarly reputation rendering evidence or refutation of explicit counter-evidence unnecessary, asserted unequivocally that 'the hijackers or those who sent them must have known perfectly well that the Israelis were already planning to release the Shi'ite and other Lebanese captives, and that a public challenge of this kind could only delay, rather than accelerate, their release'. They could proceed 'to challenge America, to humiliate Americans' because they knew that the supine media would 'provide them with unlimited publicity and perhaps even some form of advocacy'. Recall that this is the voice of a respected scholar in a respected journal, a fact that once again demonstrates the comical frenzy that passes for intellectual life.

The editors of the *New Republic* dismissed the Shi'ite plea for release of the Israeli-held hostages as 'perfect rubbish': 'Hijacking, kidnapping, murder, and massacre are the way Shiites and other factions in Lebanon do their political business'. 'Everyone knew' that the Israeli-held prisoners were scheduled for release – when Israel was good and ready.

President Reagan escalated the hysteria yet another notch, explaining that the 'real goal' of the terrorists is 'to expel America from the world', no less, while Norman Podhoretz, noting that use of force would probably have led to the death of American hostages, denounced Reagan for failing 'to risk life itself [namely, the lives of others] in defense of the national honor'. New York Mayor Edward Koch called for the bombing of Lebanon and Iran, and others struck appropriately heroic poses.[87]

But the careful reader could discover buried in news reports on the hostage crisis that two thousand Lebanese Shi'ites, including seven hundred children, fled their homes under shelling by the South Lebanon Army, who also shot at jeeps of the UN peace-keeping forces, while 'a combined force of Israeli troops and Christian-led militiamen swept into a south Lebanese village today and seized 19 Shi'ite men, a United Nations spokesman announced.'[88]

After the hijacking, Israel began to release its hostages

according to its own timetable, very likely accelerated because the TWA hijacking had focused international attention on its own vastly more significant kidnapping operation. When three hundred were released on 3 July, AP reported their testimony that they were tortured and starved, while Thomas Friedman of the *New York Times* heard only that 'we were treated well by the Israelis. . .' Finally, Reagan wrote a letter to Shimon Peres, 'saying that the Beirut hostage crisis has strengthened relations between their countries'; nothing was said about the other 'hostage crisis', which is not part of official history.[89]

Even by the standards of Western Newspeak, the Israeli actions would qualify as hostage-taking were it not that as a US client state, Israel is exempt from this charge. But it is important to stress again the limits of the Orwellian concepts of contemporary political discourse, in which such terms as 'terrorism' and 'hostage' are construed so as exclude the most extreme examples, as in Nicaragua or southern Lebanon, where entire populations are held hostage to ensure obedience to the foreign master. Such usage is obligatory, given the true nature of international terrorism and the obvious necessity to prevent any comprehension of it.

Keeping just to the Middle East, we should recognize that at some level the matter is well understood by the organizers of international terrorism. The reason for the savage attacks on southern Lebanon throughout the 1970s was explained by the Israeli diplomat Abba Eban, considered a leading dove: 'there was a rational prospect, ultimately fulfilled, that affected populations would exert pressure for the cessation of hostilities'. Translating into plain language: the population of southern Lebanon was being held hostage in order to exert pressure on it to compel the Palestinians to accept the status assigned to them by the Labor government represented by Eban, who had declared that the Palestinians 'have no role to play' in any peace settlement. Chief of Staff Mordechai Gur explained in 1978 that 'For 30 years . . . we have been fighting against a population that lives in villages and cities', noting such incidents as the bombing of the Jordanian city of Irbid and the expulsion by bombing of tens of thousands of inhabitants of the Jordan valley and a million and a half civilians from the Suez canal, among other examples, all part of the program of holding civilian populations hostage in an effort to prevent resistance to the political settlement that Israel originally imposed by force, and then proceeded to maintain while rejecting any possibility of political settlement (for example, Sadat's offer of a full peace treaty on the internationally recognized borders in

1971). Israel's regular practice of 'retaliation' against defenseless civilian targets unrelated to the source of terrorist acts (themselves often retaliation for earlier Israeli terrorism, etc.) also reflects the same conception, a departure, by the early 1950s, from Ben-Gurion's earlier dictum that 'reaction is inefficient' unless it is precisely focused: 'If we know the family – [we must] strike mercilessly, women and children included.'[90]

Gur's understanding of Israel's wars is widely shared among the military command. During the Iron Fist operations of early 1985, Defense Minister Yitzhak Rabin warned that, if necessary, Israel would conduct 'a policy of scorched earth as was the case in the Jordan Valley during the war of attrition' with Egypt. 'Lebanon is a more serious source of terror than it was in 1982', he added, with Shi'ite terrorists now holding Western Europe in fear (they did not do so prior to the summer of 1982, for unexplained reasons), so that Israel must maintain a zone in the south in which 'we may intervene'. The veteran paratroop commander Dubik Tamari, who gave the orders to level the Palestinian camp of Ain el-Hilweh by air and artillery bombardment 'to save lives' of troops under his command (another notable exercise of the fabled 'purity of arms'), justified the action with the comment that 'the State of Israel has been killing civilians from 1947', 'purposely killing civilians' as 'one goal among others'.[91]

Tamari cited as an example the attack on Qibya in 1953, when Ariel Sharon's Unit 101 killed seventy Arab villagers in their homes in alleged retaliation for a terrorist attack with which they had no connection whatsoever. Ben-Gurion pretended on Israeli radio that the villagers were killed by Israeli civilians enraged by Arab terror, 'mostly refugees, people from Arab countries and survivors from the Nazi concentration camps', dismissing the 'fantastic allegation' that Israeli military forces were involved – a brazen lie that had the further effect of putting Israeli settlements under threat of retaliation. Less known is the fact that a month before the Qibya massacre, Moshe Dayan had sent Unit 101 to drive four thousand Beduins of the Azzazma and Tarbin tribes across the Egyptian border, another step in expulsions that had been proceeding from 1950, shortly after the cease-fire. In March 1954, eleven Israelis were murdered in an ambush of a bus in the Eastern Negev by members of the Azzazma tribe ('unprovoked terrorism'), evoking an Israeli raid on the Jordanian village of Nahaleen with nine villagers killed ('retaliation'). In August 1953, Sharon's Unit 101 had killed twenty people, two-thirds women and children, at the al-Bureig refugee camp in the Gaza Strip, in 'retaliation' for infiltration.[92] The cycle of 'retaliation' (by Jews) and 'terror' (by Palestinians) can be traced back, step-by-step, for many years, an exercise that will quickly reveal that the terminology belongs to the realm of propaganda, not factual description.

Here too we might note how effectively history has been reconstructed in a more ideologically serviceable form. Thus Thomas Friedman, reviewing 'Israel's counterterrorism' strategy, writes that 'the first period, from 1948 to 1956, might best be described as the era of counterterrorism-through-retaliation, or negative feedback', though 'at least one of these retaliations became highly controversial, involving ·civilian casualties', the reference presumably being to Qibya. The record of scholarship is often hardly different.[93]

The Iron Fist operations of the Israeli army in southern Lebanon in early 1985 were also guided by the logic outlined by Eban. The civilian population was held hostage under the threat of terror to ensure that it accept the political arrangements dictated by Israel in southern Lebanon and the occupied territories. The warnings remain in effect; the population remains hostage, with no concern on the part of the superpower that finances these operations and bars any meaningful political settlement.

Wholesale terrorism, including the holding of hostages, is exempt from censure in Western Newspeak when conducted by an approved source. The same hypocrisy obtains for smaller-scale operations as well. To mention some characteristic cases, in November-December 1983, Israel 'made it clear that it would not allow Arafat's forces to evacuate the city [Tripoli, in northern Lebanon, where they were under attack by Syrian-backed forces] as long as the fate of the Israeli prisoners was in doubt'. Israel therefore bombed what were called 'guerrilla positions', preventing the departure of Greek ships that were to evacuate Arafat loyalists. Druze spokesmen reported that a hospital was hit during the bombing and strafing of 'what were described as Palestinian bases', east of Beirut, while in Tripoli, 'One already-gutted cargo ship took a direct hit and sank' and 'a freighter burst into flames when it was hit'.[94] Again, the population, as well as foreign vessels, was held hostage to ensure the release of Israeli prisoners captured in the course of Israel's aggression in Lebanon.

In Lebanon and in international waters Israel regularly carries out attacks with impunity and abandon. In mid-July 1985, Israeli warplanes bombed and strafed Palestinian camps near Tripoli, killing at least twenty people, most of them civilians, including six children under twelve. 'Clouds of smoke and dust engulfed the Tripoli refugee camps, home to more than 25,000 Palestinians, for several hours after the 2:55 p.m. attack', which was assumed to be 'retaliation' for two car-bomb attacks a few days earlier in Israel's 'security zone' in southern Lebanon by a group aligned with Syria. Two weeks later, Israeli gunboats attacked a Honduran-registered cargo ship a mile from the port of Sidon, delivering cement according to its Greek captain, setting it ablaze with thirty shells and wounding civilians in subsequent shore bombardment when militiamen returned the fire. The mainstream press did not even bother to report that the following day Israeli gunboats sank a fishing boat and damaged three others, while a Sidon parliamentarian called on the UN to end US-backed Israeli 'piracy'. The press did report what Israel called a 'surgical' operation against 'terrorist installations' near Baalbek in the Bekaa valley in January 1984, killing about one hundred people, mostly civilians, with four hundred wounded, including 150 children in a bombed-out schoolhouse. The 'terrorist installations' also included a mosque, an hotel, a restaurant, stores and other buildings in the three Lebanese villages and Palestinian refugee camp that were attacked, while Beirut news reported that a cattle market and an industrial park were also struck with scores of houses destroyed. A Reuters reporter in the bombed villages said that a second round of bombing began ten minutes after the first, 'adding to the number of those klled or wounded' since men and women had begun dragging dead and wounded from the wrecked buildings. He saw 'lots of children' in hospitals while witnesses reported men and women rushing to schools in a frantic search for their children. The leader of Lebanon's Shi'ites denounced 'Israeli barbarism', describing its attacks on 'innocent civilians, hospitals and houses of worship' as an attempt 'to terrorize the Lebanese people', but the incident passed without comment in the US, in no way affecting Israel's status as 'a country that cares for human life'. We may conclude again that the victims of this surgical bombing were less than human, as indeed they are, within the racist Western consensus.[95]

One may, again, imagine what the reaction would be in the West, including the 'pro-Arab' media, if the PLO or Syria were to carry out a 'surgical strike' against 'terrorist installations' near Tel Aviv, killing one hundred civilians and wounding four hundred others, including 150 children in a bombed-out schoolhouse, along with other civilian targets.

While the standard version in the United States is that Israeli violence, perhaps excessive at times, is 'retaliation' for Arab atrocities, Israel, like the United States, claims much broader rights: the right to carry out terrorist attacks to prevent potential actions against it, as in the justification for the Lebanon war by the dovish Knesset member Amnon Rubinstein. Israeli troops carry out what they call 'preventive gunfire' as they patrol in Lebanon, spraying the terrain with machine guns, leading Irish peacekeeping forces to block the road in protest. Quite commonly, Israeli attacks in Lebanon were described as 'preventive, not punitive', for example, the bombing and strafing of Palestinian refugee camps and nearby villages by thirty Israeli jets on 2 December 1975, killing fifty-seven people, apparently in retaliation for the decision of the UN Security Council to debate an Arab peace proposal to which Israel violently objected and which therefore has been excised from history.[96] When Israeli airborne and amphibious forces attacked Tripoli in northern Lebanon in February 1973, killing thirty-one people (mainly civilians), according to Lebanese authorities, and destroying classrooms, clinics and other buildings, Israel justified the raid as 'intended to forestall a number of planned terrorist attacks against Israelis overseas'.[97] The pattern is regular, and the justifications are accepted here as legitimate because Israel is a useful client state and its victims are considered subhuman.

The last case mentioned occurred on the same day that Israel shot down a Libyan civilian airliner lost in a sandstorm two minutes flight time from Cairo, towards which it was heading, with 110 people killed. The US officially expressed its sympathy to the families of those involved, but the press spokesman 'declined to discuss with reporters the Administration's feelings about the incident'. Israel blamed the French pilot, with the *New York Times* dutifully in tow, accepting the Israeli claim that the pilot knew he had been ordered to land but instead resorted to 'highly suspicious' evasive action – the same justification offered by the USSR for downing KAL 007[98] – so that the Israeli act was 'at worst ... an act of callousness that not even the savagery of previous Arab actions can excuse'. The official Israeli reaction was given by Prime Minister Golda Meir: 'the government of Israel expresses its deep sorrow for the loss of human life and is sorry that the Libyan [sic] pilot did not respond to the warnings given him in accordance with international practice'. Shimon Peres went further, observing that 'Israel acted in accordance with international laws'. Israel then falsely claimed that the pilot was not authorized to fly the jet plane. 'The press was forbidden to publish pictures of the destroyed plane, of the dead and the wounded,' Amiram Cohen observes in a detailed analysis of the Israeli reaction (undertaken after the KAL 007 atrocity), and 'journalists were not allowed to visit the hospital in Beersheba and to interview survivors'.

The international reaction was dismissed by the Israeli press as yet another demonstration that 'the spirit of anti-Semitism flourishes' in Europe, virtually a reflex response in the US as well when someone dares to mention or criticize an Israeli atrocity. The Israeli press insisted that 'Israel is not responsible' and that 'one must blame the (French) pilot'. It was 'a mobilized press', firm in support of the justice of Israel's actions, Cohen observes. After numerous lies, Israel confirmed that there had been an 'error of judgment', agreeing to pay *ex gratia* payments to the families of victims 'in deference to humanitarian considerations' while denying any 'guilt' or Israeli responsibility.[99] The incident was passed over quickly in the United States, with little criticism of the perpetrators of the crime. Prime Minister Golda Meir arrived in the US four days later; she was troubled by few embarrassing questions by the press and returned home with new gifts of military aircraft. As noted, the reaction was slightly different when the Russians shot down KAL 007 in September 1983,[100] though it was comparable when our UNITA friends claimed to have shot down two civilian airliners at the same time. (Thus function the criteria for 'international terrorism'.)

The record of Israeli terrorism goes back to the origins of the state – indeed, long before – including the massacre of 250 civilians and brutal expulsion of seventy thousand others from Lydda and Ramle in July 1948; the massacre of hundreds of others at the undefended village of Doueimah near Hebron in October 1948 in another of the numerous 'land clearing operations' conducted while the international propaganda apparatus was proclaiming, as it still does, that the Arabs were fleeing at the call of their leaders; the murder of several hundred Palestinians by the IDF after the conquest of the Gaza strip in 1956; the slaughters in Qibya, Kafr Kassem, and a string of other assassinated villages; the expulsion of thousands of Beduins from the demilitarized zones shortly after the 1948 war and thousands more from northeastern Sinai in the early 1970s, their villages destroyed, to open the region for Jewish settlement; and on, and on. The victims, by definition, are 'PLO partisans', hence terrorists; thus the respected editor of *Ha'aretz*, Gershom Schocken, can write that Ariel Sharon 'made a name for himself from the early 1950s as a ruthless fighter against Palestine Liberation Organization (PLO) partisans', referring to the slaughters of civilians he conducted at Al-Bureig and Qibya in 1953 (long before the PLO existed). The victims in Lebanon and elsewhere are also 'terrorists'. This must be the case, or they could not have been killed by a state so devoted to 'purity of arms' and held to a 'higher law' by the pro-Arab American press.

The terrorist commanders are even honored. When the leading contemporary US terrorist took over the Presidency in 1981, Israel's Prime Minister and Foreign Minister were both notorious terrorist commanders, while the highest position in the Jewish Agency was held by a man who had murdered several dozen civilians he was holding under guard in a mosque in a Lebanese town during yet another land-clearing operation in 1948. He was quickly amnestied, all trace of the crime was removed from the record, and he was granted a lawyer's license on the grounds that 'no stigma' could be attached to his act.[101]

Even terrorism against Americans is perfectly tolerable. The Israeli attacks against US installations (also, public places) in Egypt in 1954 in an attempt to exacerbate US-Egyptian relations and abort secret peace negotiations then in progress were ignored at the time and are barely remembered, much as in the case of the attempt to sink the US spy ship *Liberty* in international waters in 1967. Israeli bombers and torpedo boats even shot lifeboats out of the water in an effort to ensure that no one would escape, with thirty-four crewmen killed and 171 injured. The worst peacetime US naval disaster of the century until then was dismissed as an 'error' – a transparent absurdity – and is today barely known.[102] Similarly, torture of Americans by the Israeli army in the West Bank and southern Lebanon is scarcely noted in the media, with Israeli denials highlighted and verification by the US Ambassador in Israel ignored.[103] The fact that the victims were Arab-Americans no doubt serves as justification, by media standards.

What is striking about this record, which includes ample terrorism against Jews as well from the earliest days, is that it in no way sullies Israel's American reputation for moral standards unequalled in history. Each new act of terrorism, if noted at all, is quickly dismissed and forgotten, or described as a temporary deviation from perfection, to be explained by the hideous nature of the enemy which is forcing Israel to depart, if only for a moment, from its path of righteousness. Meanwhile the media are regularly denounced for their 'double standard' as they ignore Arab crimes while holding Israel to impossible standards. Respected scholars – their reputations untarnished by such absurdities – inform us soberly that 'numerous public figures in the West, even a number of Western governments' (naturally, all unnamed) have encouraged the PLO to destroy Israel.[104] Across the political spectrum in the United States and among the educated classes with remarkable uniformity and only the most marginal of exceptions, the unchallenged doctrine is that it is the terrorism of the Palestinians and their Arab allies, urged on by the Kremlin, their unremitting commitment to kill Jews and destroy Israel and their refusal to consider any political settlement, that is the root cause of the endless Arab-Israeli conflict, of which Israel is the pathetic victim. As for the United States, it is powerless in the face of 'the evil scourge of terrorism', from Central America to Lebanon and beyond.

The Jewish national movement and the state that developed from it have broken no new ground in their impressive record of terrorist atrocities, apart from the immunity they enjoy in enlightened Western opinion. For Americans, it suffices to recall 'that Adolf Hitler chose to praise the United States ... for "solving the problem" of the native races',[105] as do some of those who live by Hitler's code in Central America today, with US support. But the recent commentary on 'terrorism' in the 'civilized countries' reeks of hypocrisy and merits contempt among decent people.

But contempt, however well-merited, is not a sufficient reaction. It is also necessary to understand the motives and goals of the propaganda campaign about international terrorism designed for the 1980s by the Reagan Administration and joined with much enthusiasm by elite opinion generally. The reasons for establishing 'the evil scourge of terrorism' as the major issue of our time were transparent, though as usual inexpressible within the doctrinal system, which must pretend to take the expressed concerns seriously.[106] The Reagan Administration came into office committed to three related policies, all proposed in the latter stages of the Carter Administration, all generally endorsed with minor variations among the privileged minorities that participate in the political system, all achieved with some success:

1) transfer of resources from the poor to the rich;

2) massive increase in the state sector of the economy in the traditional American way, through the Pentagon system, a device to force the public to invest in high technology industry by means of the state-guaranteed market for the production of high

technology waste (armaments) and thus to contribute to the program of public subsidy, private profit, called 'free enterprise'; and

3) a substantial increase in the US role in intervention, subversion, and international terrorism (in the true sense of the expression).

Such policies cannot be presented to the public in the terms in which they are intended. They can be implemented only if the general population is properly frightened by monsters against whom we must defend ourselves.

The standard device is an appeal to the threat of the Great Satan, John F. Kennedy's 'monolithic and ruthless conspiracy' bent on world conquest, Reagan's 'Evil Empire'. But confrontation with the Evil Empire can be a dangerous affair, so it is preferable to do battle with safer enemies designated as the Evil Empire's proxies, a choice that conforms well to the third plank in the current political agenda, pursued for quite independent reasons: to ensure 'stability' and 'order' in our global domains. Thus, we must defend ourselves from Nicaraguans and Salvadorans who dare to resist our violence, torture and wholesale terror. In the Middle East, terrorists who may be exhibited by the compliant media as madmen bent on destruction of Western civilization are in ample supply, thanks in good measure to the persistent US rejectionism that has blocked any possibility of a meaningful political settlement of the Arab-Israeli conflict and US support for Israeli terrorism and aggression.

David Hirst observes that 'the main, or the really significant center of international terrorism [in the sanitized western sense of the term] is Lebanon. It either breeds its own terrorists, or serves as a congenial home for imported ones', either Palestinians, who 'have known little but bombardment, murder, massacre and mutilation, encircling hatred, fear and insecurity', or Lebanese whose society was given its final blow by the US-backed Israeli aggression and its aftermath; '. . . one conviction is rooted in the minds of the youth of today' among these groups: 'that under President Reagan, who has carried his country's traditional partisanship with Israel to unprecedented lengths, the US is the incorrigible upholder of a whole existing order so intolerable that any means now justifies its destruction. The terrorist impulse may be strongest among the Palestinians, but it can also be Lebanese, Arab, or – in its most spectacular manifestation – Shi'ite.' The essential point was expressed by the former chief of Israeli military intelligence, General (retired) Yehoshaphat Harkabi: 'To offer an honorable solution to the Palestinians respecting their right to self-determination: that is the solution of the problem of terrorism. When the swamp disappears, there will be no more mosquitos.'[107]

US-Israeli wholesale terrorism and aggression have surely contributed to the situation Hirst describes, predictably and perhaps consciously so, and both terrorist states are more than pleased at the outcome, which provides them with a justification to persist in their course of rejectionism and violence. Furthermore, the retail terrorism to which they have contributed so effectively can be exploited to induce a proper sense of fear and mobilization among the population, as required for more general ends. All that is required is a propaganda system that can be relied upon to shriek in chorus on command and to suppress any understanding of US initiatives, their pattern, their sources, and their motivation. On this score, policy makers need have few concerns.

Libya fits the need perfectly. Libya is weak and defenseless, so that martial flourishes and, when needed, murder of Libyans can be conducted with impunity.[108] Qaddafi is easy to hate, particularly against the background of rampant anti-Arab racism in the United States and the deep commitment of the educated classes, with only the rarest of exceptions, to the US-Israeli propaganda system. Qaddafi has created an ugly and repressive society, and he is indeed guilty of terrorism, responsible for killing fourteen Libyans according to Amnesty International, and perhaps a handful of others.

From its first months in office, the Reagan Administration arranged regular confrontations with Libya, or simply concocted Libyan plots and atrocities, as required by domestic needs. The Gulf of Sidra incident in March 1986, and the subsequent US terror attack on Tripoli and Benghazi with some one hundred killed – the first bombings in history staged for prime time television – fit the pattern perfectly, as did the servile media response.

To establish Libyan responsibility for terrorism is a simple matter, given the complicity of the media. Government charges backed with no credible evidence are headlined as 'facts', with occasional questioning permitted later in the small print after the effect has been achieved.[109] If an individual implicated in a terrorist act once paid a visit to Libya, or is alleged to have received training or funds from Libya in the past, that suffices for condemnation of Qaddafi as a 'mad dog' who must be eradicated.

The same standards would implicate the CIA in the murderous exploits of Cuban exiles over many years, among numerous other terrorist atrocities. Keeping just to 1985, one of the suspects in the bombing of the Air India jumbo jet near Ireland that was the year's worst terrorist act, killing 329 people, was trained in an anti-Communist school of mercenaries in Alabama. The terrorist action that cost the most lives in the Middle East was a car-bombing in Beirut in March that killed eighty people and wounded two hundred, carried out by a Lebanese intelligence unit trained and supported by the CIA, in an effort to kill a Shi'ite leader who was believed to have been involved in 'terrorist attacks against US installations' in Beirut.[110] By the standards of evidence used in the case of Libya, the US is the world's leading terrorist power, even if we exclude the wholesale terrorism ruled ineligible by the propaganda system, given its source.

Continuing to 1986, the most serious terrorist acts as of the time of writing were the US bombing of Libya and the bombings in Syria which, according to the radio station of Lebanon's President Amin Gemayel's Phalangist party, killed more than 150 people in April, blamed by Syria on Israeli agents operating from inside Lebanon with no reported evidence, but no less credibility than similar US charges against whoever happens to be the villain of the day – and, incidentally, not falling within 'the evil scourge of terrorism'.[111]

The most critical voices in the US agree that 'Colonel Qaddafi's open support of terrorism is a blatant evil', and 'There is no reason to let murderers go unpunished if you know their perpetrator. Nor can it be a decisive factor that retaliation will kill some innocent civilians, or murderous states would never fear retribution'[112] – a principle that entitles vast numbers of people around the world to assassinate President Reagan and to bomb Washington, even if this 'retaliation will kill some innocent civilians'. It is unlikely that more than a tiny fraction of educated Americans could comprehend these simple truths, and they are hardly likely to be expressible within the doctrinal system.

The hysteria successfully evoked in the United States by the government and the media, which leads otherwise sane people to cancel trips to Europe (where they will be far safer than in any American city), is of substantial benefit for state propaganda, helping to mobilize support for the political agenda. Furthermore, by raising the level of acceptance of US violence in 'retaliation' for terrorist acts, the US government keeps its options open for further escalation if the need arises, perhaps in Central America, to excise the 'cancer' of the Sandinistas, or in the Middle East, if Israel undertakes a 'preemptive strike' against Syria combined with a US attack, packaged for the West as 'defense against terrorism' and intended as a warning to the Soviet Union not to come to the defense of its Syrian ally.

The fraudulence and cynicism of the propaganda campaign about 'international terrorism' has been exposed to the tiny audiences that can be reached by dissident opinion in the United States, but the campaign itself has been a remarkable public relations achievement. With the mass media committed to serve the needs of the state propaganda system, systematically excluding any commentary that might expose what is unfolding before the American people's eyes or any rational discussion of it, the prospects for future successes remain impressive. This service to wholesale international terrorism contributes to massive suffering and brutality, and in the longer term carries with it serious dangers of superpower confrontation and terminal nuclear war. But such considerations count for little in comparison with the need to ensure that no threat to 'stability' and 'order' can arise, no challenge to privilege and power. There is little here to surprise any honest student of history.

Notes

1. *NYT*, 17, 18 Oct. 1985.

2. *Ha'aretz*, 22 March 1985; Chomsky, *Fateful Triangle* (*FT*, South End, 1983), pp. 54, 75, 202.

3. Yossi Beilin, *Mechiro shel Ichug* (Tel Aviv, 1985), p. 147; Gazit, *Hamakel Vehagezer* (Tel Aviv, 1985), quoted in *Al Hamishmar*, 7 Nov. 1985; Chomsky, *Towards a New Cold War* (*TNCW*: Pantheon, 1982), pp. 267-8. Israel insists that the Palestinians not only recognize it but also recognize its 'right to exist', a concept without precedent in international affairs contrived as a further impediment to negotiations.

4. When I refer to Reagan, I mean his planners and speech writers; any sentence that begins 'Reagan knows. . .' is likely to be false.

5. *Yediot Ahronot*, 15 Nov. 1985.

6. Ze'ev Schiff, *Ha'aretz*, 8 Feb. 1985; see *FT* for testimony from participants, not reported in the US.

7. Godfrey Jansen, *Middle East International*, 11 Oct. 1985, citing *LAT*, 3 Oct.

8. It appears in *Against the Current*, Jan. 1986.

9. Cf. *FT*, pp. 127. 176.

10. Bernard Gwertzman, NYT, 2, 7 Oct. 1985.

11. Beverly Beyette, *LAT*, report on International Conference on Terrorism, *LAT*, 9 April 1986.

12. Edward Schumacher, *NYT*, 27 Oct.

13. *New Republic*, 21 Oct. 1985, 20 Jan. 1986; AP, 4 April 1986.

14. Robert McFadden, 'Terror in 1985: Brutal Attacks, Tough Response', *NYT*, 30 Dec. 1985.

15. UPI, *LAT*, 28 Dec. 1985; McFadden, *op. cit*; Dershowitz, *NYT*, 17 Oct. 1985; Alexander Cockburn, *Nation*, 2 Nov. 1985, the sole notice of the transparent hypocrisy.

16. Ross Gelbspan, *Boston Globe*, 16 Dec. 1985. On *Contra* atrocities, see the regular reports of *Americas Watch* and numerous other careful and detailed inquiries, among them, *Report of Donald T. Fox, Esq. and Prof. Michael J. Glennon to the International Human Rights Law Group and the Washington Office on Latin America*, April 1985. They cite a high ranking State Department official who described the US stance as one of 'intentional ignorance'. The extensive and horrifying record is also generally disregarded by the media and others, and even flatly denied (without evidence) by some of the more extreme apologists for western atrocities; e.g., Robert Conquest, 'Laying Propaganda on Thick', *Daily Telegraph* (London), 19 April 1986; Jeane Kirkpatrick (*BG*, 16 March 1986), who tells us that 'the contras have a record of working hard to avoid harming civilians. They have done nothing that compares with the systematic brutality the Sandinista government visits on dissenters and opponents' – a shocking lie, which in no way detracts from her respectability as a regular syndicated columnist, and which is compounded by recitation of a series of long-refuted government fabrications; comparable lies and apologetics for Soviet atrocities would not be tolerated for a moment in the media.

17. *NYT*, 29 June 1985.

18. And in Israel. After Peres's accession to power, there was an increase in the use of torture in prisons, preventive detention and expulsion in violation of international law, practices that were common under the previous Labor government much lauded by left-liberal American opinion, and reduced or suspended under Menachem Begin. Dani Rubinstein, *Davar*, 4 Feb. 1986; on torture, see *Ha'aretz* 24 Feb. 1986.

19. Curtis Wilkie, *BG*, 10 March; Julie Flint, *Guardian* (London), 13 March; Jim Muir, *MEI*, 22 March; Breindel, *NYT* Op-Ed, 28 March; Nora Boustany, *WP*, 12 March 1985. A photo of the wall graffiti appears in Joseph Schechia, *The Iron Fist* (ADC, Washington, 1985).

20. *Guardian* (London) 2, 6 March 1985.

21. Ilya, *Jerusalem Post* 27 Feb. 1985; Magnus Linklater, Isabel Hilton and Neal Ascherson, *The Fourth Reich* (Hodder & Stoughton, London, 1984, pp. 111); *Der Spiegel* (27 April 1986); *NYT*, 13 March 1985. The *Spiegel* review expresses deep skepticism about US claims concerning Libyan involvement in the Berlin disco bombing that allegedly elicited the attack, and the head of the West Berlin police commission investigating the bombing, Manfred Ganschow, has explicitly denied that such evidence exists. In fact, there have been ample reasons to doubt these claims since they were announced at the White House press conference at the time of the bombing; see my 'Libya in US demonology', *Covert Action Information Bulletin*, forthcoming, for details. US journalists refrained from raising the obvious questions concerning US government claims in justification of the bombing, at the White House press conference or since; see, e.g., James Markham, *NYT*, 31 May 1986, noting various uncertainties about the disco bombing and citing Ganschow on another matter.

22. Ihsan Hijazi, *NYT*, 1 Jan. 1986; Hijazi notes that the reports from Israel differed.

23. *CSM*, 30 Jan. 1986.

24. For detailed examination of this question, see *FT* or compare, for example, what appeared in *Newsweek* with what bureau chief Tony Clifton describes in his book *God Cried* (Clifton and Catherine Leroy, Quartet, 1983), published in London. Or consider the *War Diary* by Col. Dov Yermiya, one of the founders of the Israeli army, published in violation of censorship in Israel (see *FT* for many quotations) and later in English translation (South End, 1983), but entirely ignored in the media, though it is obviously a work of considerable importance. There are numerous other examples.

25. Landrum Bolling, ed., *Reporters Under Fire* (Westview, 1985). Included, for example, is a critique of the media by the Anti-Defamation League of B'nai Brith, and other accusations which barely rise to the level of absurdity (see *FT* for analysis of these documents), but not a study by the American-Arab Anti-Discrimination Committee that presents evidence of 'a consistent pro-Israeli bias' in press coverage of the war.

26. Kifner, *NYT*, 10 March; Muir, *MEI*, 22 Feb. 1985; Mary Curtius, *Christian Science Monitor*, 27 March; Jim Yanin, *CSM*, 25 April; Yamin interview, *MERIP reports*, June 1985; David Hirst, *Guardian* (London), 2 April; Robert Fisk, *Times* (London), 26, 27 April; *Philadelphia Inquirer*, 28 April 1985. On Israeli efforts to fuel hostilities in the Chouf region from mid-1982, see *FT*, p. 418f.

27. *MEI*, 22 March 1985.

28. UPI, *BG*, 22 Sept. 1984; Olmert, interview, *Al Hamishmar*, 27 Jan. 1984; Hirsh Goodman, *Jerusalem Post*, 10 Feb. 1984; Wieseltier, *New Republic*, 8 April 1985.

29. Don Oberdorfer, 'The Mind of George Shultz', *WP Weekly*, 17 Feb. 1986; Rubin, *New Republic*, 2 June 1986; Thomas Friedman, *NYT*, 16 Feb. 1986, among many other reports. Like Wieseltier, Rubin asserts that this Syrian-sponsored 'terrorism . . . is not a cry of outrage against a Western failure to pursue peace but an attempt to block diplomacy altogether', since 'almost any conceivable solution is anathema to the Syrian government'. Rubin knows that Syria has supported diplomatic solutions close to the international consensus, but since they are remote from us rejectionism, these solutions are not 'conceivable' and do not count as 'diplomatic options', the term 'peace settlement' being reserved for us or Israeli proposals so that those who do not follow us orders are, by definition, against peace. For discussion of this useful device and others like it, see my 'Thought Control in the United States: the Case of the Middle East', *Index on Censorship*, June 1986.

30. *LAT*, 18 Oct. 1985.

31. *NYT*, 18 Oct. 1985.

32. Ze'ev Schiff, 'The Terror of Rabin and Berri', *Ha'aretz*, 8 March 1985; also General Ori Or, commander of the IDF northern command, IDF radio; FBIS, 15 April 1985.

33. Gershom Schocken, editor of *Ha'aretz*, *Foreign Affairs*, Fall, 1984.

34. Shimon Peres, *NYT*, 8 July 1983. On the atrocities in Khiam, see *TNCW*, pp. 396-7; *FT*, p. 191; Yoram Hamizrahi, *Davar*, 7 June 1984; press reports cited in the Democratic Front publication *Nisayon Leretsach-Am Bilvanon: 1982* (Tel Aviv, 1983). On Nabatiya, see *FT*, pp. 70, 187.

35. Jim Muir, *Sunday Times* (London), 14 April 1985; *CSM*, 15 April 1985; Joel Greenberg, *CSM*, 30 Jan 1986; Sonia Dayan, Paul Kessler and Geraud de la Pradelle, *Le Monde diplomatique*, April 1986. Extensive reports of torture, by former prisoners, ignored in the West, appear in *Information Bulletin 21*, 1985, International Center for Information on Palestinian and Lebanese Prisoners, Deportees, and Missing Persons, Paris.

36. Benny Morris and David Bernstein, *JP*, 23 July 1982; for comparison by Israeli journalists of life under the PLO and under Israel's Christian allies in Lebanon, a picture considerably at variance with approved doctrine here, see *FT*, p. 186f. Particularly significant is the report from Lebanon by the Israeli journalist Attallah Mansour, of Maronite origins.

37. *Economist*, 19 Nov. 1977.

38. John Cooley, in Edward Haley and Lewis Snider, eds, *Lebanon in Crisis* (Syracuse, 1979). See *TNCW*, p. 321; *FT*, pp. 70, 84.

39. Edward Haley, *Qaddafi and the United States since 1969* (Praeger, 1984), p. 74.

40. James Markham, *NYT*, 4 Dec. 1975.

41. See *TNCW*, pp. 267, 300, 461; *FT*, pp. 67, 189.

42. See *FT* and 'Thought Control in the United States'. The 1976 Arab initiative is not even mentioned in the unusually careful review in Seth Tillman, *The United States and the Middle East* (Indiana, 1982). It is mentioned by Steven Spiegel, *The Other Arab-Israeli Conflict* (Chicago, 1985), p. 306, a much-praised work of scholarship, with some remarkable commentary. Spiegel writes that the US 'vetoed the pro-Palestinian resolution' so as 'to demonstrate that the United States was willing to hear Palestinian aspirations but would not accede to demands that threatened Israel'. The commitment to US-Israeli rejectionism could not be more clear and is accepted as quite proper in the United States.

43. AP, *NYT*, 21 Feb.; Julie Flint, *Guardian* (London), 24 Feb.; Ihsan Hijazi, *NYT*, 28 Feb.; AP, 20 Feb. 1986. The only detailed account in the US, to my knowledge, was by Nora Boustany, *WP*, 1 March, though with the IDF role largely excised, possibly by the editors, since reporters on the scene knew well what was happening, as some have privately indicated.

44. Ihsan Hijazi, *NYT*, 25 March; Dan Fisher, *LAT*, 28 March; AP, 7 April; Hijazi, *NYT*, 8 April 1986.

45. Peres, *NYT*, 8 July 1983; Breindel, *op. cit.*; *NYT*, 16 Sept. 1983, 3 June 1985; Kamm, *NYT*, 26 April 1985; Friedman, *NYT*, 9 Jan., 20 Feb., 18 Feb. 1985; Brzezinski, *NYT*, 9 Oct, 1983; Reagan, press conferences, *NYT*, 29 March 1984, 28 Oct. 1983. See also the remarks by Rabbi Alexander Schindler, President of the Union of American Hebrew Congregations (Reform): the PLO 'threatened to destroy what was left of Beirut rather than surrender'; sending the Marines to oversee their departure instead of permitting Israel to finish the job was 'surely the most ignominious' assignment the Marines were ever given (UPI, *BG*, 28 Oct. 1984). These intriguing illustrations of religion in the service of state violence are omitted from the *Times* account the same day.

46. *NYT* 7 June 1983.

47. William Quandt notes further that 'the Israeli operational planning for the invasion of Lebanon against the PLO [in 1981-2] seems to coincide with the consolidation of the Egyptian-Israeli peace treaty' (*American-Arab Affairs*, Fall, 1985).

48. Philip Weiss, *New Republic*, 10 Feb. 1986.

49. Ze'ev Schiff and Ehud Ya'ari, *Israel's Lebanon War* (Simon & Schuster, 1984), p. 35; John Kifner, *NYT*, 25 July 1981. Schiff and Ya'ari claim that 'despite the great pains taken to pinpoint the targets and achieve direct hits, over 100 people were killed', including thirty 'terrorists'. The Schiff-Ya'ari book is a translation of parts of the Hebrew original; about 20 per cent of the original was excised by the Israeli censor according to Ya'ari (*Koi Hair*, 2 Feb. 1984), about 50 per cent according to the American scholar Augustus Norton, citing a 'respected correspondent – unconnected to the authors' (*Middle East Journal*, Summer, 1985). Censorship in Nicaragua, under attack by a US proxy army, arouses great

indignation in the US. The most extreme censorship in Israel, of course, is directed against Arabs, including Israeli citizens. See *FT*, p. 139f., and my *Turning the Tide* (South End, 1983, p. 73f.) for a small sample.

50. Walsh, *WP Weekly*, 4 March 1985; Wilkie, *BG*, 18 Feb. 1985.

51. *FT*, pp. 440, 448, citing Israeli press; *News from Within* (Tel Aviv), 1 Oct. 1985; *Yediot Ahronot*, 4 Nov. 1983.

52. *Ha'aretz* 25 June 1982; see *FT*, p. 200f., for further quotations and similar analyses by other Israeli commentators.

53. B. Michael, *Ha'aretz*, 13 Nov. 1983; Bachar, *Yediot Ahronot*, 11 Nov. 1983; Morris, *JP*, 5 June 1984.

54. Olmert, *Ma'ariv*, 22 Nov. 1983; Milson, *Koteret Rashit*, 9 Nov. 1983; Sharon, cited by Ze'ev Schiff, *Ha'aretz*, 23 May 1982; Milshtein, *Hadashot*, 26 Sept. 1984; Rubinstein, *Ha'olam Haze*, 8 June 1983. On Ben-Gurion's aspirations before and after the state was established, see *FT*, pp. 51, 160f.; Shabtai Tevet, *Ben-Gurion and the Palestinian Arabs* (Oxford, 1985) and the review by Benny Morris, *Jerusalem Post*, 11 Oct. 1985.

55. See 'Libya in US Demonology'.

56. *FT*, p. 199, citing an interview in *Ha'aretz*, 4 June 1982; *FT*, pp. 117, 263.

57. *Nouvel Observateur*, 4 May; *Observer* (London), 29 April; *Jerusalem Post*, 16 May; *San Francisco Examiner*, 5 May; *WP*, 8 July 1984. See my 'Manufacture of Consent'. Dec. 1984, published by the Community Church, Boston, for further details. On earlier Israeli determination to evade a political settlement, with regular US support, see *FT* and Beilin, *op. cit.* Archival materials recently released in Israel make clear that the story goes back many years. On *New York Times* successes in creating an appropriate history, in this and other areas, see my 'All the News that Fits', *UTNE Reader*, Feb./March 1986, and 'Thought Control in the United States'.

58. Friedman provided serious and professional reporting from Lebanon during the 1982 war, and occasionally does from Israel as well; see for example his report on the Gaza Strip, 5 April 1986.

59. Friedman, *NYT Magazine*, 7 Oct. 1984, *NYT*, 17 March 1985; editorial, 21 March 1985; and much other commentary and 'news' reporting: Rabin, *The Rabin Memoirs* (Little, Brown, 1979, p. 332). In keeping with his moderate stance, Rabin believes that the 'refugees from the Gaza Strip and the West Bank' should be removed to East of the Jordan; see *TNCW*, p. 234, for representative quotes.

60. *Ha'aretz*, 29 Sept. 1985 (cited by Amnon Kapeliouk, *Le Monde diplomatique* (Nov. 1985); *Koteret Rashit*, 9 Oct. 1985.

61. Julie Flint, *Manchester Guardian Weekly*, 19 Jan. 1986.

62. The *Post* does not describe this as a 'terrorist act' carried out by the 'terrorist commander' Menachem Begin.

63. Christian Williams, Bob Woodward and Richard Harwood, 'Who Are They?', *WP*, 10 Feb. 1984; editorial, *NYT*, 19 May 1976. On the reality, generally suppressed here, see *TNCW*, *FT*.

64. *New Outlook*, Tel Aviv, Oct. 1985; *Davar*, 18 July 1985. Uri Milshtein writes that contrary to the standard accounts, Israel initiated the conflict that led to the 'war of attrition' with tank firing against Egyptian positions, killing dozens of soldiers; *Monitin*, Aug. 1984.

65. Thomas Friedman, *NYT*, 31 Jan. 1986.

66. John Bulloch, 'PLO victims were Mossad agents', *Daily Telegraph* (London), 3 Oct. 1985; Shaham, *Al Fajr*, 29 Nov. 1985.

67. The PLO claim lacks credibility in this case, and Shaham has an excellent record as a responsible journalist.

68. *FT*, p. 77; David Shipler, *NYT*, 25 Nov. 1983; *NYT*, 26 Jan. 1984, last paragraph.
69. *NYT*, 30 June, 1 July; *BG*, 1, 4, 12 July; *Middle East Reporter* (Beirut), 30 June; *Observer* (London), 1 July; Jansen, *MEI*, 13 July 1984.
70. Thomas Friedman, *NYT*, 5 Feb.; the US 'refrained from making a judgment on the Israeli action', *NYT*, 5 Feb.; also Norman Kempster, *LAT*, 5 Feb. 1986.
71. *News from Within* (Jerusalem), 1 Nov. 1985.
72. *LAT – BG*, 29 June 1984. On the severe repression in the Golan, see *FT*, p. 132f.
73. See Uri Milshtein, *Monitin*, Aug. 1984, for a recent account.
74. *WP*, 40 June 1985; *Time*, 11 Oct 1982; Goodman, *NYT*, 7 Feb. 1984.
75. *FT*, p. 188f.
76. Rabin, *The Rabin Memoirs*, pp. 280-1.
77. *NYT*, 12 Oct. 1985. Meanwhile the *Times* denounces Iran, 'which has yet to extradite or punish those who hijacked a Kuwaiti airliner and killed two Americans in December, 1984', and demands that the West boycott Libya if Qaddafi continues 'to shelter hijackers'. Editorial, *NYT*, 14 May 1986. It has yet to say anything similar, or anything at all, about those who shelter the hijackers of the Soviet airliner, or about the long record of hijacking and piracy by our Israeli clients.
78. Livia Rokach, *Israel's Sacred Terrorism*, a study based on Moshe Sharett's personal diary (AAUG, 1980, p. 20f.); 'Sixty Minutes', CBS, 7 pm, 19 Jan. 1986.
79. Sune Persson, *Mediation and Assassination* (London, 1979); Michael Bar-Zohar, *Ben Gurion: a Biography* (Delacorte, 1978), pp. 180-1; Stephen Green, *Taking Sides* (Morrow, 1984), p. 38f.; Kimche, *Seven Fallen Pillars* (Secker & Warburg, 1953), pp. 272-3.
80. *Globe & Mail* (Toronto), 9 Oct. 1985.
81. *NYT*, 27 Sept. 1985, a picture caption without a story; *AWSJ*, 22 Aug., cited by Alexander Cockburn, *Nation*, 2 Sept. 1985.
82. Shultz, *BG*, 25 June 1984; *NYT*, 25 June 1984, 30 Dec 1983; AP, *BG*, 23 April 1984, *NYT*, 1 April 1984; *International Herald Tribune*, 5 May 1986; Colin Nickerson, *BG*, 3 Feb. 1985, on the convention; *Africasia*, July 1985, for details on the captured South African commandos, an episode largely ignored here; Munslow and O'Keefe, *Third World Quarterly*, January 1984. On the airliners, see *BG*, *NYT*, *WP*, 11 Nov. 1983; *BG*, 21 Feb. 1984. These barely noted incidents occurred in the midst of the mass hysteria over the shooting down of KAL 007 by the USSR, which merited seven full pages in the densely-printed *New York Times* index in September 1983 alone.
83. Dan Fisher, *LAT*, 21 June; McGrory, *BG*, 21 June; David Adams, *New Statesman*, 19 April; *NYT*, 21 June 1985.
84. *LAT*, 1 July 1985.
85. David Ignatius, *Wall St Journal*, 18 June 1985.
86. *NYT*, 21 June, 18 June, 1 July 1985.
87. Bernard Lewis, *NY Review*, 15 Aug.; *New Republic*, 8 July; Reagan, Address to the American Bar Association, 8 July (*BG*, 9 July); Podhoretz, *LAT*, 26 June; *NYT*, 2 July 1985.
88. Thomas Friedman, *NYT*, June 23; *NYT*, June 19, 1985.
89. *AP*, *BG*, 4 July; Friedman, *NYT*, 4 July; *BG*, 4 July 1985.
90. *FT*, pp. 181-2.
91. Rabin, speaking to the Knesset, *Hadashot*, 27 March 1985; Tamari, interview, *Monitin*, Oct. 1985.
92. Rokach, *op. cit.*; Uri Milshtein, *Al Hamishmar*, 21 Sept. 1983; Kennett

Love, *Suez* (McGraw-Hill, 1969), pp. 10f., 61-2.

93. *NYT*, 4 Dec. 1984. On the scholarly record, see, e.g., *TNCW*, p. 331, discussing Nadav Safran, *Israel: the Embattled Ally* (Harvard, 1978).

94. *LAT*, 24 Nov.; *BG*, 19 Dec; *NYT*, 20 Dec; *BG*, 20 Dec 1983.

95. *Globe & Mail*, 11 July; *BG*, 24 July; *NYT*, 24 July; *Boston Herald*, 25 July 1985; *NYT*, 5, 6 Jan.; *BG*, 5, 6 Jan. 1984.

96. James Markham, *NYT*, 3 Dec 1985, giving casualty estimates from Lebanese and Palestinian sources.

97. *NYT*, 23 March 1985; *NYT*, 3, 4 Dec. 1975; *Time*, 5 March 1973; *NYT*, 22 Feb. 1973, giving the figure of fifteen killed.

98. There was no supporting evidence in the case of the Libyan jet, but the Soviet allegation may be correct, though it obviously provides no justification for the atrocity; see R. W. Johnson, *Shoot-Down* (Viking, 1986), a study particularly interesting for its dissection of us government lies.

99. *NYT*, 22, 23 Feb.; editorial, 23 Feb.; 25, 26 Feb. 1973. Amiram Cohen, *Hotam*, 10 Feb. 1984. The incident was briefly recalled during the KAL 007 affair, evoking false claims by apologists for Israeli violence that Israel 'immediately accepted responsibility' and 'paid reparations'; Michael Curtis, letter, *NYT*, 2 Oct; Martin Peretz, *New Republic*, 24 Oct. 1983.

100. See note 98. For comparison of the reaction to the two events, see Robert Scheer, *Manchester Guardian Weekly*, 25 Sept. 1983; for discussion of other similar incidents, also passed over lightly here given the agents of the atrocity, see my '1984: Orwell's and Ours', *Thoreau Quarterly*, Winter/Spring 1984 and 'Notes on Orwell's Problem' in *Knowledge of Language* (Praeger, 1986).

101. On the Lydda-Ramle expulsions, see Benny Morris, *Middle East Journal*, Winter 1986; on the other cases, see *FT*, my *Turning the Tide* (South End, 1985), and sources cited; Schocken, *Foreign Affairs*, Fall 1948. On efforts to assassinate the Palestinian political leadership in 1948, organized by Moshe Dayan, see Uri Milshtein, *Al Hamishmar*, 21 Sept. 1983; *Hadashot*, 11 Jan. 1985. A recently discovered Israeli intelligence report of 30 June 1948 concludes that of the 391,000 Arab refugees (152,000 from outside the area assigned to Israel in the UN Partition recommendation), at least 70 per cent fled as a result of Jewish military operations (primarily Haganah/IDF) including direct expulsion, an apparent underestimate, Benny Morris observes in his analysis. The report also notes that this took place in the face of intense efforts of the Arab leadership to stem the flow. He also notes that the 'circumstances of the second half of the exodus', from July to October, 'are a different story'; 'after June '48 there were many more planned expulsions' (*Middle Eastern Studies* (London), Jan. 1986; interview with Haim Har'am, *Koi Ha'ir*, 9 May 1986).

102. The varying Israeli versions of this event make interesting reading. For a review of several of them (including the only account to have appeared in a major us journal, a shameful cover-up by Ze'ev Schiff and Hirsh Goodman in the *Atlantic Monthly*), see James Ennes, 'The USS Liberty: Back in the News', *American-Arab Affairs*, Winter 1985-6. Perhaps the most intriguing is that of Yitzhak Rabin, then Chief of Staff, who describes the attack on the ship as 'the most alarming development in the entire campaign', when he experienced 'sheer terror'. He then proceeds to place it very carefully on 7 June (it was 8 June), an inconceivable error, which can only be understood as an effort to obscure the apparent reason for the attack: to conceal from the us the planned invasion of Syria after the cease-fire. Rabin, *Memoirs*, p. 108f.

103. On the southern Lebanon case, see Mark Bruzonsky, *MEI*, 16 May 1985; also *BG*, 15 April; David Shipler, *NYT*, 16 April 1986. See *Houston Chronicle* (AP),

18 May, (UPI) 21 May 1984, on the case of New Mexico businessman Mike Mansour, jailed for twenty-two days and, he alleges, tortured and forced to sign a confession, which he repudiates.

104. Robert Tucker, *Commentary*, October 1982.

105. Dario Fernandez-Morera, *History of European Ideas*, 6.4, 1985.

106. On these matters, see *TNCW*, p. 47f., and my chapter in Chomsky, Jonathan Steele and John Gittings, *Superpowers in Collision* (Penguin, 1982; revised edition, 1984). See especially Edward S. Herman, *Real Terror Network* (South End, 1982).

107. Hirst, *MGW*, 20 April 1986; Harkabi, quoted by Amnon Kapeliouk, *Le Monde diplomatique*, Feb. 1986.

108. Qaddafi's execution of Libyan dissidents, his major recorded terrorist acts, might also have been prevented according to US and Israeli intelligence analysts, but with the possible consequence of revealing that the (apparently quite transparent) Libyan codes had been broken. 'An Israeli analyst put it more bluntly: "Why expose our sources and methods for the sake of some Libyans?" '; Frank Greve, *Philadelphia Inquirer*, 18 May 1986.

109. See 'Libya in US Demonology' for examples and discussion.

110. *NYT*, 27 June 1985; Attorney-General Edwin Meese stated a year later on a visit to India 'that the United States was taking steps to control private military camps that India has charged have trained Sikh extremists' (*CSM*, 25 March 1986). Bob Woodward and Charles R. Babcock, *WP*, 12 May; Philip Shenon, *NYT*, 14 May 1985, for CIA denial of involvement, 'disputed by some Administration and Congressional officials who said that the agency was working with the group at the time of the [Lebanon] bombing'.

111. Ihsan Hijazi, *NYT*, 20 April 1986.

112. Anthony Lewis, *NYT*, 21 April 1986.

6

The Essential Terrorist

Edward W. Said

As a word and concept, 'terrorism' has acquired an extraordinary status in American public discourse. It has displaced Communism as public enemy number one, although there are frequent efforts to tie the two together. It has spawned uses of language, rhetoric and argument that are frightening in their capacity for mobilizing opinion, gaining legitimacy and provoking various sorts of murderous action. And it has imported and canonized an ideology with origins in a distant conflict, which serves the purpose here of institutionalizing the denial and avoidance of history. In short, the elevation of terrorism to the status of a national security threat (though more Americans drown in their bathtubs, are struck by lightning or die in traffic accidents) has deflected careful scrutiny of the government's domestic and foreign policies. Whether the deflection will be longstanding or temporary remains to be seen, but given the almost unconditional assent of the media, intellectuals and policy-makers to the terrorist vogue, the prospects for a return to a semblance of sanity are not encouraging.

I hasten to add two things, however, that are. The noisy consensus on our Libyan adventures is, or seems to be, paper thin. The few dissenting voices are a good deal more effective in stimulating discussion and reflection (which on their own, alas, cannot prevent the destruction we are capable of unleashing) than one might have thought. A small instance of what I mean occurred recently during a Phil Donahue show whose subject was the 14 April 1986 raid on Libya. Donahue began the show by asking the audience for their opinion; he received an almost total, even enthusiastic, endorsement of 'our' righteous strike. Two of his guests were Sanford Ungar and Christopher Hitchens who, once they got going, managed quite rapidly to extend the discussion beyond the audience's unexamined assumptions and patriotic bombast. By the end of the hour, the kicking of Libyan ass in revenge for terrorism seemed to be a less agreeable, more troubling exercise than when the program began.

The second source of encouragement is related to the first. The obvious case to be made against the ugly violence and disruptions caused by desperate and often misguided people has little sustainable power once it is extended to include gigantic terror networks, conspiracies of terrorist states or terrorism as a metaphysical evil. For not only will common sense rise up at the paucity of evidence for these preposterous theories, but at some point (which is not yet near enough) the machinery for pushing the terrorist scare will stand exposed for the political and intellectual scandal that it is. The fact is that most, if not all, states use dirty tricks, from assassinations and bombs to blackmail. (Remember the CIA-sponsored car bomb that killed eighty people in the civilian quarter of West Beirut in early 1984?) The same applies to radical nationalists, although we conveniently overlook the malfeasance of the bands we support. For the present, however, the wall-to-wall nonsense about terrorism can inflict grave damage.

The difference between today's pseudoscholarship and expert jargon about terrorism and the literature about Third World national liberation guerrillas two decades ago is interesting. Most of the earlier material was subject to the slower and therefore more careful procedures of print; to produce a piece of scholar-ship on, say, the Vietcong you had to go through the motions of exploring Vietnamese history, citing books, using footnotes – actually attempting to prove a point by developing an argument. This scholarship was no less partisan because of those procedures, no less engaged in the war against the enemies of 'freedom', no less racist in its assumptions; but it was, or at least had the pretensions of, a sort of knowledge. Today's discourse on terrorism is an altogether more streamlined thing. Its scholarship is yesterday's newspaper or today's CNN bulletin. Its gurus – Claire Sterling, Michael Ledeen, Arnaud de Borchgrave – are journalists with obscure, even ambiguous, backgrounds. Most writing about terrorism is brief, pithy, totally devoid of the scholarly armature of evidence, proof, argument. Its paradigm is the television interview, the spot news announcement, the instant gratification one associates with the Reagan White House's 'reality time', the evening news.

This brings us to the book at hand, *Terrorism: How the West Can Win*, edited and with commentary, weedlike in its proliferation, by Benjamin Netanyahu, the Israeli ambassador to the United Nations. A compilation of essays by forty or so of the usual suspects – George Shultz, Jeane Kirkpatrick, Lord Chalfont, Claire Sterling, Arthur Goldberg, Midge Decter, Paul Johnson, Edwin Meese III, Jean-François Revel, Jack Kemp, Paul Laxalt, Leszek Kolakowski, etc. – *Terrorism* is the record of a conference held two years ago at the Jonathan Institute in Washington, Jonathan Netanyahu being Benjamin's brother, the only Israeli casualty of the famous raid on Entebbe in 1976. (It is worth noting that victims of 'terrorism' like Netanyahu and Leon Klinghoffer get institutes and foundations named for them, to say nothing of enormous press attention, whereas Arabs, Moslems and other nonwhites who die 'collaterally' just die, uncounted, unmourned, unacknowledged by 'us'.)

The sections into which the book is divided roll forth with a reassuringly steady acceleration: 'The Challenge to the Democracies' and 'Terrorism and Totalitarianism' are succeeded by (of course) 'Terrorism and the Islamic World', which in turn brings forth 'The International Network' and 'Terrorism and the Media'. These are followed by 'The Legal Foundations for the War Against Terrorism' and 'The Domestic Battle', yielding in place to the final, the biggest, the choicest subject of all, 'The Global Battle'. Compared with earlier works on the subject (for instance, Walter Laqueur's *Terrorism*), this one has shed all the introductory attempts at historical perspective and cultural context. Terrorism is now a fully formed object of more or less revealed wisdom.

There are some low-level oddities about this book that should be noted quickly. Very few efforts are made to convince readers of what is being said: sources and figures are never cited; abstractions and generalizations pop up everywhere; and, except for three essays on Islam, historical argument is limited to the single proposition that terrorism has never before presented such a threat to 'the democracies'. I was also struck that the verb in the book's subtitle, *How the West Can Win*, doesn't seem to have an object: win what? one wonders. So great is the number of contributors, so hortatory the tone, so confident and many the assertions, that in the end you retain little of what has been said, except that you had better get on with the fight against terrorism, whatever Netanyahu says it is.

No wonder, then, that Mario Cuomo, who consults on foreign policy with Netanyahu, an official of a foreign government, has endorsed the book in a jacket blurb, urging 'presidents, premiers, governors, mayors', to read it for its startlingly 'valuable lessons': that 'state-sanctioned international terrorism is purposeful and often conspiratorial, and that the world's democracies are targets of terrorism'. If Cuomo's presence in this august company is designed to make him appear serious and *presidentabile* by association, he really ought to reconsider for a moment, because the whole book is unfortunately staked on the premise that the Western democracies and their leaders are gullible, soft and stupid, a condition whose only remedy is that they abandon their 'Western' essence and turn violent, hard and ruthless. And if, in addition, they could be led by the Netanyahu family, Yitzhak Rabin and Moshe Arens (all of them contributors to *How the West Can Win*), their successful transfiguration would be assured. At that point, however, would a liberal Mario Cuomo stand any chance at all?

In fact, *Terrorism: How the West Can Win* is a book about contemporary American policy on only one level. It is equally a book about contemporary Israel, as represented by its most unyielding and unattractive voices. An attentive reader will surely be alerted to the book's agenda from the outset, when Netanyahu, an obsessive if there ever was one, asserts that modern terrorism emanates from 'two movements that have assumed international prominence in the second half of the twentieth century, communist totalitarianism and Islamic (and Arab) radicalism'. Later this is interpreted to mean, essentially, the KGB and the Palestine Liberation Organization, the former much less than the latter, which Netanyahu connects with all nonwhite, non-European anticolonial movements, whose barbarism is in stark contrast to the nobility and purity of the Judeo-Christian freedom fighters he supports.

Unlike the wimps who have merely condemned terrorism without defining it, Netanyahu bravely ventures a definition: 'terrorism', he says, 'is the deliberate and systematic murder, maiming, and menacing of the innocent to inspire fear for political purposes'. But this powerful philosophic formulation is as flawed as all the other definitions, not only because it is vague about exceptions and limits but because its application and interpretation in Netanyahu's book depend a priori on a single axiom: 'we' are never terrorists; it's the Moslems, Arabs and Communists who are.

The view is as simple as that, and it goes back in time to the fundamental and inaugurating denial in Israel history: the buried fact that Israel came to exist as a state in 1948 as a result of the dispossession of the Palestinians. In the early 1970s there was, I believe, a subliminal recognition on the part of Israel's leaders that no conventional military option existed against the Palestinians, who number 650,000 inside Israel, 1.3 million in Gaza and the West Bank and two million in exile, and that therefore they would have to be done away with by other means. That recognition was certainly the result of the emergence of post-1967 Palestinian nationalism as a force resisting Israel's occupation of historical Palestine in its entirety.

The principle of 'armed struggle' derives from the right of resistance accorded universally to all peoples suffering national oppression. Yet like all peoples (including, of course, the Jews) the Palestinians resorted on occasion to spectacular outrages, in order to dramatize their struggle and to inflict pain on an unremitting enemy. This, I have always believed, was a political mistake with important moral consequences. Certainly Israeli violence against Palestinians has *always* been *incomparably* greater in scale and damage. But the tragically fixated attitude toward 'armed struggle' conducted from exile and the relative neglect of mass political action and organization inside Palestine exposed the Palestinian movement, by the early 1970s, to a far superior Israeli military and propaganda system, which magnified Palestinian violence out of proportion to the reality. By the end of the decade, Israel had co-opted US policy, cynically exploited Jewish fears of another Holocaust, and stirred up latent Judeo-Christian sentiments against Islam.

An interesting article by the Israeli journalist Amnon Kapeliouk in the February 1986 issue of *Le Monde diplomatique* suggests that it became a conscious aim of Israeli policy in the mid-1970s to delegitimize Palestinian nationalism in toto by defining its main expression – the PLO – as terrorist, the better to be able to ignore its undeniable claims on Israel. The major consequence of this policy was, of course, the 1982 Israeli invasion of Lebanon, allegedly carried out to defeat terrorism but in reality designed to settle the fate of the West Bank and Gaza, particularly given the fact that the PLO had scrupulously observed a cease-fire between July 1981 and June 1982.

Yet one of the complexities of the 1982 invasion was that it showed the West a side of Israel hitherto well hidden. All the more reason, therefore, to efface the picture of Sabra and Shatila by waging a full-scale ideological and cultural battle against terrorism – a battle whose main thrust has been, first, its selectivity ('we' are never terrorists no matter what we may have done; 'they' always are and always will be), and, second, its wholesale attempt to obliterate history, and indeed temporality itself. For the main thing is to isolate your enemy from time, from causality, from prior action, and thereby to portray him or her as ontologically and gratuitously interested in wreaking havoc for its own sake. Thus if you can show that Libyans, Moslems, Palestinians and Arabs, generally speaking, have no reality except that which tautologically confirms their terrorist essence as Libyans, Moslems, Palestinians and Arabs, you can go on to attack them and their 'terrorist' states generally, and avoid all questions about your own behavior or about your share in their present fate. In the words of Benjamin Netanyahu:

> The root cause of terrorism lies not in grievances but in a disposition toward unbridled violence. This can be traced to a world view which asserts that certain ideological and religious goals justify, indeed demand, the shedding of all moral inhibitions. In this context, the observation that the root cause of terrorism is terrorists is more than a tautology.

To reduce the whole embroiled history that connects 'us' with terrorists (or Israelis with Palestinians) to Midge Decter's tiny, scornful phrase, 'the theory of grievances', is to continue the political war against history, ours as well as theirs, and leave the problem of terrorism unsolved.

Consider now the rigorous selectivity of this approach. Julie Flint, a reporter for *The Guardian* of London, described an Israeli intervention in Lebanon in early March 1986 just as Farrar, Straus was getting the Netanyahu compilation ready for the bookstores. Looking for two missing Israeli soldiers, an Israeli military unit accompanied by South Lebanese Army men (Israeli mercenaries) entered the village of Shakra: 'Throughout the week, every day at daybreak, the Israelis herded all Shakra's men into the courtyard of the local school for interrogation. "We've spent the whole time sitting on the ground," Mr Nassar [a young merchant in the town, just returned from several years' absence] said. "If we stood up they hit us." ' Flint's report continues in terrifying detail; I shall cite it here at length because it is not likely to be found in any American publication, so powerful are the restraints against printing material that openly discredits the

Israelis and compromises their antiterrorist stance. It should be set against the items regularly produced by the US media that purport to describe the US-Israeli view of 'terrorism', for example, the handouts given to and dutifully reproduced by Thomas Friedman of *The New York Times*. (A particularly egregious instance was an article on 16 February 1986, in which we were treated to such solecisms as the Israeli intelligence notion of the 'terrorilla'.) The evidence from Shakra undermines, to say the least, Netanyahu's definition of terrorism as applied exclusively to the PLO and the KGB:

> The Irish [UN] troops tried to send in water, milk and oranges, but the Israelis and the SLA men threw it all on the ground. Then on Friday, the routine changed: men, women and children – the youngest a day-old baby – were all locked in the courtyard and interrogated in two schoolrooms. Villagers say the first interrogation was with Israeli soldiers and the second with SLA thugs – in a room where bloodstains were still to be seen last week on the floor and on two school desks. Scattered all over the small room were objects villagers said were used in the interrogation – chair legs, wooden sticks, cigarette butts in ash trays still sitting on electric stoves, electric coils, and nails with which the interrogators reportedly pierced ears. Throughout the day, the Irish were refused access to the detainees, although screams could be heard and several people could be seen badly hurt in the schoolyard. In the late afternoon, five men were thrown into the street outside the school, all crying and some unable to stand upright. They were taken to the hospital. Although Unifil declines to discuss the 'full documentary evidence' in its medical report, reporters who visited the five saw they had been brutally beaten and burnt on the back with cigarette ends. Radwan Ashur, a student, had badly damaged hands; friends said his interrogators walked over them in army boots. Another man had his penis burnt with a cigarette lighter. A short way from his school, young men including Mr Nassar, were assembled at night by the village pond. They said they were thrown into it and then, dripping wet and their hands tied behind their backs, were made to lie until dawn on the floor of an unfinished shop. 'You have to tell us everything about this town,' Mr Nassar was told. He replied: 'I don't know anything. I've just come from Liberia'. After the Israelis finally departed late on Saturday having failed to find their men, the security report for Shakra showed that 55 men and six women, one of them pregnant, had been taken away, three houses had been dynamited and many others looted and wrecked, their doors blasted off with grenades. Several dozen cars were stolen.

The point about this little episode (which features the innocent civilians whom the United States loves to defend) is not that it occurs daily, or that such behavior has been characteristic of the Israeli state from the very beginning (as revealed by revisionist Israeli historians Tom Segev and Benny Morris, among others), or that it is increasing in viciousness as the spurious excuse of 'fighting terrorism' serves to legitimize every case of torture, illegal detention, demolition of houses, expropriation of land, murder, collective punishment, deportation, censorship, closure of schools and universities. The point is that such episodes are almost completely swept off the record by the righteous enthusiasm for deploring Arab, Moslem and nonwhite 'terrórism'.

In this enthusiasm a supporting role is played by the accredited experts on the Islamic world. Note here how, unlike those scholars of Latin America, Africa and Asia whose naïveté leads them to express solidarity with the peoples they study, the guild of the Middle East Orientalists seems to have produced only the likes of Bernard Lewis, Elie Kedourie and the utterly ninth-rate P.J. Vatikiotis, each of whom contributes a slice of mendacity to Netanyahu's smorgasbord. Far from offering insights about their area of specialization (which provides them with a living) that might promote understanding, sympathy or compassion, these guns-for-hire assure us that Islam is indeed a terrorist religion. So untoward and humanly unacceptable is this position that *The New York Times*'s John Gross refused to recognize it in his review of this book. He therefore especially commended Lewis's view – Gross paraphrases freely – 'that there is nothing in Islam as a religion that is especially conducive to terrorism'. But had he read past the second paragraph of Lewis's essay, he would have found the great man saying that 'it is appropriate to use Islam as a term of definition and classification in discussing present-day terrorism'.

Gross and Lewis are symptomatic of the whole deformation of mind and language induced by 'terrorism'. Gross is so ideo-logically infected with the antinomian view that, on the one hand, no respectable scholar can say racist things and, on the other, one can say anything about Islam and the Arabs if one is a respectable scholar, that he just gives up on reading critically. Lewis, who is by now reckless with the confidence inspired by having *The New York Times*, *The New York Review of Books*, *The New Republic* and *Commentary* more or less at his disposal, serves up one falsehood or half-truth after another in his essay. Islam, he tells us, is a political religion, a unique thing. Whereas, he intones, Jesus sacrificed himself on the cross and Moses died before he entered the Promised Land, Mohammed (clever fellow) founded a state and governed it. Those three millennial facts alone are supposed to have determined the whole of Christian, Jewish and Islamic history and culture ever since. Never mind that Jewish and Christian leaders have – to this day – founded and governed states, or that Jews and Christians (quite ignoring the charity of Christ or the misfortunes of Moses) fought battles in the name of Christianity and Judaism that were as bloody as anyone else's. What matters, says Lewis, is that at the present time there is 'the reassertion of this association of politics and Islam', as if it isn't clear that Israel is perhaps the most perfect coincidence of religion and politics in the contemporary world, or that Jerry Falwell and Ronald Reagan time and again connect religion and politics. No, not at all, it is only Moslems, unregenerate combiners, like their founder, of politics and religion, who are guilty of this atavism. It can make you quite angry to read such nonsense.

Terrorism: How the West Can Win is thus an incitement to anti-Arab and anti-Moslem violence. It further inflames an atmosphere in which it is considered natural that when Leon Klinghoffer is senselessly and brutally murdered, *The New York Times* devotes 1,043 column inches to his death, but when Alex Odeh, no less an American, is just as senselessly and brutally murdered at the very same time in California, he gets only fourteen column inches. Have we become so assured of the inconsequence of millions of Arab and Moslem lives that we assume it is a routine or unimportant matter when they die either at our hands or at those of our favoured Judeo-Christian allies? Do we really believe that Arabs and Moslems have terrorism in their genes?

The worst aspect of the terrorism scam, intellectually speaking, is that there seems to be so little resistance to its massively inflated claims, undocumented allegations and ridiculous tautologies. Even if we allow that the press, almost to a man or woman, is so traduced by moronic notions of newsworthiness, spectacle and power that it cannot distinguish between isolated and politically worthless acts of desperation and orchestrated attempts at genocide, it is still difficult to explain how or why it is that those who should know better either say nothing or leap on the bandwagon. Only a handful of people, like Noam Chomsky and Alexander Cockburn, seem willing to ask publicly why facts are never discussed or how it has become customary to judge evidence entirely on the basis of what race, party or creed delivers it up. If you say that the United States supplied Israel with the cluster bombs used to kill Palestinian children in Beirut, you, and by

extension your statement, are dismissed, not because the statement is untruthful but because you are 'a Palestinian (or Arab or
Moslem) spokesman', as if that fact doomed you irremediably to
spreading terrorist lies. But no one says to Claire Sterling and
Jillian Becker that their unverifiable claims about 'international
terrorist conventions' and various 'terrorist agreements', for which
no proof or contents are ever given, are unacceptable as evidence.
And other Orientalists do not challenge Lewis and Kedourie for
the bilge they regularly spill out on Arab or Islamic culture, which
would be considered the rankest racism or incompetence in any
other field.

Past and future bombing raids aside, the terrorism craze is
dangerous because it consolidates the immense, unrestrained
pseudopatriotic narcissism we are nourishing. Is there no limit to
the folly that convinces large numbers of Americans that it is now
unsafe to travel, and at the same time blinds them to all the pain
and violence that so many people in Africa, Asia and Latin
America must endure simply because we have decided that local
oppressors, whom we call freedom fighters, can go on with their
killing in the name of anticommunism and antiterrorism? Is there
no way to participate in politics beyond the repetition of
prefabricated slogans? What happened to the precision, discrimination and critical humanism that we celebrate as the hallmarks of
liberal education and the Western heritage?

Do not try to answer those questions straight out. Instead, get
hold of any treatise, article, television transcript, editorial, public
proclamation or book on terrorism (virtually any one will do;
they're interchangeable) and ask the author questions you would
ask someone who argued that the universe was being run from an
office inside the Great Pyramid. The world's, and our, problems
will not disappear at all: they'll become fully apparent as now,
under the sign of terrorism, they are not. The main task for
American intellectuals is not to attack Libya or denounce Soviet
communism, but to figure out how this country's staggering power
can be harnessed for communal coexistence with other societies,
rather than for violence against them. Certainly such a task cannot
be helped by trading in metaphysical abstractions while we charge
about the world as if we were the only people who counted. Nor
will it be helped by declaring ourselves to be in a perpetual state of
siege, partners in this protracted insanity with the Middle East's
diehard rejectionists.

PART THREE

The 'Liberal' Alternative

7

Michael Walzer's *Exodus and Revolution*: A Canaanite Reading

Edward W. Said

Michael Walzer's *Exodus and Revolution* (Basic Books) is principally a contemporary reading of the Old Testament story. Yet it also
touches on revolutionary politics and biblical and narrative
interpretation; and it refers to the relationship between secular and
religious realms, between 'paradigms' and actual events, between a
particularly Jewish and a more generally Western history. This
may seem rather a heavy load for so small and apparently modest a
book, but it is a major part of its interest, and indeed of Walzer's
skill as a writer, to say things with an appealing simplicity while in
fact alluding to many considerably more complex issues. The
result, however, is not so much an unsatisfactory as an unsatisfying
book, though I hasten to add that Walzer sets his reader's critical
faculties very intensely to work, surely a testimonial to how
provocative his subject is.

The essential lines of Walzer's argument are quickly rehearsed.
Unlike narratives of recurrence and return, the Exodus story is
linear, Walzer says, and moves from bondage and oppression in
Egypt, through the wanderings in Sinai, to the Promised Land.
Moses is not an Odysseus who returns home, but a popular leader
– albeit an outsider – of a people undergoing both the travails and
novel triumphs of national liberation. What we have in Exodus,
therefore, is the 'original form of progressive history' – and,
Walzer adds, while other slave revolts in antiquity established no
really new or influential type of political activity, 'it is possible to
trace a continuous history from Exodus to the radical politics of
our own time'.

Walzer's exposition is interspersed with references to later events and to thinkers explicitly indebted to Exodus. Readers of his first book, *The Revolution of the Saints*, will not be surprised to see some of the seventeenth-century Protestant radicals discussed there referred to again in *Exodus and Revolution*, in addition to various American Black leaders of the civil rights movement and Latin American liberation theologians. Two of the main features of this constellation of affiliated political ideologues are, first, that they all draw upon divine authority for 'radical hope' even as they stress 'this worldly endeavor', and second, that none of them is theoretically systematic or, in the literal sense, revolutionary. Rather, Walzer says, these traits express what he is himself committed to, 'the Jewish account of deliverance and the political theory of liberation'.

Specific to both of these is the covenant, which in the Old Testament is made with God but which Walzer reinterprets as 'a founding act' that creates 'a people' and the possibility of 'a politics without precedent in [the people's] own experience'. More advantages of the covenant are that 'the people' become a 'moral agent'. Thus for the people, solidarity with the oppressed is a moral obligation. Less pleasant (and less easy to gloss over) is the people's candidly stated need to defeat counterrevolution – that is, worshippers of the Golden Calf and, in the Promised Land, the unfortunate native inhabitants who by definition are not members of the Chosen People. Walzer's main point, however, is that culmination of Exodus in the attainment of a Promised Land is really the birth of a new polity, one that admits its members to a communal politics of participation in political and religious spheres. It isn't entirely clear what useful or positive role God can play in these spheres, once they have become the social property, so to speak, of the citizenry in a secular state; Walzer's indifference to the problem is odd, but one can at least understand it.

Walzer concedes that Exodus politics – the phrase is his, and he uses it to distinguish a particular political outlook and style – can lead, as indeed, it has led in Jewish and Christian history, to messianism and millenarianism. These riotous chiliastic movements are very distant from the relatively sober and apparently attractive notions professed by believers in the kind of Exodus politics endorsed by Walzer. He also concedes that the best part of the Exodus experience occurs at the beginning; problems of many sorts, all of them self-made, come in immediately after that to qualify, and perhaps even cancel, the beginning's promise. In any event, according to Walzer, we are fully entitled to reject anything about Exodus that smacks of mere territorialism, since what matters is the 'deeper argument' proposing 'that righteousness' (and not the coarse act of holding the Promised Land) 'is the only guarantee of blessings'. In applying these notions to modern Zionism, Walzer seems to align himself with those Israelis who want a compromise over the territories occupied by Israel since 1967, and he cites Gershom Scholem in support of the view that Zionism is not a messianic movement but a historically – as opposed to religiously – redemptive one.

Along the way Walzer offers a number of insights that expand and illuminate the Bible's relatively speedy narrative course. Of these his commentary on 'murmurings' – the anxieties, difficulties and restive stirrings among the Jews being forced to actions beyond ordinary tolerance – is the freshest and most perceptive. But, as with much else in this work of one hundred and fifty pages, one wishes for more detail and amplification in its author's account of modern styles of radical politics, particularly when he draws rather challenging distinctions between Moses's Levites and Lenin's vanguard party as élite leaders of a popular movement. The former he says can be 'read' as avatars of social-democratic leadership, whereas the latter quite obviously cannot. Yet the evidence he offers for such a charitable reading (unlike Lincoln Steffens's, who thought Leninism and Exodus supported each other) is comparatively meager; it doesn't in itself convince one that Moses's kindness or his lawgiving magnanimity are enough to inhibit later clerical bloodthirstiness and zeal. Nevertheless, Walzer's readers are likely at first to go along with many of his suggestive, rather than exhaustive, arguments because they are, I think, inherently attractive.

A 'relaxed and easygoing vision' of reality, said Ronald Dworkin of one of Walzer's previous books: the same vision is very much in evidence in *Exodus and Revolution*. Homey, egalitarian, melioristic, as in the book's final sentences, a summary of

> what the Exodus first taught, or what it has commonly been taken to teach, about the meaning and possibility of politics and about its proper form:
>
> - first, that wherever you live, it is probably Egypt;
> - second, that there is a better place, a world more attractive, a promised land;

- and, third, that 'the way to the land is through the wilderness'. There is no way to get from here to there except by joining together and marching.

As you read Walzer and mull over his various agreeable conclusions and affirmations, you begin to wonder how the world has become so malleable and so possible a place. Not that Walzer actually *says* it is a possible place; on the contrary, he insists on its complexity and difficulty at almost every opportunity. No: what bothers you is the world of Walzer's discourse, the verbal space in which his discussions and analyses take place, as well as the political locale isolated by him for reflection and hypothesis. Then you begin to realize how many extremely severe excisions and restrictions have occurred in order to produce the calmly civilized world of Walzer's Exodus. In itself, the strategy of *découpage* is unavoidable. Every author who pretends to rationality obviously has to do some cutting and delimiting in order to manage his or her subject, but although these tend to occur offstage, they are certainly well within critical reach, and require fairly close inspection if the main onstage action is to be fully comprehended.

Walzer's 'relaxed and easygoing' work is the result of a very curious and, to my mind, extremely problematic antithetical mode, insistent and uncompromising in places, indifferent and curiously forgiving in others. Take as perhaps the most obvious instance the cluster of descriptive references with which he endows Exodus: it is Western, Jewish, liberating, complex, this-worldly, linear, clear. Compared with that of Lewis Feuer's *Ideology and the Ideologists* (referred to once in a passing note by Walzer), the Exodus of Walzer's study is tremendously circumscribed; Feuer is anxious to show the presence of the Exodus 'myth', as he calls it, in *all* revolutionary ideology, Western and non-Western, progressive and reactionary alike, the more easily to reveal its multiple short-comings. But the grounds for Walzer's assertions of Exodus's various discrete and positive qualities are kept obscure and, I think, unexamined. Why is Exodus 'Western', for instance? Why is it of use to seventeenth-century English revolutionaries? to some Latin American liberationists and not to others? to some Black leaders but not to others? Walzer has no answer that is not tautological, and he does not really propose the questions.

The effect of Walzer's chatty style is to disarm those who might look for evidence, argument, proof and the like – particularly in the writing of an author whose numerous strictures on Michel Foucault (*Dissent*, Fall 1983) include the objection that Foucault's studies are 'often ineffective in what we might think of as scholarly law enforcement – the presentation of evidence, detailed argument, the consideration of alternative views'. Nor can *Exodus and Revolution* be taken as a poetic or metaphoric excursus through an Old Testament text. Walzer's political and moral study is addressed to us 'in the West' and his prose is dotted with *us*'s and *ours*, the net result of which is to mobilize a community of interpretation that relies for illumination upon a canonical text believed to be central, true, important as giving 'permanent shape to Jewish conceptions of time'. And, he adds, 'it serves as a model, ultimately, for non-Jewish conceptions too'. *Ultimately* in this sentence plays a crucial tactical role, as of course does the plural in 'Jewish conceptions of time'. Walzer signals that there are in fact more issues than can be dealt with by 'us' here and now; if we had the time, we could ultimately discover how important Exodus was as a model for various nonspecified non-Jewish views of temporality. *Ultimately*.

Let me call this tactic inclusion by deferral, in order next to bring in its accomplice, avoidance. Remember that at the same time that he uses these tactics, Walzer is making very strong assertions about revolution, progress, peoplehood, politics and morality: it is not as if he were just an avoider and a deferrer. In fact, a fog is exhaled by his prose to obscure those problems entailed by his arguments but casually deferred and avoided before they can make trouble. The great avoidance, significantly, is of history itself – the history of the text he comments on, the history of the Jews, the history of the various peoples who have used Exodus, as well as those who have not, the history of models, texts, paradigms, utopias, in their relationship to actual events, the history of such things as covenants and founding texts.

Walzer spends no time at all on what brought the Jews to Egypt (in Genesis) nor on the great degree of wealth and power which because of Joseph they achieved there. It is quite misleading simply to refer to them as an oppressed people when Genesis 46 and 47 tell in some detail of how 'they had possessions therein, and grew, and multiplied exceedingly'. The Old Testament gives the strong impression that the Jews had come to Egypt, an earlier promised land, at the invitation of Pharaoh to seek their fortunes, that is, as compradores; when Egypt fell on hard times, so too did the Jews and because they were foreign they were the targets of local rage and frustration. This history is hardly comparable with that of American Blacks or contemporary Latin Americans. I suspect that Walzer uses the rhetoric of contemporary liberation movements to highlight certain aspects of Old Testament history and to mute or minimize others.

The most troubling of these is of course the injunction laid on the Jews by God to exterminate their opponents, an injunction that somewhat takes away the aura of progressive national liberation which Walzer is bent upon giving to Exodus. The greatest authority on the history of class politics in the ancient world, G.E.M. de Ste. Croix, Fellow of New College, Oxford, says the following in his monumental study, *The Class Struggle in the Ancient Greek World*:

> I do not wish to give the impression that the Romans were habitually the most cruel and ruthless of all ancient imperial powers. Which nation in antiquity has the best claim to that title I cannot say, as I do not know all the evidence. On the basis of such of the evidence as I do know, however, I can say that I know of only one people which felt able to assert that it actually had a divine command to exterminate whole populations among those it conquered; namely, Israel. Nowadays Christians, as well as Jews, seldom care to dwell on the merciless ferocity of Jahweh, as revealed not by hostile sources but by the very literature they themselves regard as sacred. Indeed, they continue as a rule to forget the very existence of this incriminating material.

Not only does Walzer refuse to meet these matters head on; what little he does say slides away from the facts, as we shall see in a moment. He also cuts out from consideration all of the material in Numbers and Leviticus (extensions of Exodus) in which we find Jahweh urging revoltingly detailed punishments for offenders against His Law. It seems to me inescapably true that during moments of revolutionary fervor, *all* the monotheistic religions proposed unforgiving, merciless punishment against actual or imagined enemies, punishments formulated by perfervid clerics in the name of their One Deity. This is as true of early Islam as it is of Pauline Christianity and of Exodus. Simply to step past all of that into a new realm called 'Exodus politics' will not release you fröm the problem. In other words, it seems unlikely to expect that the kind of secular and decent politics Walzer salvages from Exodus could coexist with the authority of the sole Divinity plus the derivative but far more actual authority of His designated human representatives. But that *is* what Walzer alleges. Walzer also claims rather lamely that commandments like 'thou shalt utterly destroy them' should not be taken literally. Similarly, he avers, 'the original conquest and occupation' of the land plays only 'a small part' in Exodus politics. It is difficult to know here what

Walzer is talking about, so anxious is he to disconnect from, and yet connect with, the essential parts of Exodus that have inspired the text's later users, from Indian-killing Puritans in New England to South African Boers claiming large swatches of territory held by Blacks. Maybe it is true (although Walzer provides no evidence) that the conquest of Canaan was 'more like a gradual infiltration than a systematic campaign of extermination'; but he seems unperturbed that for the Jews 'the Canaanites are explicitly excluded from the world of moral concern'. This does not suggest a very elevated model for realistic politics, and it isn't clear how the dehumanization of anyone standing in Moses's way is any less appalling than the attitudes of the murderous Puritans or of the founders of *apartheid*. To say that 'thou shalt utterly destroy them' is a command that 'doesn't survive the work of interpretation; it was effectively rescinded by talmudic and medieval commentators arguing over its future applications' is, I regret to say, to take no note of history *after* the destruction of the Temple in which Jews were in no position at all collectively to implement the commandment. Therefore, I think, it is Walzer who is wrong, not 'the right-wing Zionists' in today's Israel whom he upbraids for being too fundamentalist. The text of Exodus *does* categorically enjoin victorious Jews to deal unforgivingly with their enemies, the prior native inhabitants of the Promised Land. As to whether that should be 'a gradual infiltration' or 'a systematic campaign of extermination', the fundamental attitude is similar in both alternatives: get rid of the natives, as a practical matter. In either case, Israel's offending non-Jewish population is 'excluded from the world of moral concern' and thus denied equal right with Jews.

Walzer offers no detailed, explicit or principled resistance to the irreducibly sectarian premises of Exodus, still less to the notion of a God as sanguinary as Jahweh directly holding them in place. Walzer accepts those unpleasant but surely not simple facts as givens and then goes on to protest that he finds in Exodus a realistic, secular paradigm for 'radical politics'. Not being as amphibious as Walzer, the unbelieving or atheistic reader, such as myself, cannot so quickly adjust to this odd new element, which combines sacred and profane in equal doses. In the positivist calendar, August Comte unsurprisingly accorded Moses the dubious privilege of having founded the first theocracy. As a salve for the secular conscience, however, Walzer again and again offers the startling propositions that Exodus is nevertheless really secular and progressive, is about liberation and against oppression. According to him, no other text has either the priority or the force of this one, and, to repeat, 'it is possible to trace a continuous history from the Exodus to the radical politics of our own time'.

As we have seen, Walzer's 'continuous' lines come from what remains after inconvenient fact and divagations have been lopped off all around them. His dismissal of the Helots' struggle against their Spartan overlords is an example of how one such fact, which considerably lessens the uniqueness of Exodus's liberationist power, gets eliminated. Helots, Walzer says, didn't leave 'us' an account of what they meant by deliverance, as if in itself leaving 'an account' qualified you for entry into the rolls of honor. Only the Jews in Exodus did, which is why they were ultimately the model for radical politics. The sturdily anti-clerical de Ste. Croix, however, enables us to dismiss such an exaggerated comparison as the preposterous ahistorical cant it is by stating not only that the Helots were far more unfortunate as 'state serfs' than any other ancient people, but that they were legendary in classical antiquity and after for articulating their unified struggle 'to be free and an independent entity'.

Once you begin a catalog of the exceptions to Walzer's claims for Exodus, much less remains of his argument about the book's paramount importance for future movements of liberation. Vico, Marx, Michelet, Gramsci, Fanon either mention the book not at all or only in passing. Many Black and Central American theorists do mention it; but a great many more do not. Certainly Exodus is a trope that comes easily to hand in accounts of deliverance, but there isn't anything especially 'Western' about it, nor – to judge from the various 'non-Western' tropes of liberation from oppression – is there anything especially progressive that can be derived from its supposedly Western essence. All oppressed peoples dream of liberation after all, and most tend to find rhetorical modes for mobilizing themselves, imagining a better future and justifying to themselves the vengeance they intend to take not only on their former masters but also on their future underlings.

Given recent history, one would have thought that Walzer might have reconsidered the whole matter of divinely inspired politics and coaxed out of it some more sobering, perhaps even ironic, reflections than the ones he presents. With examples readily at hand of a crazy religious leadership at the head of substantial political movements in Israel, Lebanon and Iran (all of them pulling references out of their common monotheistic tradition in order to eliminate opposition) can he be seriously recommending that we use Exodus as 'realistic' or 'progressive'? Yes, he can. Perhaps it is the Exodus narrative itself he find appealing as a work of art. If so, he says hardly anything about it that hasn't been said more artfully by various literary theorists – Northrop Frye, Frank Kermode, Paul Ricoeur, Hayden White, scholars whose uses of the Bible are exhilarating in their technical as well as aesthetic ingenuity.

No: Walzer's Exodus offers the opportunity for him to assert and stress the inaugural priority of a text as a matter of consolidation and conviction, not of persuasion or of proof. As for the relationship between Exodus and its subsequent users, Walzer included, that, like so much else about this curious contemporary performance, is hinted at in telegraphic allusions. The theoretical question of how ideological texts like Exodus relate to actual events (*cf*. Gramsci's famous 1917 treatment of the Bolshevik revolution, 'The Revolution Against "Das Kapital" ') is not even considered. Then too Walzer's insistence on seventeenth-century Puritan ideology, which he cites as confirmation of Exodus's millennial power, denudes the phenomenon of its fascinating seventeenth-century context in the period's politicized philo-Semitism, recently studied in 'Philo-Semitism and the Readmission of the Jews to England, 1603-1655' (Clarendon Press, Oxford, 1982), a monograph by David S. Katz. Walzer also ignores the quite potent negative reaction against Moses and Exodus to be found in the writings of some Puritan figures, as he does also Moses's quite fanciful apotheosis in writers like the eighteenth-century Bishop Warburton. Above all, I think, Walzer's work relegates the notion of a genuinely secular political option to nullity; he seems to be saying that only the salutary inflections in Exodus could bring forth a wholesomely progressive politics, thereby sweeping the board improbably clean of zealotry, vicious sectarianism, tyrannical theoretical systems and the sheer disorderly tumble of historical events. Reading Walzer you could not know that a whole ideological radical literature, Western and non-Western, had offered millions of adherents ideas for which his reading of Exodus makes no allowances. Why is Walzer so undialectical, so simplifying, so ahistorical and reductive?

The first answer is that he really is not. His argument in *Exodus and Revolution* has an altogether different, and quite complex, trajectory from the one presented to a surface reading.

To begin with, Walzer is deeply and symptomatically anti-Marxist: he will have none of the labor theory of value, of relations of production, of historical materialism. Informed by his espousal of what he calls Jewish (that is, religious) conceptions of time, the anti-Marxism in Walzer is not difficult to understand. Yet Walzer continues to aver his radicalism as well as his attachments to a 'secular and realistic politics', the basis for which he locates in Exodus.

Now there is nothing in *Exodus and Revolution* to suggest that Walzer's attitude toward current Jewish studies is a very developed one. From what I know of Jewish studies as a field most influenced by Gershom Scholem and today having some bearing on literary theory, it doesn't seem to me that Walzer even tries to make a contribution to the field or to engage with other scholars working in it. I say all this tentatively because, on the one hand, Walzer doesn't offer his readers very many clarified insights as to his fundamental interests in the hermeneutical problems of canonical texts, and because, on the other hand, the Jewish material in Walzer's work is made to pull in the chariot, so to speak, of a resolutely political (and not philosophical) agenda, its path marked by repeated words and phrases: *progressive, moral, radical politics, national liberation, oppression.*

Considered as a group, the provenance of these is not Exodus. The terms enter American and European political vocabulary after the Second World War, usually in the context of colonial wars fought against movements of national liberation. The power of 'liberation' and 'oppression' in the works of those Third World militants like Cabral and Fanon, who were organically linked to anticolonial insurrectionary movements, is that the concepts were later able to acquire a certain embattled legitimacy in the discourse of First World writers sympathetic to anticolonialism. The point about writers like Sartre, Debray and Chomsky, however, is that they were not mere echoes of the African, Asian and Latin American anti-imperialists, but intellectuals writing from within – and against – the colonialist camp.

Although most commentators recognize that that period is now practically over (largely because the anticolonial movements were victorious), only a little attention has been devoted to the ideological aftermath in Europe and America. A 'return' to Judeo-Christian values was trumpeted; the defense of Western civilization was made coterminous with general attacks on terrorism, Islamic fundamentalism, structuralism and communism; a pantheon of aggressive new culture heroes emerged, including Norman Podhoretz, Jeane Kirkpatrick, George Will and Michael Novak. Much retrospective analysis of the colonial past focused on the evils of the newly independent states – the corruption and tyranny of their rule, the betrayed promise of their revolutions, the mistaken faith placed in them by their European supporters. The most striking revisionist has been Conor Cruise O'Brien, whose total about-face found him an entirely new audience (to some degree already primed by the Naipaul brothers) extremely eager to hear about the evils of black or brown dictators and the relative virtues of white imperialism. Other former anticolonialists like Gerard Chaliand contented themselves with chronicling the history of their disappointments.

The revival of anti-imperialist and liberationist language in discussions of Nicaragua and South Africa is one major exception to this pattern. The other major exception has been the rhetoric of liberal supporters of Israel. I speak here of a rather small but quite influential and prestigious group which, since 1967, has conducted itself with – from the perspective of students of rhetoric – considerable tactical flexibility. All along, in the face of considerable evidence to the contrary, members of this group have tried to maintain Israel's image as a progressive and wholly admirable state.

Consider that all of the Third World national liberation groups identified themselves with the displaced and dispossessed Palestinians, and Israel with colonialism. Historically, Zionist writers did not generally describe their own enterprise as a national liberation movement; they used a vocabulary specific to the moment of their vision of history – in the early twentieth century – which, while it contained important secular elements, was primarily religious and imperialist. The concepts of chosen People, Covenant, Redemption, Promised Land and God were central to it; they gave identity to a people scattered in exile, they were useful in getting crucial European support and in the setting up of institutions like the Jewish National Fund, and, as is the case in all such situations, they were a focus for heated discussion, intense partisanship, contested political theories. After the Second World War the appeal of Zionism to the British Labour Party, the Socialist International, or to any number of Western liberal supporters – in whose ranks, surprisingly, one could find anti-imperialists like Sartre and Martin Luther King – was determined by European sympathy with the dominant Weizmann-Ben-Gurion (and not Jabotinsky-Begin revisionist) trend within Zionism. This trend was perceived as socially progressive and morally justifiable in a form that Europeans and Americans could immediately understand. When R. H. S. Crossman, Paul Johnson or Reinhold Niebuhr spoke of Zionism (and later of Israel), it was because the Jewish presence in Palestine was viewed as an extension of like-minded undertakings in Europe and, much more significantly, as restitution for the horrors of European anti-Semitism. Arabs were routinely seen as corrupt, backward, irrelevant.

After 1967, it became difficult to portray the Israeli occupation armies in Gaza, the West Bank, Sinai and the Golan Heights as furthering a great social experiment. And it has not often been noted how strange the anachronism, how ironic the disjuncture, that enabled the emergence of a new and eccentric colonial situation at exactly the same time that classical colonialism was being defeated nearly everywhere else. Eccentric because while they were settler-colonists like the French or British in Africa, Israeli Jews were different in essential ways: they had a traditional tie to the land, they had an unimaginable history of suffering, they were by no means an overseas offshoot of a metropolitan Western power. In 1967 however, the American intervention in Vietnam was at its height, and so for progressive supporters of Israel it became directly imperative to separate Israel in the Occupied Territories from America in Indochina, and to find coherent reasons for excusing the first while condemning the second.

Walzer played a pioneering role in this effort. With Martin Peretz (to whom *Exodus and Revolution* is dedicated) he wrote a landmark article in *Ramparts* (July 1967). Its title, 'Israel Is Not Vietnam', comprehended half a dozen points, all of them showing the way in which Israel was not like France, the United States or Britain in their nasty colonial adventures. The article did not change the opinions of too many on the Left – to whom the article was explicitly addressed – and Peretz later withdrew his financial support from *Ramparts*. In any event, the article is important not only because Walzer used his Left credentials to speak with and to the Left, but also because the piece codified the mode of analysis he would later use.

The steps Walzer takes are worth listing. One: he finds a contemporary situation that could, if it isn't immediately addressed, affect Israel's standing adversely. In *Exodus and Revolution* it is the discredited appearance both of Jewish fundamentalism and continued colonial rule over many Arabs and Arab land. Two: he does that initially by appearing to condemn something close at hand, which progressives can also condemn without much effort and for which an already substantial consensus exists. In *Ramparts* it was Western colonialism; in *Exodus and Revolution* it is Zionist extremists like Gush Emunim and Rabbi Kahane. Three: he shows how certain rather provocative aspects of Jewish and/or Israeli history and/or related episodes in, say, American or French history, do not all fit the condemned instances, although some obviously do. Thus since Kahane, like Begin and Sharon, does not resemble Moses, Moses's stature as a fine leader is enhanced and hence he qualifies along with contemporary Israelis like Gershom Scholem and members of the Labor Party. Four (the really important intellectual move): Walzer formulates a theory, and/or finds a person or text – provided that none is totally general, too uncompromising, too theoretically absolute – that provides the basis for a new category of politico-moral behavior. The book of Exodus as interpreted by Walzer does fit the need quite perfectly, especially by allowing him to appropriate the language of national liberation and apply it anachronistically to the ancient Jews. Similarly, as we shall see presently, Albert Camus's position on French colonialism is made by Walzer to stand for the role of the 'connected' intellectual. Five: he concludes by bringing together as many incompatible things as possible in as moral-sounding as well as politically palatable a rhetoric as possible. The desired effect is that both the generosity and the 'relevance' and not the inconsistency of the procedure will be noted.

Operations of this sort cannot survive critical analysis. *Exodus and Revolution* proves their fallibility in all sorts of ways. The nagging question is how Walzer can continue to claim that his positions are progressive and even radical. He seems unconscious of the degree to which Israel's military victories have affected his work by imparting an unattractive moral triumphalism – harsh, shortsighted, callous – to nearly everything he writes, despite the veneer of radical phrases and protestations. The results have often been extraordinarily disturbing, but not, apparently, to him; here and there a disquiet will briefly disturb his style, but all in all Walzer is at ease with himself and always has been. In 1972, for example, he argued that in every state there will be groups 'marginal to the nation' which should be 'helped to leave'. Saying that he had Israel and the Palestinians in mind, he nevertheless conducted this discussion (that coolly anticipates by a decade Kahane's bloody cries of 'they must go') in the broadly sunny and progressive perspectives of liberalism, independence, freedom from oppression. In his book *Just and Unjust Wars*, he insists on the difference between the two kinds of war, yet finds excuses for Israeli recourse to such actions he otherwise condemns as preemptive strikes and terrorism. His political articles in Peretz's *New Republic*, especially during the 1982 Israeli invasion of Lebanon, are full of such tactical paradoxes. In 1984 he rewrites the history of the Algerian war by praising Camus, the archetypal trimmer, for his loyalty to the *pied-noir* community (one of 'the two Algerian nations', as Walzer calls them), for his rejection of 'absolutist' politics, and for his unwillingness completely to condemn French colonialism. Walzer's unstated thesis is that the one hundred and thirty years of Algerian enslavement and consequent demands for Algerian liberation were somehow *less* of a moral cause than that of Camus's community of French settler-colonialists.

But Walzer's recuperation of Camus's lamentable waffling is even more interesting as an example of the relentless application of step four (the creation of a new category of politico-moral behavior). An essay by Walzer which appeared in the Fall 1984 issue of *Dissent*, the socialist magazine he edits with Irving Howe, reveals a good deal more about Walzer in the process than it does about Camus. Walzer says that Camus was impressive because 'he was committed to a people, the FLN intellectuals to a cause'. I shall leave aside for now the astonishing highhandedness of this judgment of the Algerian resistance and return to it later. According to Walzer, the people Camus wrote for were his own, and insofar as it has been viewed as the critic's role to write of his/her own people as 'the others', Camus, to his immense credit, does not fit the prescription. So much, by way of backhanded dismissal, for Benda's *trahison des clercs*. Camus wrote of what was intimate for him as 'a connected social critic', connected, that is, to his people, the colonizing *pieds-noirs* of Algeria. Thus he was effective in touching their consciences in ways that intellectuals who have taken critical distance from the people could not be. Moreover, Walzer adds, Camus, the writer of 'intimate criticism', was always aware of how what he wrote might expose his family 'to increased terrorism'. Therefore he was sometimes reduced to silence, even though 'the social critic can never be alone with his people; his intimacy can't take the form of private speech; it can only shape and control his public speech'. In short, much more than those French intellectuals like Sartre and Aron, who condemned French colonialism outright, Camus the temporizer and political 'realist' was heroic. He remained, in Walzer's approving formulation, '*what he was*'.

The backing and filling as well as the complaisant sophistry mobilized for this redefinition of the responsible intellectual's role are quite remarkable. Not only does Walzer advocate just going along with one's own people for the sake of loyalty and 'connectedness': he also begs two fundamental questions. One:

whether the position of critical distance he rejects could not also, at the same time, entail intimacy *and* something very much like the insider's connectedness with his or her community? In other words, are critical distance and intimacy with one's people mutually exclusive? Two: whether in the end the critic's togetherness with his/her community might be less valuable an achievement than condemning the evil they do together, therefore risking isolation? These questions raise others. Who is more effective as a critic of South African racial policy, a white South African militant against the régime, or an Afrikanner liberal urging 'constructive engagement' with it? Whom does one respect more, in the accredited Western and Judaic traditions, the courageously outspoken intellectual or loyal member of the complicit majority?

Much of Walzer's recent political and philosophical writing validates the notion of a double standard, one applied to outsiders, another to the members of the intellectual's own community or, to use an important word for him, sphere. Ronald Dworkin was right to say, in the *New York Review of Books* (13 April 1983), that Walzer's moral theory depends on 'a mystical premise' that 'there are only a limited number of spheres of justice whose essential principles have been established in advance and must therefore remain the same for all societies'. In a sense, *Exodus and Revolution* is a book about the establishment of such a sphere for the Chosen People who are inscribed in a Covenant and owners of a Promised Land presided over by God. Hence one's realization that Walzer's idea about 'Exodus politics' turns out to be very snobbish and exclusive indeed.

Walzer has regressed to an odd position on the concept of equality. He has modified it by saying that social goods ought to be considered as having different valences within their separate spheres (education, medicine, leisure, office), not in absolute terms. The key terms once again are 'members' in and 'strangers' to a community, and although Walzer does not refer to Jews and non-Jews, it is difficult not to arrive at the conclusion that his reflections as a Jew on Israel have 'shaped and controlled' his other thought. Thus, for him, the views that members have rights that strangers don't, or can't have, come from the very same political ground on which Israel, as the 'state of the Jewish people' – and not of its citizens, 20 per cent of whom are not members of 'the Jewish people' – is constructed. An additional complication, unattended to by Walzer's philosophy, is that whereas any Jew anywhere is entitled to Israeli citizenship under the Law of Return, no Palestinian anywhere, whether born in Palestine before

1948 or not, has any such right. I refer here to over two million Palestinian refugees, those people (with their recent descendants) who like the Canaanites were originally driven out of their native land by Israel on the premise that they were 'explicitly excluded from the world of moral concern'.

Yet the secular facts are not so neat, so clear and so simple, for 'spheres' do not just exist, nor do they simply acquire the authority of natural facts, nor are they accepted uncomplainingly by 'strangers' who feel their rights have been denied. Spheres are made and maintained by men and women in society. My feeling about Walzer is that his views on the existence of separate spheres have been shaped not so much by Israel as by those of Israel's triumphs which he seems to have felt have been in need of defense, explanation, justification. If Jews were still stateless, and being held in ghettos, I do not believe that Walzer would take the positions he has been taking. I cannot believe that he would say, for example, that communities have the right to restrict land ownership or immigration so that Jews (or Blacks, or Indians) couldn't participate equally in an absolute sense. Not at all. But now that Israel holds territories and rules inferior people, he does not question such practices against non-Jews. Rather he speaks about the intimate connectedness of Camus and the role of 'members' in a state, as well as that of people marginal to it. As for the root problem – why the discrimination instituted by Jews in power should be any more just than the discrimination against Jews by non-Jews in power – that elicits no comment.

It would be wrong and unfair to single out Walzer in all this, since the adjustments and the compromises he has made are part of a general retreat among Left and liberal intellectuals during the past few years. We are at the point now where it is nearly impossible to discern individual themes within the chorus of revised views that blares out from the pages of formerly Left or liberal publications like the *New Republic*. Nowadays religion and God have returned, along with realism; utopia and radicalism are dirty words; terrorism and Soviet communism have acquired a kind of metaphysical purity of horror that eliminates history entirely; competition and the laws of a free market have replaced justice and social concern.

Certainly the peculiarity of Walzer's position (about which, with a few exceptions, he has not been stridently polemical) is that it is still advanced, and honored, as a Left position. It is at bottom a position retaining the vocabulary of the Left, yet scuttling both the theory and critical astringency that historically gave the Left its moral and intellectual power. For theory and critical astringency, Walzer has substituted an often implicit but always unexamined appeal to the concreteness and intimacy of shared ethnic and familial bonds, the realism, the 'moral' responsibility of insiders who have 'made it'. Still, as I have said, if like the Canaanites you don't happen to qualify for membership, you are excluded from moral concern. Or, in Walzer's other surprisingly disparaging, dismissive judgment, you are relegated to a mere cause, like the FLN intellectuals.

If this is the difference between Exodus politics and the politics of causes, then I'm for the latter. For not only does Exodus seem to blind its intellectuals to the rights of others, it permits them to believe that history – the world of societies and nations, made by men and women – vouchsafes certain peoples the extremely problematic gift. of 'Redemption'. Another of the many endowments Walzer bestows on Exodus insiders, Redemption, alas, elevates human beings in their own judgment to the status of divinely inspired moral agents. And this status in turn minimizes, if it does not completely obliterate, a sense of responsibility for what a people undergoing Redemption does to other less fortunate people, unredeemed, strange, displaced and outside moral concern. For this small deficiency Walzer has a reassuring answer too: 'to be a moral agent', he says, 'is not to act rightly but to be capable of acting rightly'. While it is not blindingly clear to me how national righteousness – a highly dubious idea to begin with – derives from such precepts, I can certainly see its value as a mechanism for self-excuse and self-affirmation.

Little of such writing derives from 'radicalism' or from 'righteousness'. Walzer's Exodus book is written from the perspective of victory, which it consolidates and authorizes after the fact. As a result, the book is shot through with a confidence that comes from an easy commerce between successful enterprise in the secular world and similar (if only anticipated) triumphs in the extra-historical world. As to how radicalism and realism square with Walzer's astonishing reliance upon God, I cannot at all understand. I have no way – and Walzer proposes none – for distinguishing between the claims put forth by competing monotheistic clerics in today's Middle East, all of whom – Ayatollah Khomeini, Ayatollah Begin, Ayatollah Gemayel (and there are others) – say that God is indisputably on their side. That the Falwells, the Swaggerts, the Farrakhans in America say much the same thing piles Pelion on Ossa, and leaves Walzer unperturbed, urging a remarkable amalgam of God and realism upon us, as we try to muddle through.

But the one thing I want Walzer to remember is that the more he shores up the sphere of Exodus politics the more likely it is that Canaanites on the outside will resist and try to penetrate the walls banning them from the goods of what is, after all, partly their world too. The strength of the Canaanite, that is the exile position, is that being defeated and 'outside', you can perhaps more easily feel compassion, more easily call injustice injustice, more easily speak directly and plainly of all oppression, and with less difficulty try to understand (rather than mystify or occlude) history and equality. I have read Walzer for many years and I have always admired his intellect, although I have fundamentally disagreed with his politics. I have always wanted to say to him that the defense of spheres and peoplehood based on exclusion and displacement of others who are deemed to be lesser is not what intellectuals ought to be about. I have also wanted to say that ideologies of difference are a great deal less satisfactory than impure genres, people, activities; that separation and discrimination are often not as estimable as connecting and crossing over; that moral and military victories are not always such wonderful things. But having read him again recently, I now realize that *Exodus* may be a tragic book in that it teaches that you cannot both 'belong' *and* concern yourself with Canaanites who do not belong. If that is so, then I thank Walzer for showing me that, and allowing me – and I hope others – to remain unconvinced by what he says, and to resist.

PART FOUR

Scholarship
Ancient and Modern

8

Palestine: Ancient History and Modern Politics

G. W. Bowersock

In the southeastern corner of the Mediterranean there was a province of the ancient Roman Empire that was known simply as Arabia. The Romans had taken over the territory from a race of gifted Arab traders whose kingdom provided the boundaries for the province. For at least three hundred years under these Arabs and for another two hundred or so under the Romans, this part of the Middle East constituted an administrative and cultural unity. In today's perspective it is almost inconceivable that Roman Arabia could have survived the uprisings, civil wars, and invasions of the Hellenistic and Roman periods. But it did.

The region had an odd shape, at least to modern eyes, although natural contours and lines of communication provided coherence. In terms of modern geography this Arabia encompassed the whole of the Sinai peninsula, the Negev desert, all of the modern kingdom of Jordan, the southern part of the present republic of Syria, and the so-called Hejaz in the northwest part of the kingdom of Saudi Arabia. To look at the territory in another way, it stretched from Suez across the southern part of the Holy Land and included everything on the eastern bank of the Jordan that lay opposite the present state of Israel. Access to the eastern side of the Jordan valley could be gained either by sea at Aqaba or by land through the Saudi Arabian Hejaz. Commerce with Damascus had connections therefore with both the sea and the inland trade routes of the Arabian peninsula. This north-south link was simultaneously and peacefully connected with an east-west link across the Araba depression south of the Dead Sea to the

Mediterranean at Gaza or farther southwest across the northern part of the Sinai peninsula. For more than five hundred years a geopolitical entity of major importance in the Middle East of classical times was thus spread across land that is now divided up among no less than five nations. These are Egypt, Israel, Jordan, Saudi Arabia, and Syria.

Some fifteen years ago it occurred to me that there was need for a systematic historical study of this area in Roman antiquity, and from then until now, in such time as I could find, I devoted myself to writing that history. Since the work, *Roman Arabia*, has at last appeared, this may be an appropriate moment to reflect on the interrelationship of past and present in the Middle East. Any historian knows that the past can be exploited politically in contemporary conflicts, but nowhere is this so obvious as in the Middle East.

In visiting the region, I found myself inevitably passing back and forth from one country to another, often with considerable inconvenience. Much of Roman Arabia became part of the larger area known in the Byzantine age as Palestine. The use of the term Palestine, which means literally the land of the Philistines, can serve as a salutary reminder of the ancient unity of the two sides of the Jordan valley. That grand old man of Greek history, Herodotus, had already used the expression Syria Palestine for the whole coastal region from Lebanon to Egypt, and it was taken over by the Roman emperors as a new name for Judea in the second century. Two centuries later, Palestine became an even more comprehensive designation. The Byzantine rulers had three Palestines, of which the Second was the northernmost, occupying the territory south of Lebanon around Haifa. The region around Jerusalem was named First Palestine, while Third Palestine incorporated a large piece of old Arabia – the Sinai, Negev, and the eastern bank of contemporary Jordan south of Amman. The term Palestine accordingly evokes an ancient geographical and administrative coherence, and for later antiquity it represents an even more unified pattern than the province of Arabia. In other words, to the old Arab kingdom on both sides of the Jordan was ultimately added the whole of Judea to make up the ancient concept of Palestine, divided into three numbered segments.

It was not an accident that historians had so long neglected the history of this region in Roman times. Many distinguished explorers and travelers had collected an immense quantity of material, often at great personal risk. But a coherent history of the

region somehow seemed not to be anywhere available. By the end of the first decade of this century the results of exploration in Syria and Trans-Jordan were already so abundant that an enterprising historian could easily have written a substantial work at that time. Expeditions from France, Germany, and America had been so frequent and thorough that in many cases there was extensive duplication in the reports. But for seventy years the material remained in a raw and undigested state, and naturally in the interim there were further revelations.

The long delay in taking seriously the history of the Middle East under the Roman and early Byzantine emperors can be explained in several ways. Through the efforts of western travelers and archaeologists, Biblical archaeology acquired a stranglehold on the study of the ancient Middle East. Until recently the majority of Western specialists in the excavation of the region thought that history ended with Alexander the Great and that even he was a deplorably late and decadent figure. On the Eastern side the indigenous populations showed little inclination to pursue the study of foreign domination in their own homeland. Furthermore, among Arabs the time before the prophet Mohammed had been traditionally considered an age of ignorance, and even now it is designated by the Arabic world *jahiliyya*, which means precisely that. To be sure, the prehistoric epochs of the *jahiliyya* proved somewhat more palatable because they included the achievements of an indigenous ancestral population.

But perhaps more important than anything else in subtly deflecting historical research was a reluctance to confront the fact of an Arabian state and subsequently an even more extensive Palestinian state in the Middle East. These states were parts of the international community of Rome and Byzantium but without the sacrifice of their cultural and economic independence. Since the establishment of modern Israel, research in this area has become trickier still. A decade ago an Israeli scholar reminded me of the basic truth that archaeology is politics in that country, and therefore I suppose it is scarcely surprising to find that in all of Israel there is only one archaeologist who is concerned with pre-Islamic Arab culture, and he is someone who has been made to feel very much alone.

And so the difficulties of comprehending the underlying unity of the ancient province, whether in the form of Arabia or of greater Palestine, were made almost insurmountable by the conditions of today. In antiquity traders passed regularly from the great city of Petra across the Araba depression through the Negev and on to Gaza or points farther west. Only the reckless would attempt that journey in either direction now. I have made the journey from the old Roman city of Philadelphia, which is the modern Jordanian capital of Amman, across the new Allenby Bridge to Jerusalem, but only with my papers in good order. There is no more instructive experience for a student of the Middle East, in any period of its history, than this journey from the Jordanian plateau down into the tropical vegetation of the valley and ultimately into the dry seascape at which one makes the passage over to Jericho. On the whole everyone puts a good face on the problems of travel in the area, but for an ancient historian each barrier is a constant reminder that there was nothing comparable in former times.

The politics of archaeology are everywhere. The late Yigael Yadin was both an eminent archaeologist and a political figure. The intermingling of his two careers is nicely exemplified by the care with which he brought to public attention his discovery of authentic letters of the Jewish rebel Bar Kokhba. These letters survive from the time of the Jewish revolt against Roman rule in the reign of Hadrian. To a dispassionate eye they scarcely show that famous figure as an inspiring leader (I once called him a pious thug), but nonetheless Yadin was pleased to introduce him to the Israeli public as nothing less than the first president of Israel. This was a disingenuous rendering of the title *nasi*, or prince, which the rebel took for himself.

Meanwhile, although the Bar Kokhba letters had been given prompt and broad publicity, another important discovery made by Yadin and his fellow archaeologists has remained unpublished for nearly twenty-five years. At the beginning of the 1960s in a cave in the Judean desert Yadin recovered a set of thirty-five personal documents concerning a Jewish woman by the name of Babatha who had fled into the wilderness for security during the disturbances launched by Bar Kokhba. As we can tell from the few tantalizing excerpts and summaries that have been published, these documents concern the legal affairs of this woman over a period of some forty years. She and her family not only observed the transition from Arab kingdom to Roman province in the territory known as Arabia: she and her family had actually lived there at one time. It is clear that the relation between Jews and Arabs in the territory south of the Dead Sea was a harmonious one. It is amply apparent that in the archive of Babatha we have precious documentation for a social coherence in Palestine that mirrored the administrative and geographical unity. It scarcely matters whether it is by accident or design that neither Yadin nor any other Israeli scholar has seen fit to publish this extraordinary material. In a society in which archaeological discoveries are often extensively reported, the fact that it remains unpublished to this day is eloquent enough.

If archaeology is politics, so inevitably is history. Once again the treatment of Bar Kokhba's revolt is indicative. Apologists have often written that the terrible punishment visited by Hadrian upon the Jews at the end of the revolt was the erection of a pagan temple upon the very site of the Jewish temple that had been destroyed in the days of Vespasian. And yet eyewitness observers in antiquity tell us plainly that no such temple stood on that site in late antiquity. All that was there was a statue of the emperor, whereas the pagan temple in question was located at a considerable distance. Since the truth is not politically helpful, it has been quietly suppressed.

Another good example of the politics of history can be seen in the modern treatment of traditional accounts of the Phoenicians. From the time of Herodotus until the Roman emperors it was believed in both the Phoenician cities of the Mediterranean coast and the cities of the Arabian Gulf that the original Phoenicians had actually come from the Gulf. This tradition has seemed so surprising to Western historians that they have preferred either to forget it or to reverse it and send the Phoenicians as colonists to the Gulf. Yet the Phoenicians themselves accepted the tradition. In this persistent refusal to take seriously the ancient story of Phoenician origins, we are confronted once again with a manipulation of the past.

One constantly stumbles over the obstacles thrown up by the deliberate fragmentation of a fundamentally unified region. If Palestine, together with Syria to the north, constituted between them a cohesive and relatively stable area in Roman and Byzantine times, this was not, as some would undoubtedly suspect, because the Romans imposed the structure. They inherited it from the indigenous populations. In taking over Syria well before the Romans annexed Arabia, the Seleucid monarchs did relatively little to alter the cultural and administrative patterns they inherited. And when both Syria and Palestine were firmly within the sphere of Roman and Byzantine influence, the concept of a combined Syria-Palestine as an overall geographical and cultural unity became a reasonable one. In fact, the only real threat to this conjunction came from the dynasty of Zenobia at Palmyra. It was clearly her design to replace the influence of Rome with that of Palmyra, but not to question or disrupt the essential unity of the region.

The fragmentation of recent times has precipitated endless tragedy. Diplomats and negotiators keep hoping that problems can be resolved by carving up pieces to satisfy the various interested parties. But at least to a historian of the Middle East in the Roman period, such a procedure seems, to borrow Alcibiades' expression for Greek democracy, acknowledged folly. In historical perspective the convulsions of the region in the last decade represent a frantic and bloody effort to recapture some of the lost coherence, to restore the natural balance. The Syrian presence in Lebanon, the Israeli invasion of the same nation, not to mention the Israeli seizures of land from Jordan and Syria, all point to a primordial effort to eliminate, from one side or the other, the unstable and unwise fragmentation of the area. But unfortunately the decision made more than thirty years ago to introduce an entirely new population into a part of the coastal territory of Palestine has wiped out the possibility of ever restoring a coherence or natural balance. Whatever balance is to be achieved in the immediate future will necessarily be unnatural.

Under these circumstances it is reassuring to find that in many countries of the Middle East there is an increasing interest in the long-forgotten history of the Roman and Byzantine ages. Those were times in which the indigenous cultures found ways to flourish in the shadow of large international powers. The old Western emphasis on Biblical archaeology and Biblical history has been far less edifying for the natives of the region. The persistent use of the term Holy Land marked the predisposition of Westerners involved in the Middle East for more than a century. In other words, the turning away from Biblical history to that of Rome and Byzantium represents not merely a shift in scholarly interests but an important accommodation of historical research to the demands of the present.

The new directions of pre-Islamic studies in several Arab nations can be seen in their projects and publications. The Department of Antiquities in Saudi Arabia has already undertaken a vigorous program of excavation and research, and plans are under way for a major expansion of museum facilities throughout the kingdom. A conference on the pre-Islamic history of Saudi Arabia took place in Riyadh seven years ago, and publication of the papers is imminent. A spectacular excavation by the professor of archaeology in the University of Riyadh has opened up a major site of Hellenistic-Roman times in the center of the Arabian peninsula. This is at a place known as Qaryat al-Faw.

The Department of Antiquities in the kingdom of Jordan has also provided enlightened support for research and excavation in pre-Islamic fields, with particular attention to the culture of the Nabataeans, who were the Arabs that preceded the Romans in the region. The Jordanians have organized several international conferences on the history of the country, and the Department of Antiquities publishes an excellent periodical with annual reports on new discoveries. Similarly in Syria today there is strong encouragement of research in non-Biblical history. An excellent archaeological journal, together with support from the Antiquities Department, has prepared the way for a major publication on the history of Syria. This work, in many volumes, will contain contributions from scholars in the West as well as in the Middle East, and it will be disseminated in French and Arabic.

All of this means that the history of the Middle East between the end of the Biblical period and the coming of the Prophet has now become, after centuries of neglect, an important area of research. This development is clearly linked to an effort on the part of the various nations to reassess their traditional role in the area by restoring a forgotten element to the tradition. In view of more sensational events in the contemporary Middle East, it has been easy to forget that this awakening of interest in Rome and Palestine has proceeded through a close and cordial relationship between historians and archaeologists of both East and West.

The situation in Israel is different. For obvious reasons Biblical archaeology still dominates, and the quality of work in the Roman and Byzantine fields does not match the level of Biblical studies. The problem arises from the isolation in which Romano-Byzantine specialists are obliged to work. Archaeology is a big business in Israel, but very little support goes to the study of Nabataean Arabs or the cult of Roman emperors. As we have already seen, one substantial discovery that illuminates both Rome and the Arabs has been allowed to remain unpublished for a quarter of a century. Even those who have devoted their careers to the study of the Roman East have acquired strange perspectives on the situation. One Israeli archaeologist has postulated a curious defense system in the northern extremity of the Negev desert, even though most foreign archaeologists seem unable to discern the evidence for this system. More remarkable still is that scholar's notion that there should have been a linear defense inside an individual Roman province. Such a thing belongs on a frontier. It is as if one were to have a major barrier of fortresses running through central New York State. But this scholar has seen fit to make his proposal because he assumed there would be threats to the Jewish population from the Arabs of the desert. That is to perpetuate an old fallacy by failing to recognize the unity of the Roman Middle East. Arabs and Jews at that time were not in conflict.

It is sad to find political pressures causing distortions of this kind in writing history, especially when a cooler appreciation of the facts would be salutary. The earliest Israeli scholars, who were already mature when the nation was founded, did not suffer from this myopia and set a standard to which one can only hope the Israelis will return. I think particularly of Michael Avi-Yonah, whose treatment of the history of Palestine in a standard German encyclopedia remains invaluable. It is accurate, thorough, and dispassionate. The other extreme is represented by an American scholar with strong ties to Israel, who published not long ago a brief article discussing the history of the region around Jerusalem. It had been inhabited at one time by Edomites. Since that scholar is aware that Edomites and Israelites were traditional enemies in the Biblical period and afterward, he automatically assumed that the Edomites must have been Arabs. Inasmuch as the Biblical tradition makes the Edomites closely related to the Israelites and traces their hostility to sibling rivalry, one can only assume that such a scholar operates on the general assumption that any enemy of Israel is an Arab. That is clearly a pernicious notion.

Tampering with history in the interests of the present is just as reprehensible as any other kind of misrepresentation. Honest mistakes can be expected anywhere and at any time, but the tendentious falsification of the past is another matter. I have the impression that just as the study of Roman Arabia and Roman Palestine has become more attractive to scholars in the Arab world, it has appeared increasingly threatening to those in Israel. There are a few scholars there who soldier on without the recognition they deserve, and once in a while, as in a recent issue of the journal *Cathedra*, there is an extensive review of problems concerning Roman Palestine. But even in that publication one cannot help noticing that the main preoccupation is with the defenses of the area and not with the cultural, social, or economic life that bound it together.

*   *   *

The manipulation of ancient history for present purposes is an unusually bold deception. Most of the evidence is in the public domain, and the conclusions that are promulgated are therefore always subject to scrutiny and control by others. If one finds a willingness to tamper with the facts where the facts are publicly known, then it becomes difficult to have confidence in conclusions that are presented on the basis of evidence that is kept secret. This is the problem that confronts an ancient historian who reads the reports that come out of Israel about the massacres in Lebanon or the treatment of the Arabs on the West Bank. The recent report of an international commission to inquire into violations of international law by Israel during the invasion of Lebanon has regrettably done little to allay one's fears.[1] The Israeli authorities refused to collaborate with this international commission, and, in view of its composition, their concern was certainly understandable. But silence is not an adequate response.

The past is at the same time, therefore, the present in the modern Middle East, as it is in most countries with a long historical tradition. America is most unusual in its lack of feeling for the contemporaneity of ancient history, but the reason is evident: America has no ancient history. It is easy for many observers to miss the contemporary significance of what is going on in areas that might seem exclusively scholarly. Archaeology and history are indeed politics. They are part of the fabric of the modern world. If there were any interest in Israel today in the social world of Babatha and her family among the Arabs of the second century AD, the thirty-five documents she left behind would have been published long ago. After fifteen years of studying Babatha's world, I have become persuaded that to neglect her testimony is to suppress it.

Until recently the archive of Babatha was the single most important piece of new evidence on the relation between Jews and Arabs in post-Biblical times. A few years ago another remarkable discovery was made in the Negev desert. A stone turned up with writing in the script of the Nabataean Arabs. The text, although in a single script, appears to have been written in two distinct languages, one Nabataean and the other Arabic. The finder of this inscription is inclined to date it to the middle of the second century AD, and it would therefore constitute by far the earliest example of the Arabic language. It is obviously significant that the inscription was lying in the Negev desert. The stone is weathered and brittle. Its significance for pre-Islamic scholarship could be enormous. In any other country with a serious interest in archaeology this object would have been removed to a protected place for safekeeping. More than that, one might have expected some publicity for so important a discovery. But there has been no publication of the inscription, and it still lies today under the desert sun.

Notes

1. *Israel in Lebanon: The Report of the International Commission*, Ithaca Press (London), 1983.

9

Territorially-based Nationalism and the Politics of Negation

Ibrahim Abu-Lughod

I

Within less than a decade the Question of Palestine in its basic formulation would be a hundred years old. The past nine decades have witnessed major transformations of the territorial, demographic and political dimensions of that Question. Palestine as an administrative/geopolitical unit has passed from Ottoman *de jure* control to that of a British Mandate to an entirely Israeli controlled land. Its population today represents a much larger mix of people: in terms of religious identity the majority are Jewish; in terms of ethnicity in all probability the majority are derived differentially from Arab origin, and in terms of national identity it is divided along a political dimension of Israeli Jews and Palestinian Arabs engaged in a major contest for either political power or acceptable sharing of *de jure* control.[1] Although British colonial control of the land lasted less than three decades, that period presaged the major transformations that occurred subsequently. Two decades after the dismemberment of Palestine, Israel occupied the remaining parts that became known as the West Bank and Gaza. That occupation awaits termination; whether it will terminate by its legal transformation as some Israelis wish or whether it becomes the site of an independent Palestinian State as Palestinians, backed by an international consensus, press for is a function of the balance of national and international power.

Despite these objectively changed realities what is remarkable is how little the discourse on Palestine has changed; from its beginning the Question of Palestine has revolved around three fundamental issues: 1) Land; 2) People; and 3) Political Sovereignty of the people and land of Palestine. These three issues constitute the essence of the politics of negation in which the protagonists have thus far engaged: historically Palestinian Arabs – and other Arabs as well – negated the Zionist claims of the reality of a Jewish People whose national fulfillment requires a homeland (State) in Palestine. Zionist Jews, and later on Israel, negated the Palestinian Arabs' right to Palestine and the establishment of a Palestinian State therein. Britain as a colonial power then and now negated the Palestinian right to self-determination entailing the establishment of a Palestinian State and affirmed, no matter how it equivocated, the right of the Jewish people to found a Jewish homeland in Palestine. Since 1948, a time when practically all other colonial possessions were achieving their independence, Israel, with considerable support first from Britain and later from the United States, has consistently denied the Palestinian right to self-determination. Its denial is rooted in its conceptualization of both Palestine and its people. Much of contemporary rhetoric reflecting certain political stances is anchored in the historic discourse on the Question of Palestine.[2]

II

Irrespective of how Zionism is defined, its projection of Palestine as the future site of the Jewish homeland (State) was not disputed even when other alternatives were considered. Zionist leaders understood that the Palestine of the period was part of a multinational Empire, and their efforts were directed first toward the Ottoman State, whose sovereignty comprehended Palestine, to obtain its consent; failing in that effort they turned their attention to other powers, and eventually Britain made its commitment in the form of the Balfour Declaration of 1917 'to facilitate the establishment of a homeland for the Jewish people . . . in Palestine'. Zionist/Ottoman/European concession politics are not relevant to my discussion. What is relevant is what is entailed in the term Palestine as a geographic space where European Jews of Zionist persuasion wished to establish their homeland (State). Whereas Zionists, like others, referred to Palestine in an historic sense, the Palestine of the late nineteenth and early twentieth centuries was a territorial domain but not a distinct administrative/

geopolitical unit. As a territorial domain it was part of the Ottoman Empire; administratively it did not exist as a unit governed by a representative of the Ottoman Government. It was, much like the rest of the Eastern Arab provinces of the Ottoman State, part of other *Wilayats* or included autonomous districts (*Sanjaks*). Thus certain parts of the Palestinian seashore areas were part of the Wilayat of Beirut whereas Jerusalem was an autonomous Sanjak. At no point in the long history of the Ottoman/Islamic State did Palestine exist as a geopolitical/administrative unit. Yet in the long discussions preceding the formulation of the Balfour Declaration it appeared that Zionists and others understood that Palestine stood for a particular domain despite ·the imprecision of its geographic expanse or limit. The historic conception of Palestine as well as its imprecise limit were to contribute to the negative discourse among the protagonists.

As an administrative/political unit Palestine is an artifact created by British colonialism much in the same way that practically all African States (and the Eastern Arab States) were set up by European colonialism. While African States do not seriously challenge the legitimacy of the established statehoods, in some important ways both Palestinian Arabs and Israeli Jews are reluctant, for very different reasons, to acknowledge it. As such Palestine became what it is precisely when the British Mandate was imposed on the territory in 1922. Briefly, Britain and France concluded an agreement, known as the Sykes-Picot, in 1916, by which they decided to carve up the Eastern Arab Provinces of the Ottoman Empire; whereas France was allotted what came to be known as Syria and Lebanon – by an arbitrary mix of various administrative districts – Britain was allotted – again by an arbitrary mix of administrative districts – what came to be known as Iraq, Transjordan and Palestine.[3] What is forgotten today, in part because we take for granted that what exists has always been there, is the fragility of that design. It is virtually impossible to single out any of these 'successor' states that did not contest the legitimacy of the parts or the entirety of the geopolitical map of the region. The Turkish Republic contested both Britain and France (representing Iraq and Syria) on the issue of the northwestern frontier regions of both; it accommodated Britain in the former and eventually France ceded Syria's Alexandretta (Hatay) to Turkey. The northern frontier of Palestine was eventually settled between Britain and France. France alienated part of its Syrian (Tripoli) area to the Lebanon. And just as France, the Mandatory for Syria and Lebanon, was able to impose its will in its domain, Britain imposed, for its own reasons, its will in Iraq, Transjordan and Palestine. An important consideration which made it necessary for Britain, as the Mandatory power, to settle the issue of the precise definition of Palestine early on clearly related to its many conflicting commitments. In addition to the Sykes-Picot agreement, Britain had made certain, admittedly controversial, commitments to the Sharif Husayn of Mecca when he on behalf of the Arabs declared the Arab Revolt in 1915. The Arab understanding of these commitments would have entailed the establishment of an Independent Arab State which would have included Palestine. But another agreement, namely the Balfour Declaration, essentially negated Britain's Arab commitment. But the territorial meaning of the Balfour Declaration was at best ambiguous. Whether Britain was impelled by its knowledge of what the Zionists understood by Palestine and therefore had to provide its own is not relevant for my analysis. What is not in doubt is that Britain settled the issue of what constituted Palestine as a geopolitical Mandate when that was approved by the League of Nations in 1922. The Annex to the approved Mandate for Palestine took into account Article 25 relative to the Eastern Frontier of Palestine and specifically excluded the area East of the River Jordan as a potential site for land acquisition or European/Jewish migration; the Balfour Declaration was held not to apply to Transjordan. Since it is common knowledge that the Palestinians at that time as well as other Arabs rejected the whole scheme of the Mandate and rejected the Balfour Declaration, and in the absence of any concerted Transjordanian pressure, Britain's exclusion of Transjordan as a potential site of European Jewish migration has to be ascribed to the meaning of Palestine which was provided by the World Zionist Organization. At the request of the Peace Conference in 1919, the Zionist Organization presented a map[4] of the territory which it construed to be the site of the projected 'national home of the Jewish people'. It claimed that Britain's commitment in the Balfour Declaration applied to that area. It would not come as a surprise now to identify the territory in question: it does include the Palestine of the Mandate but also includes certain parts of Southern Lebanon and Syria (Golan) and considerable parts of Transjordan. At a minimum then, the Zionist understanding of Palestine is that it included important segments of the area east of the Jordan River. Needless to say, this Zionist understanding has no historical – distant or modern – counterpart. The geopolitical unit so identified by the World Zionist Organization may make good economic or strategic sense but it is not premised on a historical foundation.

Clearly Britain did not attach much importance to the geopolitical map. of the Zionists; it proceeded to exercise its Mandatory authority over the two territories – Palestine and Transjordan – as if in fact they were separate units. The fact that both shared a High Commissioner, with a 'resident' adviser in Amman, did not invalidate the distinctness of the two areas politically, administratively and in other matters.

Relevant to this discussion is the statement presented by Mr Herbert Samuel, the first British High Commissioner, to the League of Nations on the administration of Palestine and Transjordan between 1920-25. The statement is sufficiently clear on the distinctness of Transjordan and its emergence and leaves no doubt that Palestine did not include Transjordan in prior periods. He reported:

When the war ended, Trans-Jordan found itself within the administrative area which had been entrusted to His Highness the Emir Feisal, the third son of King Hussein of the Hedjaz; his capital was at Damascus. In July, 1920, the Emir came into conflict with the French authorities, who exercise the mandate for Syria, and left the country. At that moment Trans-Jordan was left politically derelict. The frontier between the two mandatory zones, as agreed between Great Britain and France, cut it off from Syria, but no authority had been exercised from Palestine. The establishment of a direct British Administration was not possible, since Trans-Jordan was part of the extensive area within which the British Government had promised in 1915, in the course of negotiations with the Hedjaz, to recognise and support the independence of the Arabs. Nor would His Majesty's Government have been prepared in any case to send armed forces to maintain an administration. These conditions having arisen soon after my arrival in Palestine, I proceeded to Trans-Jordan in August, 1920. I held a meeting with the leading inhabitants, and, as no centralized government was at that time possible, I took steps to establish local councils in the three districts into which the country is divided by its natural features. These councils assumed the administration of affairs, with the assistance of a small number of British officers who were sent from Palestine for the purpose.

A few months later, His Highness the Emir Abdulla, the second son of King Hussein, arrived in Trans-Jordan from the Hedjaz. He had with him a small force, and he expressed hostile intentions with regard to the French authorities in Syria. The Secretary of State, Mr Churchill, was at that time in Palestine. A conference with the Emir was held at Jerusalem, and an agreement made, under which the mandatory power recognized him, for a period, as administrator of

Trans-Jordan, with the condition that any action hostile to Syria must be abandoned. In 1922 the Emir visited London, the arrangement was confirmed, and in April, 1923, I was authorized to make the following announcement, at Amman, the capital of the territory: 'Subject to the approval of the League of Nations, His Majesty's Government will recognize the existence of an independent Government in Trans-Jordan under the rule of His Highess the Emir Abdulla, provided that such Government is constitutional and places His Britannic Majesty's Government in a position to fulfill its international obligations in respect of the territory by means of an agreement to be concluded between the two Governments'. Owing to various causes, the discussion of the terms of such an agreement has been postponed from time to time, and has not yet been undertaken. The Government of the Emir has continued, however, to receive recognition and support. . .

The territory is now governed by His Highness the Emir, through a small council of ministers. A British representative resides at Amman and advises the Government in the conduct of its affairs, acting under the direction of the High Commissioner for Palestine. The relations which have been maintained with the Emir and his ministers are, and have been throughout, close and friendly.[5]

It is evident from the above that Transjordan was as much of an artifact as Palestine was – and as Syria and Lebanon in their own form; such specific formations were deliberately created by a competitive colonial system to serve the colonial interests of France and Britain; it did not in any serious way reflect the interests or the values of their Arab inhabitants. It is not accidental that the entire colonial scheme was challenged by both Arabs and Zionists. The Arab Nationalists – those who adhered to the ideal of an independent Arab State comprising the entire region – contested the legitimacy of the 'territorial' basis of Statehood, contested the imposed Mandate system and contested Britain's right to promise the alienation of Palestine. The Zionists contested Britain's definition of Palestine and its exclusion of Transjordan from the Palestinian Mandate.

The Zionist and later on the Israeli discourse stresses the 'fact' that Israel emerged on only a very small part of Palestine – less than a third – by which they mean the entirety of Palestine and Transjordan; hence the term 'the partitioned State'.[6]

The Zionists have been consistent in their claim. I will illustrate its 'constancy' by referring to specific instances separated by time. David Ben-Gurion, Israel's first Prime Minister, and Moshe Sharett (Shertook), Israel's first Foreign Minister, often referred to the partition of Palestine in 1922 and referred to the scheme of establishing a Jewish State in 'Western Palestine'. In his testimony before the Peel Commission (1937), Valdimir Jabotinsky, leader of the Revisionists, insisted on the right of the Jews to the entire area – 'Palestine on both sides of the Jordan'.[7] While Israel officially is more circumspect in its pronouncements, its official spokesmen often refer to Jordan as a Palestinian State and claim that Palestinians already therefore have a state of their own.

A series of advertisements that appeared in major American newspapers in the course of 1983 claimed openly that Jordan is Palestine. The series was presumably paid for by 'private' sponsors who support Israel but have been reported to be acting on behalf of certain sectors of Israel's leadership.[8]

Though rightly discredited as spurious scholarship, Joan Peters's *From Time Immemorial* (1984) gave much publicity to the Zionist definition of Palestine as including Transjordan (and, throughout, her work utilizes seriously flawed data that specifically refer to 'Western Palestine'). Perhaps Israel's preference for a solution to the Palestinian-Israeli conflict in terms of what has become known as the 'Jordanian' option reflects the same understanding.

What can be concluded from the above discussion? Whereas Palestinian Arabs (and other Arabs as well) accepted a de facto definition of Palestine as the territory so carved by the British Mandate in which the specific Palestinian aspiration for a territorial state took concrete form – an acceptance now enshrined in Articles 1 and 2 of the Palestinian National Charter – the Zionist/Israeli definition is more flexible and broader. Zionist historical presentation and contemporary Israeli discourse suggest strongly that Palestine includes the territory lying on both sides of the River Jordan. In that sense, the territorial issue continues to inform the politics of negation.

III

Joan Peters's work was viewed, initially, with seriousness – although its first review in the *New York Times Book Review* section (13 May 1984) by John Campbell raised the issue of 'credibility' without taking a position – and scholars addressed themselves to one of its principal allegations, namely the existence of a Palestinian people. Though they faulted her handling of statistical data which she evidently both distorted and 'created' without even bothering to consult the only official censuses of Palestine or the serious academic studies based on these censuses, many did not address themselves to the intimate connection between her claims and the historic position of the Zionist movement on the peoplehood of Palestine. In an important way there was literally nothing new – save the appearance of 'hard data' – in Joan Peters's claims. Even if one does not have recourse to history, former Prime Minister Golda Meir's statement 'that there is no such thing as a Palestinian people, they do not exist' made in 1969 ought to have alerted readers to another constant in the politics of Palestinian-Israeli negation. The Palestine that emerged from the wreckage of the First World War had a population in excess of seven hundred thousand persons, the vast majority of whom were indigenous to the land – the exception were European Jewish settlers numbering less than eighty thousand.[9] Had it not been for the constant demographic/political debate that characterizes the Question of Palestine, neither the origin nor the political rights of the indigenous population would have been seriously questioned. But the discourse on the issue, largely as a consequence of Zionist/Israeli presentations, inevitably and adversely affected the consideration of these matters. It was Chaim Weizmann who summed up the early Zionist formulation of the twin issues of land and people. At a Zionist meeting in Paris in April 1914, he made the following remark: 'In its initial stage, Zionism was conceived by its pioneers as a movement wholly depending on mechanical factors: there is a country which happens to be called Palestine, a country without a people, and on the other hand, there exists the Jewish people, and it has no country. What else is necessary, then, than to fit the gem into the ring, to unite this people with this country?' He went on to indicate that their efforts went into 'buying' the country from its 'owners', the Turks.[10] Whereas Weizmann referred to early Zionists, Golda Meir's statement of 1969 and that of the weight of Joan Peters's work indicate that contemporary Zionists are not averse to repeating the same postulate. The intent of the image thus transmitted was, and is, clear: the establishment of the projected Jewish State by trans-planting European Jewish settlers onto the land would not be at the expense of an extant population. Yet even in 1897 Theodor Herzl, the formulator of political Zionism, knew that Palestine had a population of some sort; but he thought that Jewish colonization would in fact help improve the standards of that population, much in the same fashion that European colonialism was viewed as benefiting the Afro-Asian people it had colonized; and for the unwanted population he thought that they would need to be 'spirited away' without much fanfare. Thus when Zionists confronted the reality of another people on the land, they imputed a certain 'quality' to that population that would justify either subordination or 'transfer'. This was in fact the second major theme which Zionism developed in its attempt to negate the Palestinian people who were clearly opposed to the projected aspirations of the Zionist movement.

The Palestinians were often referred to as Arabs; the term had, at that time as well as later on, two negative connotations. One, by far the more benign, was that they are part of the surrounding Arab region which was variously described as 'backward', 'underdeveloped', 'uncivilized' etc. The other, less generous, referred to them as either nomadic or Beduin. In either case they would benefit greatly from the act of Jewish settlement as Herzl suggested and as Zionists continued to stress in their statements throughout the period of the Mandate. The perceived disparity in achievement of the two protagonists became in time the basis upon which the hypothetical emigration of Arabs from other regions was asserted.

But the third dimension – the identity of the inhabitants – was ignored altogether, a negation that today appears in the terminology used by Israel to refer to the 'residents of Judea and Samaria' as if such a population does not have either a cultural or national identity. Consciously or otherwise it appeared that the Zionists, and to some extent the British and later on Israel, resorted to such negation in an effort to delegitimize the people in question to make it easier to denude them of their political rights. An important index of the success of this concerted effort to deny the Palestinian/Arab identity of the affected population or to undervalue it is the omission of any reference in the Balfour Declaration to either a national or cultural designation of Palestine's population whose civil and religious rights were to be protected by its terms; on the other hand the Declaration was very specific about the Jewish people.

My suggestion is that the Palestinian people's right to self-determination was contested in large measure by both Zionists/ Israel as well as the British colonial administration for reasons that differed only in detail. What they had in common was an agreed-upon definition that the inhabitants of Palestine were part of another people (the Arabs), and whereas Britain alleged that it had fulfilled its promises to the Arabs in general, the Palestinians could find their expression within the Arab framework. Weizmann, when thinking of the Palestinians, thought of them as Arabs and he suggested that every people has a natural homeland: the Jewish homeland was in Palestine whereas the Arab homeland was elsewhere – the centers are Damascus, Baghdad etc. – and the Palestinians belong there and not in Palestine. The latest iteration of the same postulate by Joan Peters is more explicit in that she attributes the Palestinian presence in Palestine to recent times, primarily as a consequence of the improvement of the land by Jewish settlers and thus its 'attractiveness' to Arab immigrants. As the conflict developed between Palestinian Arabs and Palestinian Jews, the Arab identity of the Palestinians was utilized to undermine their political rights by contrasting Jewish, Western and Arab values. While the emphasis on the Arab backwardness continued, additional negative attributes were imputed to the Arabs, ranging from anti-democratic, authoritarian, fanatical (religious or national) tendencies, to collaboration with the Fascists and Nazis and ultimately to being anti-Semitic. On those issues, Joan Peters's work is merely the latest codification of the historic presentations by the Zionist movement, and relies primarily on the earlier work on such issues by C. Alroy, E. Kedouri, S. Haim, Bernard Lewis and lesser protagonists.

A less negative reading of the Palestinian people would have of course produced an entirely different portrait. Historians of the Middle East, less involved with advancing the political interest of the Zionist movement, have noted that Palestine, regardless of its geographic expanse is, and has been, part of the Arab region; its people have been largely Arab in terms of cultural identity since the seventh century when the entire region was transformed culturally and religiously. But as a people who have stayed on a land centrally located in that region and of obvious religious significance to Jews and Christians as well as Moslems, they represent a natural mix of ethnicities, traditions and histories; that within the Arab national community, Palestinians were both Arabs – regardless of their faith – and people of a specific land. Since territorial identity – derived from a territorial state – is very recent in origin, the Palestinian identity of the premodern period, similar to that of other Arabs, was based upon their religious, cultural and geographical – town, village or tribal background. To speak of territorial identity is to commit an anachronism which Palestinians and their adversaries often do to legitimate a modern political 'right'.

That Palestine has absorbed other people is as true as that it has been a place of emigration. It is virtually impossible to find a single Arab State in the modern period that does not contain citizens whose ancestors have not hailed from some other domain within the Islamic or Arab world. The fact that the Ottoman domain was in theory and practice the domain of a multinational community enabled people from one part of the Empire to move to another for commerce, education, employment and so forth. That Palestine contained and contains today Arabs and descendants of non-Arab Moslems is not exceptional; it is typical of the region. What would have been unnatural was an insularity that would have prevented ordinary human interaction, migration and settlement. Not only did some Egyptians settle in Palestine after the departure of Ibrahim Pasha's army – and chroniclers of the nineteenth century, Arab and non-Arab, noted that fact – but others drawn from what became Lebanon and Syria settled there as well. The reverse of this was equally true. Palestinians had settled in other parts of the Ottoman domain and can be identified as such even today. The late Lebanese Prime Minister, Mr Sami al-Sulh, occasionally would point out in the context of discussions of Arab unity that he was born in the Palestinian city of Akka.

Geography, traditions, history and politics played their part in the structuring of Palestinian consciousness and in the eventual formation of a distinct Palestinian/Arab identity. With its successful emergence, the battle for political sovereignty in Palestine was joined between Palestinian Arab and Zionist Jew.

IV

Anxious to 'prove' a historical basis for Palestinian independence, Palestinians often refer to the effort of the Palestinian leader Dhaher al-Umar to wrest control of much of Palestine from the Ottomans in the late eighteenth century. It is true that Lebanese nationalists ascribe similar motives to the Shihabis in Lebanon and territorial nationalists elsewhere in the Arab region find convenient antecedents. What is not contested is that the Ottoman Empire did experience serious 'provincial' challenges to its authority almost everywhere. But to attribute these challenges to 'national, territorially based consciousness' is an altogether different and murky issue. What is also not contested is that the Arab national revolt against the Ottomans before and during the First World War was led by a coalition of activist 'leaders' drawn from different Arab Provinces. Palestinian figures appeared on the list of those either imprisoned or hanged by the Turkish leader Jamal Pasha in the course of the First World War. Clearly they were engaged in a struggle for Arab independence, animated by a form of Arab nationalism. That broad national consciousness continued to inform the political struggle as did that waged against European colonialism of the interwar period and eventually translated itself into what became known as the Arab League. With perhaps the exception of Egypt all of the Arab independence movements became territorially based only after the political map of the Eastern Arab provinces was drawn by European colonialism. In that sense, Palestinian nationalism as a movement that anchored its demand for self-determination and independence in Palestine *per se* can be dated to the period of the Mandate and subsequently.

There are some studies of Palestinian national development in the Mandate period that obviate the need for detailed analysis. Suffice it to say that specific processes of political, social, cultural and economic integration were initiated that were consolidated later on, giving Palestinian nationalism its particular manifestations. These were strengthened by other processes that characterized the Palestinian experience in the post-dismemberment period. The Palestinian experience with dispossession, exile, occupation, subjugation and ethnocide is now sufficiently national in scope that it underpins the Palestinan drive towards independence and sovereignty as much as the previous processes of national integration informed the politics of the Mandate period. Significant as these may be, what is perhaps more relevant to our discussion of the politics of negation is how the Palestinians address themselves to the competing claim for political sovereignty of the Israeli State.

Whereas the Palestinians met Zionist negation with a limited affirmation, in that they always insisted that Jews could live in a Palestinian Arab State as a minority, the Palestinian formulation of the post sixties period exhibits a higher level of affirmation. There is no question today that the Palestinians have recognized the reality of a Jewish people's presence in Palestine – illegal as it might be construed. And accordingly the Palestinian call for the establishment of a non-confessional democratic State in the whole of Palestine – its feasibility notwithstanding – signalled that the Jewish presence in Palestine was irreversible and therefore had to be accommodated. The only question is how to reconcile that presence with the equally valid presence of the Palestinians on the same land. The initial Palestinian answer entailed essentially a shared political sovereignty over the whole of Palestine. The unacceptability of this formulation to Israeli Jews prompted the

Palestinians to provide another alternative. From 1977 onward, the Palestinians pressed for two sovereignties on the same land, one Palestinian Arab and the other Israeli Jew. The premise underlying both alternatives is reasonably clear: there are two distinct peoples – regardless of their origin, cultural and religious identities, etc. – on the land of Palestine in search of political sovereignty. The historic politics of negation would deny one of these two peoples their aspiration; the politics of affirmation would meet the national territorial requirements of both. Only in the context of the politics of mutual affirmation could the historic conflict between Palestinian Arab and Israeli Jew be resolved. Only in that context could genuine appreciation of the other prevail.

Notes

1. Janet L. Abu-Lughod, 'The Demographic War Over Palestine', in *The Link* (New York: Americans for Middle East Understanding), December 1986.

2. See, *inter alia*, the following general works: I. Abu-Lughod, ed., *The Transformation of Palestine* (Evanston, IL: Northwestern University Press, 1976); Aruri, *Occupation: Israel Over Palestine* (Belmont, MA: AAUG Press, 1983); H. Cattan, *Palestine and International Law* (London: Longman 1974); Marc Heller, *A Palestinian State?* (Cambridge, MA: Harvard University Press, 1984); David Hirst, *The Gun and the Olive Branch* (London: Faber & Faber, 1979); A. M. Kayyali, *Palestine: A Modern History* (London: Croom Helm, not dated, late seventies); W. T. Mallison and S. Mallison, *The Palestine Problem* (London: Longman, 1986); Edward W. Said, *The Question of Palestine* (New York: Times Books, 1979); Christopher Sykes, *Crossroads To Israel, 1917-1948* (New York: World Publishing, 1965).

3. For background and discussion see, among others, the following: George Antonius, *The Arab Awakening* (London: Hamish Hamilton, 1939); A. L. Tibawi, *A Modern History of Syria Including Lebanon and Palestine* (London: Macmillan, 1969); and his *Anglo-Arab Relations and the Question of Palestine* (London: Luzac, 1978).

4. The map is reproduced in, among others, Ben Halpern, *The Idea of the Jewish State* (Cambridge, MA: Harvard University Press, 1961), p. 278. Contrast with the approved Mandate map on p. 279.

5. Samuel's statement is reproduced in Lee O'Brien, American Jewish Organizations and Israel (Washington, DC: IPS, 1986), pp. 23-4.

6. This term served as the title of Amos Perlmutter's book, *Israel: The Partitioned State*, NY: Charles Scribner's Sons, 1985.

7. Ben-Gurion's and Shertook's characterizations appear in, among others, Department of State, *Foreign Relations of the United States*, vol. V, (Washington, DC, 1971), pp. 125ff. Jabotinsky's statement is reproduced in Arthur Hertzberg, ed., *The Zionist Idea* (New York: Meridian Books, 1955), p. 562.

8. The text of the statements was uniform. For an illustration see the text which appeared in *New York Times*, 25 March 1983 and Warren Rickey's 'Jordan as Palestine', in *Christian Science Monitor*, 6 April 1983, where he provides some

information on the proclivities of Mr Richard Jacoel, the 'sponsor' of these advertisements.

9. See Janet Abu-Lughod's analysis, 'The Demographic Transformation', in I. Abu-Lughod, *The Transformation of Palestine*, op. cit.

10. Weizmann's statement is reproduced in Hertzberg, ed., *The Zionist Idea*, p. 575.

10

Palestinian Peasant Resistance to Zionism Before World War I

Rashid Khalidi

I

It is axiomatic that history is written by the victors. And it is a corollary that it is more likely to be written about the strong than the weak, and that the views and exploits of those able to read and write are more frequently recorded by historians than those of the illiterate.

Both of these inherent historical biases have bedeviled the modern historiography of Palestine. This has not always been intentional. Over the past four decades, much source material for writing Palestinian history has been lost, destroyed, or incorporated into the state archives of Israel, where it is inaccessible to many Palestinian and Arab historians. The unsettled situation of the Palestinian people, whether under occupation or in the diaspora, has meant that other existing archives, research institutions and universities have been denied the stability, organized existence and peace of mind which are the prerequisites for their proper functioning.[1]

Partly in consequence of these circumstances, there has been a dearth of sound historical scholarship by Palestinians.[2] Thus most writing about Palestinian history has been done by non-Palestinians, who by and large have lacked an intimate familiarity with the indigenous sources, the individuals concerned, and the social and cultural context of Palestinian politics. Irrespective of any bias such foreign scholars may have had, this situation has naturally had a major effect on what has been written, and particularly the perspective from which it is written. While a cross-cultural approach is often extremely valuable, and can provide insights otherwise unavailable, nothing can substitute for people writing their own history, and indeed the two processes can and should be complementary.

Thus, the purview and perspective of much work on Palestine has paid more attention to certain sources and subjects than to others. One example is Yehoshua Ben Arieh's *Jerusalem in the 19th Century: The Old City*, much of which treats the city's Arab population (according to Ben Arieh, Arabs were a majority of its population during most of the period he covers) using no Arabic or Ottoman sources.[3] Similarly, Isaiah Friedman's *The Question of Palestine 1914-1918*, subtitled *A Study of British-Jewish-Arab Relations*, in practice deals only with the British and Jewish sides of this triangle, again using no Arabic or Ottoman sources.[4]

Further, when the Arabs have been the primary subject, the urban and literate sectors of the population have perhaps naturally tended to be the focus of attention, as in the most respected works on Palestinian political history during the 1920s and 30s by Yehoshua Porath and Ann Mosely Lesch, which depend on Arabic, Zionist and Western sources.[5] In others, more use has been made of Zionist sources than Arab ones. This is true even with examples of sound scholarship and great originality focusing on the Palestinians such as Neville Mandel's *The Arabs and Zionism before World War I*, which relies primarily on press reports preserved in the Central Zionist Archives, rather than on the Arabic newspapers themselves, for an analysis of the Arab press.[6]

There are partial justifications for some of these apparent methodological weaknesses. As has already been pointed out, Israeli and Western archives contain more material than some existing Arab ones. In other cases, accessibility and convenience have perhaps wrongly determined which sources were used. Moreover, it is to be expected that the Arab urban population, which was the most vocal, politically active, and most extensively represented in the existing written record, would be the object of the most intense scholarly scrutiny. Finally, the population of the countryside was poor, illiterate and largely inaccessible, and as such left few records of its own.

But regarding issues like land sales, peasant dispossession and resistance, and the impact of Zionist settlement on the rural majority of the Palestinian population, some of these justifications ring hollow. While the British and Zionist records are central sources for any such analysis, and while attention must be paid to the newspapers and activities of the urban Arab notables, what happened at the village level should be the primary focus. This can be followed from non-traditional sources, as did Ya'kov Firestone in his pioneering work using material from outside the formal archives,[7] or through using these archives with special attention to the rural areas, as did Ylana Miller in her *Government and Society in Rural Palestine, 1920-1948.*[8]

Such an approach is essential in any work dealing with demography, land and the peasantry in Palestine. It goes without saying that it is totally absent in a travesty such as Joan Peters's *From Time Immemorial*, which makes sweeping and categorical judgments in all these fields. A book based on the selective and tendentious use of sources, systematic misquotation, plagiarism, and other unscholarly methods would not deserve mention but for the dignitaries who have praised it, the noted scholars whose aid was acknowledged by the author but who have refrained from disassociating themselves from it, and the respected publications which have failed to reveal the dimensions of this scandal.[9]

Such an approach is absent as well in nominally more serious works which reiterate Peters's themes. Thus, Arieh Avneri's *The Claim of Dispossession*, subtitled *Jewish Land Settlement and the Arabs 1878-1948*, purports to show that there was no dispossession of Palestinians, in large part because there were no 'Palestinians' in the commonly accepted sense of the word. He asserts rather that much of the Arab population of the country drifted into it in recent times. Slightly more coherent than Peters, Avneri too treats this subject using Western and Hebrew sources, to the exclusion of Arabic or Ottoman ones.[10] In three hundred pages he never dignifies the indigenous population or the sovereign authority until 1918 with so much as a single quotation from a source generated by them. In cases such as Peters's and Avneri's, the society being studied is an object rather than a subject of history. It can be described by others, but cannot describe itself.

The assertions of these polemicists have been demolished by scholars such as Porath and Alexander Schölch, who have carefully studied Palestinian society using Arabic and Turkish materials, together with Western and Zionist sources.[11] Contentions like those of Peters and Avneri are tenable only from a perspective which denies credibility to the sources produced by the society being studied. In the words of Edward Said, for such writers the Palestinians do not have 'permission to narrate',[12] which from the authors' perspective is rigorously logical, since they don't exist!

While it is impossible at this temporal remove to record in detail what passed in the countryside of Palestine before 1914, what follows is an attempt to reconstruct certain key interactions from a variety of sources, with the objective of providing a perspective which is too often absent.

II

According to one widely-propagated view, awareness in the Arab world regarding Zionism began only during the late Mandate period, and since then has been artificially fostered by a succession of protagonists for a variety of reasons. This view is groundless. In fact, such awareness goes much further back in time, as is shown by a careful study of Arab society and politics before World War I. For during that period, Zionism was the subject of extensive journalistic comment and public controversy throughout the Arab provinces of the Ottoman Empire and in Egypt, and ultimately became a major issue in both local and Ottoman politics.[13]

The extent of the opposition within Palestine itself to Zionist immigration before 1914 has received recognition in several studies.[14] Less attention has been paid to the effect of developments in Palestine during this period on the thinking of the elites of the rest of Syria, Egypt and the other Arab lands under Ottoman rule, at a time when Arabism, the forerunner of Arab nationalism, was born and grew into an effective political movement.

Following the re-imposition of the Ottoman Constitution in 1908, political, intellectual and journalistic activity flourished throughout the Empire after decades of the despotism of Sultan 'Abd al-Hamid. This relatively liberal era continued until 1914, during which period there was a major expansion of the Arabic-language press in the entire region, intensive activity of political parties and secret societies, and important intellectual developments. At the same time, following the turn of the century, the Arabs of Palestine were dismayed by the impact of increasing Zionist colonization, as mounting persecution of Eastern European Jews sent waves of new settlers to Palestine in the second *'aliya*. The newcomers, moreover, were more deeply imbued with political Zionism than earlier Jewish settlers, and more intent on creating a new, purely Jewish society in Palestine.

The Palestinian reaction to this increased Zionist activity during the years from 1908 to 1914 was strong. For the first time, many Arabs realized that Zionism aimed ultimately to create a Jewish polity in place of the existing Arab one, while in the countryside increased land purchases and the replacement of Arab wage-laborers on Jewish estates by Jewish workers angered many *fellahin*. The intensity of these reactions helps explain the role played by the Palestine question in Arab politics then and afterwards. And while it was the response of the literate urban Palestinian upper classes expressed in the press, in the Ottoman Parliament, and elsewhere which most affected thinking in other Arab countries, it is clear that at the root of their fears about Zionism was the experience of those *fellahin* who were the first to clash with the Zionist settlers.

As has been shown by Owen and Issawi, economic and social changes in the lands of the Eastern Mediterranean were increasingly rapid in the late nineteenth century.[15] Simultaneously, the local political patterns of the mid-nineteenth century had been significantly transformed by 1908, and even more by 1914. Underlying many of these changes was the tendency towards the privatization of land ownership and its concentration in fewer hands after the promulgation of the Ottoman Land Code in 1858. This law was only put into effect in Syria and Palestine very slowly, over a period of decades. It required the registration in the name of individual owners of agricultural land, most of which had never previously been registered and which had formerly been treated according to traditional forms of land tenure, in the hill areas of Palestine generally *masha'a*, or communal usufruct. The new law meant that for the first time a peasant could be deprived not of title to his land, which he had rarely held before, but rather of the right to live on it, cultivate it and pass it on to his heirs, which had formerly been inalienable if taxes were paid regularly.

Under the provisions of the 1858 law, communal rights of tenure were often ignored, as many peasants with long-standing traditional rights failed to register out of fear of taxation and other state exactions, notably conscription. Instead, members of the upper classes, adept at manipulating or circumventing the legal process, registered large areas of land as theirs.[16] As far as lands in Palestine were concerned, the biggest beneficiaries were the merchants of the coastal cities of Beirut, Jaffa and Haifa. Their new wealth was a by-product of the incorporation of the region into the world economy, with the attendant opening up of new means of communications, and the growth in trade and in agricultural production related to the improvement in security in the countryside in the 1870s and 80s.

Simultaneous with this socio-economic transformation, there was taking place a cultural, educational and linguistic revival in *bilad al-Sham* (Syria, Palestine and Lebanon), which was closely connected with the rise of Arabism, the precursor of Arab nationalist thinking. The renaissance of the Arabic-language press was central to this revival and to the new patterns of thought which came with it. Although forced abroad by the censorship enforced by Sultan 'Abd al-Hamid in the years after 1878, journalism by individuals from this area continued to flourish in Cairo. An ever-growing number of Arabic newspapers, magazines and technical and scientific journals were published in Egypt by such writers, bringing to the Arab world the latest thinking of Europe, the newest ideas of Islamic reform, the first glimmerings of Egyptian and Arab nationalism, and other currents of thought.

After 1908, *bilad al-Sham* and other regions of the Ottoman Empire made the transition from a regime of authoritarian despotism to one of parliamentary democracy and relative freedom of speech. In the first year following the re-imposition of the Constitution, thirty-five new newspapers were founded in the cities of this region, while in Palestine alone eight newspapers and twenty-one periodicals were established and prospered between 1908 and 1914, not counting dozens of other shorter-lived publications.[17]

The number of schools and with them the rate of literacy was also rising, albeit slowly, in Syria and the other Ottoman regions. This was partly a result of the expansion of the network of missionary schools sponsored and financed mainly by the Great Powers: thus by 1914 there were almost eighty thousand students in French and Russian schools alone in Syria and Palestine. It was also due to the efforts of the central government and of the local population to open new, modern-type schools, both under 'Abd al-Hamid and during the constitutional era. A total of 221 state schools of all levels had been established by World War I in the Beirut *vilayet*, which included the Acre and Nablus districts of Northern Palestine, as well as the districts of Beirut, Tripoli and Latakia. According to 1914 Ottoman figures, in Palestine alone there were ninety-eight state and 379 private Muslim schools.[18]

It can therefore be argued on the basis of such indicators as the growth of the press and the spread of education that while the society within which Jewish immigrants settled at the turn of the century was still backward, it was far from stagnant. Indeed it was changing and beginning to acquire a sense of self-awareness. Most of these changes, and the most visible reaction to Zionist settlement, could be found among the urban notables and a small but growing middle class. However, change was taking place as well among the peasant majority of the Palestine population. Some scholars have argued that 'for all practical purposes the masses were politically, socially and intellectually non-existent',[19] and that it was 'the reactions of the political elite among the Arabs to Zionism, ... and not those of the peasant masses, which was significant'.[20] Contrary to these views, it can be argued that the reaction of the peasantry was central to the struggle over Zionist colonization in Palestine.

Although most peasants were illiterate, they were aware of events in their immediate region and often farther afield: certainly land sales and transfers involving removal of the traditional Arab cultivators in favor of newcomers would have been widely noticed by the rural population. The illiteracy of the peasants nevertheless meant that their responses had to be expressed in a written form by others. We are thus left with little direct record of these responses, except as they were expressed by the literate urban members of the community who rarely perceived them first-hand, or via outbursts of violence by the peasants against Jewish colonists. From a study of both sets of reactions, and the interaction between them, it is clear how and why events in Palestine aroused such widespread concern in the rest of the Arab world.

III

There are no exact figures regarding the size of the Jewish population of Palestine before World War I. According to studies based on Zionist sources, it appears to have been about 80-85,000 in a total population of almost seven hundred thousand.[21] According to the same sources, before 1914 the great majority of Palestinian Jews lived in the cities and towns; only twelve thousand or so lived on the land, nearly all of them in about forty-four agricultural colonies established since 1878.

It is this rural minority of the Jewish population which concerns us, however. This was first because unlike most of the urban majority of Jews in Palestine at this time who were generally religiously-oriented and apolitical, many of those in the countryside had explicit political objectives. Secondly, they came into the closest contact with the majority of the Arab population of Palestine, the peasantry. This naturally occurred because, as can be seen from a map recording the location of the first Jewish colonies,[22] these were generally sited in the fertile lowlands of the coastal plain, Eastern Galilee, or of Marj Ibn 'Amer (the Plain of Jezreel), the valley running southeast from Haifa to Beisan. By and large these areas were already fairly heavily populated by Arabs, although less so than the hill regions.

The situation in these lowland areas where the collision between Arab and Jew first took place must be explained. The sandy soil of the coastal plain was ideal for labor-intensive citrus culture for export, which expanded rapidly in the decades before 1914, drawing workers to these formerly sparsely inhabited areas. Meanwhile, the population grew in other lowland regions in the Galilee after the 1860s as greater security from Beduin depredations allowed the more stable hill villages to expand their cultivation into the valleys. These processes were noticed by prosperous urban merchants, who managed to acquire title to large areas of these fertile lands, in some cases settling new Arab cultivators on them. Soon afterwards, Zionist settlers began to be drawn to them.

By 1914, therefore, Palestine's Arab population of over six hundred thousand was spread relatively densely over the country, in the hills as well as the lowlands.[23] Thus from a very early stage in the process of Zionist colonization, the steps which accompanied the establishment of a new Jewish colony – purchase of land, often from an absentee landlord; expulsion of tenant cultivators; and the settlement of Jewish immigrants – frequently led to confrontations with the local populace.

There were exceptions to this pattern when the land concerned had formerly been sparsely-populated or uncultivated (though even in such cases it may have been subject to customary grazing rights which the inhabitants were naturally loath to surrender). But most land purchased before World War I, especially after the turn of the century, was fertile and therefore inhabited, and *fellahin* with long-standing traditional rights of tenure were displaced in the process of Jewish settlement. The *fellahin* naturally considered the land to be theirs, and often discovered that they had ceased to be the legal owners only when the land was sold to Jewish settlers by an absentee landlord who had acquired it in the decades following the implementation of the 1858 land law.

This process can be illustrated by a detailed discussion of two cases, those of the purchases in the Tiberias region in 1901-2 (which had a bloody sequel in 1909), and 'Afula in 1910-11, and by mention of a third at Petah Tiqva in 1886, which is summarized by Mandel. The Petah Tiqva incident involved a clash settled by the intervention of Ottoman troops and the arrest of many *fellahin*. In the melée, a settler was killed and several others wounded by peasants aggrieved because land which they considered theirs had been sold to the colony after they forfeited it to money-lenders and the local authorities. Moreover, the latter 'had sold the Jews more land than was actually theirs to sell'. As Mandel's account makes clear, it was only some years after the purchase had taken place that 'for the first time some of the peasants were confronted with the fact that they no longer owned the land'.[24]

The example of Petah Tiqva in 1886 confirms a pattern stretching back to the early years of Jewish colonization in Palestine. Mandel mentions four similar incidents during the same period involving disputes over ownership. These culminated in settlers at Gedera being 'harassed for years' from 1884 on; in an 1892 raid on Rehovot 'reminiscent of the attack on Petah Tiqva'; and in lengthy property disputes at Nes Ziyyona and Hadera. Mandel notes that in most of these early cases, Arab animosity eventually died down when the *fellahin* were able to lease back some of their lands, and obtained permanent or seasonal work in other parts of their former properties.

The pragmatic and unideological settlers of the first *'aliya* were thus in effect treating the *fellahin* little differently than had their former Arab landlords, disappropriating but in most cases not fully dispossessing them. This changed definitively with the second *'aliya* early in the twentieth century, when the idea of the 'conquest of labor' – meaning replacing Arab workers with Jewish ones – took hold, and a new, exclusivist form of colonization began.[25]

The twentieth-century incidents in the Tiberias region and at 'Afula, especially the latter, are significant because of the major effect they were to have in the context of Ottoman and Arab nationalist politics. Moreover they are also apparently the first cases where the replacement of Arab labor with that of Zionist settlers was a source of friction. Both incidents are unusual in that they became the subject of major controversy and serious disturbances at the time, and are among the few for which sufficient data are readily available. They are nevertheless typical of a clear pattern of peasant resistance to colonization, as the Petah Tiqva incident and the four others from the nineteenth century just mentioned indicate, and as will be apparent from some of the figures regarding Zionist land purchase before 1914 cited below.

Although much nonsense of the Peters variety has been propagated to the effect that Palestine was empty and desolate on the eve of Zionist settlement, there was little doubt in the minds of the first settlers and of those responsible for purchasing land for Jewish settlement that this was not the case. In the words of the famed writer Ahad Ha'am in 1891:

> We abroad are used to believing that Eretz Israel is now almost totally desolate, a desert that is not sowed, and that anyone who wishes to purchase land there may come and purchase as much as he desires. But in truth this is not the case. Throughout the country it is difficult to find fields that are not sowed. Only sand dunes and stony mountains that are not fit to grow anything but fruit trees – and this only after hard labor and great expense of clearing and reclamation – only these are not cultivated.[26]

The inevitable consequence of this situation, in terms of what had to be done with the Arabs who tilled the land the Zionists coveted, was clearly perceived by Dr Arthur Ruppin, the foremost land expert of the Jewish Agency. He wrote in 1930, by which time the principle of the 'conquest of labor' had been firmly established in Zionist ideology, and with it therefore the necessity not simply to disappropriate the tillers of the land by buying title to it and moving in Jewish farm owners and managers to supervise Arab *fellahin*, but to dispossess the latter in order to make room for Jewish tillers of the soil. Ruppin declared:

> Land is the most necessary thing for our establishing roots in Palestine. Since there are hardly any more arable unsettled lands in Palestine, we are bound in each case of the purchase of land and its settlement to remove the peasants who cultivated the land so far, both owners of the land and tenants.[27]

'Removal' of the owners of the land was usually accomplished quite easily since, as a result of the accumulation of much fertile land in the hands of a relatively small number of urban merchants and notables after implementation of the 1858 Land Code, the tiller of the land was often different from the owner. But the resistance of *fellahin* to being uprooted from land on which they and their ancestors had worked and lived for generations was not so easily overcome. In their eyes, the transfer of formal, legal ownership did not mean they could be deprived of what they believed were inalienable rights of usufruct. Given their perspective, neither abstract legal principle nor compensation, which was frequently offered, were very convincing.

Sometimes, the *fellahin* accepted compensation from Jewish settlement bodies, presumably feeling themselves unable to stand up to the new owners of the land and their official backers. But at other times, the *fellahin* resisted their dispossession, on occasion with violence. In such cases, it was necessary for the purchasers to depend on the power of the state, whether the Ottoman Empire, or, later on, the British Mandatory authorities, to enable them to take control of the land. In both situations, lingering resentments remained, often expressing themselves in acts of violence against the new settlements.

The 1901-2 attempt of the Jewish Colonization Association (JCA) to 'remove the peasants who cultivated the land so far' from a tract of about seventy thousand dunams in the Tiberias district (the largest single piece of land thus far purchased for Jewish settlement in Lower Galilee) met with stiff resistance from the Arab inhabitants of the villages of al-Shajara, Misha and Melhamiyya, who were to be dispossessed by this purchase. Of this land, over sixty-thousand dunams had been purchased from the big Beirut merchant family of the Sursuqs, and their business partners, the Tuenis and Mudawwars. Some seven hundred had been bought from local landlords, and three thousand from some of the *fellahin* themselves.[28]

According to the account of the incident by H.M. Kalvariski, an official of the JCA, the peasants not only refused to be removed from their lands; the JCA agent who had engineered the land deal, a Mr Ossovestky, 'was shot at; troops were brought and many tenants were arrested and taken to prison'. Through the forcible intervention of the authorities, lands cultivated by inhabitants of the three villages were seized and they were prevented from tilling them. Over the next three years, the Jewish agricultural settlements of Sejera, Kafr Tavor, Yavniel, Menehamia and Bet Gan were set up on these lands.[29]

Although this was ostensibly a routine conflict between new land-owners and the traditional occupants of the land, with the state naturally intervening decisively on behalf of the former, there were two unusual factors involved. The first was obviously that the new owners of the land were foreigners who intended to supplant the indigenous tenant farmers; the second was that these newcomers were supported by a regime which the local population was beginning to see as alien for the first time.[30]

Thus, in a situation where an Ottoman government which was increasingly coming to be seen as Turkish-dominated forced Arab peasants to accept the sale and transfer of their land to Zionist colonists, it was of some significance that the Arab *qaimmagam* (district officer) of Tiberias, Amir Amin Arslan, should oppose the transaction on nationalist grounds. This he did, Kalvariski noted, in spite of the indifference to the issue's national aspects of his Turkish superior, Rushdi Bey, the *vali* of Beirut. Rushdi Bey acted according to the letter of the law in ultimately seeing to it that the new owners of these lands were able to take possession of their property. But the opposition of an Arab government official presaged Arab opposition in the years which followed to both Zionist settlement endeavors, and to a Turkish-dominated government which took no apparent interest in a question of vital and growing interest to the Arabs of the Empire.

According to Kalvariski's account, even after implementation of the *vali*'s orders, Arslan continued to 'resist the de-Arabization of the district'; he perhaps also gave discreet encouragement to the small bands of peasants angry at the loss of their land who afterwards harassed the new settlers.[31] For the time being there was little else he could do besides insisting that compensation be paid to the evicted tenants, whose will to resist had been broken by the Ottoman government's repression on behalf of the JCA. Such aggrieved *fellahin*, with their former Arab landlords, the Ottoman state and the new Jewish settlers all ranged against them, were within a few years to find public advocates for their mute resistance.

The 1908 revolution led to the re-imposition of the 1876 Constitution, which guaranteed freedom of speech and provided for the election of a parliament. Among the deputies elected to represent the Beirut *vilayet* was the former *qaimmagam* of Tiberias, Amir Amin Arslan, who won a 1909 by-election. In the Ottoman Parliament he became an active member of a large group of deputies representing the Arab provinces, who as time went on grew increasingly sensitive to the questions of Zionism and Arab nationalism. At the same time, with the expansion of education, the lifting of press censorship, and the flowering of the Arabic-language press, ideas which had been long suppressed came to the surface and spread.

In the newly-free press, the issue of Zionism soon became a subject of extensive comment, and a focus of criticism of the Ottoman authorities.[32] Parallel with increasingly negative coverage of Zionism in the Arabic press, after the revolution there were more attacks on Jewish settlements, particularly those in the Galilee around al-Shajara which had been the scene of the 1901-2 incidents involving Amir Amin Arslan. Here new problems arose in 1909 as disputes over land which had 'persisted for years' erupted and peasants 'challenged boundaries which had been agreed upon a decade earlier'.[33]

The resulting clashes were so serious, involving three killed and several wounded on both sides over the course of a few days, that the previously secret Jewish para-military organization, *Hashomer* ('the guardian'), was formally and publicly established, after the settlers received permission from the Ottoman authorities to arm themselves. This was the culmination of a process which had been going on for several years, and which also fell under the rubric of the 'conquest of labor', whereby Jewish immigrants of the second *'aliya* had gradually been taking over duties as armed watchmen at Jewish settlements, replacing the Arabs who had formerly performed these duties. In doing so, they were taking on the defense of newly-acquired land from its dispossessed former cultivators, who firmly believed they still had rights to it: in microcosm, this was the essence of the conflict in Palestine.

In his book *The Making of Israel's Army*, Gen. Yigal Allon describes *Hashomer* as the nucleus of the Haganah, itself the forerunner of the Israeli armed forces.[34] The roots of the military institution which has been central to the Zionist enterprise throughout most of its history therefore lie in simmering armed peasant resistance to Jewish settlement on land which the *fellahin* stubbornly persisted in considering theirs. Mute and inarticulate though it was, this resistance was considerable enough, at least in areas of extensive land purchase from absentee landlords, to necessitate the creation of what Ze'ev Schiff, in his history of the Israeli army, calls a 'highly disciplined' armed force, and the precursor of that army.[35]

Important as had been the al-Shajara incidents in 1901-2 and their sequel in 1909, repeating as they did the pattern of the clashes in Petah Tiqva and other settlements in the late nineteenth century, a far greater impact was created by events in the village of 'Afula, only some fifteen miles away from al-Shajara in the neighboring district of Nazareth. In 'Afula, as in al-Shajara eight years earlier, an Arab *qaimmagam* supported *fellahin* threatened with dispossession, and unsuccessfully resisted his Turkish superior in opposing the transfer of land legally sold by an absentee landlord to the Zionists.

Although the end result for the *fellahin* involved was the same, dispossession and homelessness, the 'Afula purchase marked the beginning of an overt and articulate anti-Zionist campaign, which was based on the widely publicized details of this case of dispossession. This campaign developed over the next two years until it had encompassed the provinces of *bilad al-Sham*, the Arabic press, and the Ottoman parliament.

The details of the 'Afula transaction are simple. The village lands totalled about ten thousand dunums (a dunum is about one thousand sq. meters, or ¼ acre) situated in the middle of the fertile Marj Ibn 'Amer. Halfway between Nazareth and Jenin, 'Afula was only a small part of the vast ownings in various parts of this valley of the Sursuqs of Beirut, who in 1872 had purchased some 230,000 dunums from the Ottoman Government for the paltry sum of LT 20,000, and altogether seem to have owned well over a quarter of a million dunums. According to one source, the family's annual returns from its properties in Marj Ibn 'Amer equalled their original purchase price, while another put their annual income from these properties in 1883 at $200,000.[36]

In late 1910, Elias Sursuq agreed to sell the lands of 'Afula to the Jewish National Fund (JNF), headed by Arthur Ruppin. According to Mandel, this was 'some of the best agricultural land in Palestine',[37] and the JNF set about immediately occupying and settling its new property. There was immediate, stiff resistance, however, from the *fellahin* of 'Afula, their resolve apparently stiffened by the changing mood in Palestine and other parts of the Empire regarding Zionism, and by the effect of earlier examples of dispossession in nearby parts of Lower Galilee over the preceding years. In addition to the five settlements established between 1901 and 1904 on the land whose sale Amir Amin Arslan had opposed, another five had been set up in the same area between 1905 and 1910, and all were settled mainly by immigrants of the second *'aliya*.

Another factor encouraged the resistance of the peasants of 'Afula: this was the support of the Arab *qaimmagam*, or district governor, of Nazareth. Shukri al-'Asali was a member of a prominent Damascus family who had received his higher education at the Mulkiya College in Istanbul and had thereafter held a number of government posts in different parts of *bilad al-Sham*. Upon hearing of the sale, al-'Asali refused to hand over the title deed to the property to the new owners, in spite of a directive to comply from the *vali* in Beirut, where the transaction had been arranged.

The *qaimmagam's* refusal to go along with the sale led to further representations in Beirut, this time by Ruppin himself, and to a renewal of the order from the *vali* to hand over title of the 'Afula lands to its new owners. At this point al-'Asali went further than had Arslan, in December 1910 writing an open letter signed 'Salah al-Din al-Ayyubi' [Saladin] bitterly critical of Zionism, which he published in the important Damascus opposition paper *al-Muqtabas*. This and two other articles about 'Afula published in February 1911 accused the Zionist movement of separatist objectives in Palestine, and hinted strongly that they were prompted by motives not compatible with loyalty to the Ottoman Empire.

All three articles had a large readership, as they were reprinted in the Haifa paper *al-Karmil,* and in the Beirut dailies *al-Mufid, al-Ittihad al-'Uthmani* and *al-Haqiqa,* where they helped fuel the ongoing controversy over Zionism. In these and other journalistic writings by al-'Asali, the issue of peasant dispossession was prominently featured and linked to patriotic themes: there are historical connections linking the people to the land going all the way back to Saladin, and thus expelling its original peasant tenants and replacing them with foreigners is treason, al-'Asali wrote in one of these articles.[38]

Shukri al-'Asali's next step was even more radical. Upon being informed that at the orders of the local agent of the JNF, a band of thirty armed members of *Hashomer* had been sent to occupy the lands of the 'Afula villagers, the *qaimmagam* immediately sent a large body of troops to the scene to drive them away. This was all he could do, for the new owners had both the law and their potent financial capabilities on their side, and the Turkish *vali* in January 1911 overruled his insubordinate actions, allowing the establishment in that month of the settlement of Merhavia on the disputed lands.

The resistance of the dispossessed peasants of 'Afula, whose land and homes had been sold out from under their feet by the Susuq family in Beirut, continued even after the sale had been completed. Attacks on Merhavia by the former cultivators of the land were frequent. In the words of an authority on Zionist land purchase, Alex Bein, these attacks were due to 'the natural resentment of the former cultivators'.[39] In an armed clash in May 1911, an Arab was killed near the settlement, provoking elements of the local population to lay siege to Merhavia for two days until the local authorities moved in and jailed several of the settlers.

Shukri al-'Asali's role did not stop there. Basing his election campaign on the 'Afula affair, he ràn for and won a seat for Damascus in a hotly-contested January 1911 by-election. His electoral platform pledged him to fight Zionism 'to his last drop of blood', on the basis of his experience in the 'Afula case. Once elected, al-'Asali was to play a key role not only in the opposition to Zionism in the Ottoman Chamber and outside, but in galvanizing members of the Arab parliamentary bloc in its opposition to the nascent Turkish nationalism of the ruling Committee of Union and Progress (CUP).[40] He had all the more impact because he was one of the editors and part-owner of the Damascus newspaper *al-Muqtabas*, one of 'the most influential Arabist journals of its day thanks to his efforts and those of another co-owner and editor, Muhammad Kurd 'Ali.

In large part as a result of al-'Asali's actions, the 'Afula incident became a cause célèbre in *bilad al-Sham*, with dozens of articles appearing in newspapers in Damascus, Beirut, Haifa and elsewhere over a period of well over a year. In the press and during debates in the Ottoman parliament after al-'Asali's arrival there, it served as a striking illustration of charges regarding the ruling CUP's failure to take into account Arab concerns made by Arabs restive over what increasingly seemed like Turkish domination of the Empire. From the press accounts and descriptions of al-'Asali's speeches during the election campaign and later on in the Ottoman Parliament, it is clear that it was the spectacle of Arab peasants resisting expulsion from their homes and lands to make room for foreign colonists which gave this incident its potent impact.

Again and again in the press coverage, the voices of the illiterate *fellahin* who cultivated the land come through in descriptions of the 'Afula affair. This is true even in an article defending his actions in ordering the handing over of the land to its new owners by the *vali* of Beirut, Nur al-Din Bey. He stated that after Elias Sursuq began proceedings to sell the land, the peasant proprietors begged him to urge the government to exercise its right of eminent domain, or failing that to 'sell it to the inhabitants of the villages for a similar price'. This was refused by higher authorities in Istanbul, he stated, on the grounds that Sursuq had the absolute right to dispose of his property as he chose.[41]

Similarly, the lasting bitterness caused by the expulsion of these *fellahin* is visible in small local news items in the following months in *al-Muqtabas* noting that settlers in the Tiberias area, including those of 'Afula, had sent telegrams to the authorities, accusing the local inhabitants of being motivated by a spirit of hostility, accusing the government of weakness, and demanding action.[42] Another article, in *al-Karmil*, argued that it was only because the government failed to do its job in resisting foreign colonial penetration that hostility to the settlers had developed among the Arabs of Palestine. When the Zionists took over lands, it added, there was naturally resistance to this, with the peasants fighting back, and the colonists killing them in the resulting clashes and then sending telegrams of protest to the authorities.[43] The ongoing resistance to their dispossession by the peasants is visible in other incidents reported in *al-Karmil*, such as one in June 1911, months after the 'Afula deal had gone through, in which settlers there accused the inhabitants of a neighboring Arab village, who undoubtedly included some of those who lost their homes and lands as a result of the sale, of destroying crops and property to the value of 3100 Turkish pounds.[44]

The sharp, continuing controversy sparked off by the 'Afula sale, an otherwise minor incident, underlines the importance of the dispossession and consequent resistance of the Palestinian peasantry in making the issue of Zionism a central one in Arab political discourse before 1914. As has been shown by Mandel and others, there were many other reasons for this strong response to political Zionism among the Arabs of Palestine and neighboring lands. But the intensity of the post-1908 reaction can be explained only by the cumulative effect of a series of land purchases from absentee landlords involving expulsions of *fellahin* and ensuing clashes. This is what brought the urban elite to a realization of the full import of Zionism: not only was land being purchased; its Arab cultivators were being dispossessed and replaced by foreigners who had overt political objectives in Palestine.

This phenomenon was particularly important in Galilee after the turn of the century, where twelve of the fifteen Jewish settlements established in Palestine between 1901 and 1912 were located. In this fertile region much land had recently come into the hands of absentee landlords, most of them newly prosperous Beirut merchants, for whom land was an investment, and who were willing to sell when the price was right. Tension rose also because of the new freedom of expression in the Empire after 1908, which encouraged open expressions of hostility to Zionism, and to the Ottoman authorities for their laxness in dealing with it. It also increased after 1903 with the arrival of immigrants of the second *'aliya*, committed to the 'conquest of labor' and the replacement of Arabs by Jews in as many occupations as possible.

The coalescence of all these factors made the 'Afula clashes between Arab *fellahin* and Jewish settlers more significant than the many others which preceded it and which had followed a similar pattern.

Nur al-Din Bey had stated in his response to al-'Asali over the issue of 'Afula that 'property which is at the disposal of someone can be used by him as he wishes, if there are no legal obstacles; this right is guaranteed by the basic laws of all states'.[45] For the Ottoman state, this was a simple matter of property rights: Elias Sursuq could sell his land to whom he pleased. The fact that the Ottoman citizen he was selling the land to was an intermediary for the Zionists was in effect not the business of the state, any more than was the fate of the dispossessed peasants, or the historic nature of the parcel in question (al-'Asali had quoted medieval Arab historians to the effect that 'Afula was the site of a fortress erected by Saladin after his defeat of the Crusaders at nearby Hittin in 1187).

All of these considerations combined with growing concern among the elite of Palestine and other parts of *bilad al-Sham* over the development of the Zionist movement in Europe (there was intensive coverage in the press in *bilad al-Sham* and Egypt of the Zionist congresses, particularly the tenth held at Basle in August 1911).[46] The result was a potent mix, made all the more incendiary by the growth of Arabist sentiment among that elite. Zionism, it was charged, was being tolerated and even encouraged by the Turkish-dominated CUP because of its lack of concern for the Arab provinces. These charges may or may not have been justified: some leaders of the CUP, such as Cavid Bey, the Minister of Finance, were apparently sympathetic to the Zionists, while others were less so. However, they were widely believed, and constituted a potent weapon in the conflict between the Arabist tendency among the Arab elite and the CUP.

IV

To conclude an assessment of the significance of peasant resistance to land sale and dispossession, it is necessary to attempt to establish some facts about land sales to the Zionists before 1914. The majority of sellers are often described simply as 'absentee landlords', and a controversy marked by fierce polemics has grown up around this point. A table listing land purchased according to former owners (the most authoritative published source extant) is contained in *The Land System in Palestine* by Dr Avraham Granott, the eminent Zionist land expert. He was Managing Director of the JNF (the main land purchasing agency for the Zionist movement) from 1922 until 1945, after which he became Chairman of its Board of Directors. Based on incomplete Jewish Agency figures, the table gives details regarding 682,000 dunums purchased to 1936, or about half of Zionist land purchases in Palestine until 1948.[47]

As for the period before 1914 which concerns us, Granott's table provides figures regarding 245,581 dunums purchased between 1878 and 1914 (59 per cent of the total of 418,100 dunums acquired by Jews in Palestine by World War I). Granott divides the purchases into four categories according to 'previous owners', as follows: 25% from 'large absentee landlords', 25% from 'large resident landlords', 37.5% from 'various sources' (such as the Ottoman Government, large foreign companies and churches) and 12.5% from the *fellahin*.[48] For the entire period covered by the table (1878-1936) the figures are even more heavily weighted towards absentee and large landowners: in the same four categories the percentages are 52.6, 24.6, 13.4 and 9.4 respectively.

It would appear that for the period until 1914 the trends indicated by Granott were even more pronounced, and more heavily weighted towards non-Palestinian absentee landlords. This emerges from parcel-by-parcel pre-World War I land sale figures in a table in an unpublished work written by a parliamentary colleague of Shukri al-'Asali, Ruhi al-Khalidi (the deputy for Jerusalem). Covering sales to Jewish institutions from 1878-1907, it can be supplemented by data from newspapers of the period, and other published soures.[49] The resulting figures are considerably more detailed than those of Granott. They list by name the vendors of a total of 247,466 dunums, or 60% of all the land purchased to that point, and the twenty-two Jewish colonies established on this land, including many of the oldest and largest ones, and every one of those which were the scenes of the cases of peasant resistance we have surveyed. These sources yield the following results regarding those selling land:

143,577 dunums (58%): Non-Palestinian absentee landlords
  88,689 dunums (36%): Palestinian absentee landlords
  15,200 dunums (6%): Local landlords and *fellahin*

The first group includes foreigners, foreign diplomats, Beirut merchants, as well as Turks who were government officials. This and the second group sold 94% of the land which changed hands before 1914 for which we have detailed figures. If these figures are representative (and Granott's similar figures strongly indicate that they are), they show that a far higher proportion of land sales were undertaken by absentee landlords, both Palestinian and non-Palestinian, than some scholars have indicated. It would further-more seem that the role of non-Palestinian absentee landlords was decisive in this regard in the pre-1914 period.

Extrapolating from the two sets of partial pre-1914 figures on land sales presented above, and adding to them further figures for the succeeding decades, it is possible to come `to tentative conclusions about land sales for the entire period to 1948. In his book *The Land System in Palestine 1917-1939*, Kenneth Stein lays particular stress on sales of land to Jews by Palestinians, particularly notables who often played a prominent role in nationalist opposition to Zionism. There can be little doubt that under the kind of economic pressure combined with financial inducements which Stein describes, Palestinian landlords, both absentee and resident, as well as *fellahin* cultivators, often sold land. Nevertheless the overall picture is in fact more complex than he paints it.

Stein himself notes that 'during the 1920's more than 60 per cent of the land purchased by Jews was bought from Arab absentee landlords residing outside of Palestine'.[50] The actual proportion is very likely much higher than 60 per cent, in view of the fact that over 240,000 dunums, or nearly half of the total of 510,000 dunums sold during the period 1920-29, was made up of an enormous piece of land encompassing most of the fertile Marj Ibn 'Amer, which was sold by the Sursuq family of Beirut and a number of their partners in 1924-25. Together with the other lands in the Marj Ibn 'Amer (such as 'Afula), sold to the Zionists before 1914 by the Sursuqs and their business partners in a few Beirut families related to them, such as the 'Aryans and the Tuenis, this single bloc in one region amounts to 313,000 dunums, or over 22 per cent of all the land purchased by Jews in Palestine until 1948. This would seem to contradict Stein's assertion that the Marj Ibn 'Amer sale had 'important significance, but certainly not the political value given it by many writers'.[51]

More importantly, for the over four hundred thousand dunums sold before 1914 and the over five hundred thousand dunums sold in the 1920s, the available figures (which, it must be repeated, apply to only a portion of these totals) suggest that well over 60 per cent of the land acquired by the Zionists before 1930 was sold by non-Palestinians. Inasmuch as these nine hundred thousand dunums are the bulk of the 1.39 million dunums purchased and registered by the Zionists until the end of the Mandate,[52] these partial figures have major implications for the whole question of land sales from the beginning of modern Jewish settlement in Palestine and until 1948. Although many Palestinian landlords and *fellahin* sold land, whether out of greed and lack of patriotism, or because of need and without knowing who would ultimately control it, the great bulk of land would indeed seem to have been sold by non-Palestinian absentee landlords.

V

In light of the data just presented, it seems clear that opposition to land sales to the Zionists, particularly sales by absentee landlords (both Palestinian and non-Palestinian), was an important shared element in cementing the link between Arabist members of the elite who opposed Zionism on grounds of principle, and the *fellahin* whose resistance caught the popular imagination and thereby played a vital role in mobilizing opinion in Palestine and the Arab world. This opposition united both the peasants, who tried desperately to cling to their land, or retaliated against the Zionist settlers in a blind, Luddite fashion if they lost it, and the urban intellectuals and notables who only realized what Zionism implied when they beheld the dispossession al-'Asali decried. The result was a new shared urban-rural perception of Zionism among Palestinians as a new type of Zionist settlement, beginning with the second *'aliya*, which for the first time witnessed Jewish settlers actually taking over not just ownership, but also cultivation, of the land on a large scale. This new phenomenon quickly engendered a local response among embittered *fellahin*, which in turn helped to shape the first systematic expressions of anti-Zionism in Palestine and the Arab world.

Such a pattern of interaction between rural resistance and urban opposition to Zionism has already been established for the Mandatory period. Thus, the funeral in Haifa in November 1935 of the first articulate public apostle of armed resistance, Shaykh 'Iz al-Din al-Qassam, who died in combat with British troops, became an enormous public demonstration.[53] This in turn helped to spark the 1936 general strike and the 1936-39 Palestinian Arab revolt. In the words of the best study of al-Qassam, that of Abdullah Schleifer, his death 'electrified the Palestinian people'.[54] Al-Qassam appealed in particular to the uprooted landless peasants who drifted from Galilee into the northern port city of Haifa. These first recruits to organized armed resistance were in many cases thus the same people who had been dispossessed or displaced by Zionist colonization activity in Galilee. In Schleifer's words: 'Many of his followers were former tenant farmers recently driven off the land by the land purchases and Arab labour exclusion policies of the Jewish National Fund. . .'.[55] At the other end of the social scale, urban leaders of the secular nationalist Istiqlal Party like Akram Zu'aytir were deeply affected by al-Qassam's funeral, as he recorded in his diary at the time.[56] It can be seen that this pattern of *fellahin* resistance affecting the rest of Palestinian society, clearly established for the Mandatory period, in fact stretches back before 1914.

Because those we have focused on could not speak for themselves in the sources which are left to us after seven or eight decades, we have seen their actions through a glass darkly, largely via records left by foreigners who did not speak their language or understand their culture, who had little sympathy for them, and who often were their enemies. As for their countrymen, the urban elites of Palestine, they too have left us little which can help us to establish a full picture of what was happening on the land in Palestine at the very outset of the conflict between Zionist settlers and Palestinian Arabs. Even regarding some issues where more information should be available, such as land purchase, we are forced to use fragmentary and incomplete data.

But it has been possible to discern a pattern of alienation of land from its cultivators, sometimes into the hands of Arab absentee landlords, and sometimes from them to Zionist land purchasing agencies. A largely mute process of resistance arose, particularly where alienation and disappropriation was followed by dispossession. In older Zionist colonies, as the settlers were transformed into gentlemen farmers employing Arab labor, some Arab resentment was appeased as the *fellahin* found jobs or were able to rent back their lands as tenant farmers. But a new and more serious process began with the second *'aliya* in 1903 and the concomitant effort to establish an exclusive Jewish economy in Palestine.

After 1908, peasant resistance was echoed by members of the urban upper classes newly conscious of their identity as Arabs, chafing at what many of them perceived as Turkish control, and newly able to express themselves in the press and in party politics. This potent mix thus established a pattern which was already firmly set by 1914. All the elements were already in place for the bitter and protracted disputes over the questions of land sales and peasant dispossession and the resulting violence which were the main features of the Mandate period.

Although only further research in the Ottoman, British and Israeli archives can produce conclusive results as far as many of these questions are concerned, it is apparent that there is more than enough evidence to show that Arab attacks on early Jewish settlements were more than 'marauding' or 'banditry' as many Israeli writers would have it.[57] Frequently, they were rather the result of a real process of dispossession which, in the cases for which we have evidence, can be conclusively documented not in the words of the victims but rather on the basis of contemporary Zionist sources and recent research based on them. Like many of the powerless in history, we are forced to tell their story in the words of those who victimized them. This does not make it any less vivid, or less valid as a picture of what was happening in Palestine before 1914.

Notes

1. In spite of conditions in Beirut, the PLO's Palestine Research Center and the unaffiliated Institute for Palestine Studies produced some significant research until Israel's 1982 invasion disrupted their functioning, and indeed much Palestinian intellectual production. The Center's historical archives were seized by occupying Israeli forces, but were returned as part of the November 1983 prisoner exchange with the PLO. The war also disrupted a UNESCO project for a Palestinian Open University, as well as the academic atmosphere at the five Beirut universities where many Palestinian scholars had become established. The Israeli occupation causes continuing problems for West Bank universities like Bir Zeit, al-Najah and Bethlehem.

2. Exceptions include 'Arif al-'Arif, author of *al-Nakba*, a study of the 1947-49 war and of other major works; Ihsan al-Nimr, a historian of the Nablus region; and 'Abd al-Latif Tibawi, author of a number of works on the great powers and Palestine; Muhammad 'Izzat Darwaza, a noted historian of Arab and Palestinian nationalism; and Walid Khalidi, an authority on the events of 1947-48. See Tarif Khalidi, 'Palestinian Historiography: 1900-1948', *Journal of Palestine Studies*, 10, 3 (Spring 1981), pp. 59-76. Younger scholars working in the field include Elias Sanbar, author of *Palestine 1948: L'expulsion* (Paris: Livres de la Revue d'Études Palestiniennes, 1984); Emile Sahliyeh, *The PLO after the Lebanon War* (Boulder: Westview, 1986); Musa Budeiri, *The Palestinian Communist Party, 1919-1948* (London: Ithaca, 1979); and Muhammad Muslih, whose *Palestinian Nationalism in its Arab Setting* is forthcoming from Columbia University Press.

230

3. Jerusalem and New York: Yad Izhak Ben Zvi Institute and St Martin's Press, 1984.

4. London: Routledge and Kegan Paul, 1973.

5. These are the standard works on the subject: Porath's *The Emergence of the Palestinian-Arab National Movement, 1919-1929* (London: Frank Cass, 1973) and *The Palestinian Arab National Movement 1929-1939: From Riots to Rebellion* (London: Frank Cass, 1977); and Lesch's *Arab Politics in Palestine, 1917-1939* (Ithaca: Cornell University Press, 1979).

6. Berkeley: University of California Press, 1976.

7. See, e.g. his 'Crop-Sharing Economics in Mandatory Palestine', *Middle Eastern Studies*, XI, 1 (January 1985), pp. 3-23; part 2, XI, 2 (April 1975); pp. 188-203; and 'Production and Trade in an Islamic Context: Sharika Contracts in the Transitional Economy of Northern Samaria, 1853-1943', *International Journal of Middle East Studies*, VI, 2 (April 1975), pp.185-209; part 2, VI, 3 (July 1975), pp. 308-24.

8. Austin: University of Texas Press, 1985. Outstanding examples of scholarship using a combination of archival and other sources to investigate issues at this level are the studies by Alexander Schölch, Sarah Graham-Brown, Salim Tamari and Avi Plascov in Roger Owen, ed. *Studies in the Economic and Social History of Palestine in the Nineteenth and Twentieth Centuries* (London: Macmillan, 1982).

9. The controversy over Peters's book, published by Harper and Row in 1984, and lavishly praised by Barbara Tuchman, Saul Bellow, Arthur Goldberg, Theodore White and other luminaries, spilled over into the columns of the *New York Times* in 1985-86. The gross lapses in the research on this book were first documented by Norman Finkelstein and William Farrell, and published in *In These Times* on 11 September 1984, and the *Journal of Palestine Studies* in its Fall 1984 issue respectively.

10. New Brunswick, NJ: Transaction Books, 1984.

11. Israel's most respected historian of the Palestinians, Porath dismissed Peters's book in a scathing review entitled 'Mrs Peters's Palestine', in the *New York Review of Books*, 16 January 1986, pp. 36-9. Using Ottoman and Western sources, Schölch has established certain key points about Palestinian demography, rebutting some of the outrageous claims made on this subject:: 'The Demographic Development of Palestine, 1850-1882', *International Journal of Middle East Studies*, 17 (1985), pp. 485-505.

12. 'Permission to Narrate', *Journal of Palestine Studies*, XII, 3 (Spring 1984), pp. 27-48.

13. The importance of Zionism as an issue in the politics of the era is dealt with in several chapters of Neville Mandel, *The Arabs and Zionism*, and chs. 4-6 of Rashid Khalidi, *British Policy Towards Syria and Palestine, 1906-1914* (London: Ithaca Press, 1980). It is the focus of Rashid Khalidi, 'The Role of the Press in the Early Arab Reaction to Zionism', *Peuples Méditerranéeans/Mediterranean Peoples*, 20 (July-September 1982), pp. 102-24, which establishes that over six hundred articles on Zionism were published in a sample of seventeen important Cairo, Beirut, Haifa and Damascus newspapers from 1909 until 1914.

14. Mandel's is the first book-length attempt to deal with this problem, and does so competently. It is also one focus of earlier works by Palestinian historians such as 'Abd al-Wahhab Kayyali, *Palestine: A Modern History* (London: Croom Helm, 1978), and Naji 'Alush, *al-Muqawama al-'Arabiyya fi Filastin, 1917-1948* [The Arab resistance in Palestine, 1917-1948] (Beirut: Palestine Research Center, 1967).

15. Roger Owen, *The Middle East in the World Economy, 1800-1914* (London: Methuen, 1981); Charles Issawi, *An Economic History of the Middle East and Northern Africa* (New York: Columbia University Press, 1982). For a study focused on a key part of this region which illustrates these changes see Laila Fawaz, *Merchants and Migrants in Nineteenth-Century Beirut* (Cambridge, Harvard University Press, 1983).

16. This process is well described in Avraham Granott, *The Land System in Palestine: History and Structure* (London: Eyre and Spottiswoode, 1952), pp. 72-77. As Managing Director of the Jewish National Fund, Granott was perhaps the foremost expert on Zionist land purchase, having been deeply involved in such transactions throughout the Mandate. See also Doreen Warriner, *Land Reform and Development in the Middle East: A Study of Egypt, Syria and Iraq*, 2nd ed. (London: Oxford University Press, 1962), pp. 60-70, and the works of Y. Firestone, cited in note 7.

17. For details see Rashid Khalidi, 'The Press as a Source for Modern Arab Political History', *Arab Studies Quarterly*, 3, 1 (Winter 1981), pp. 22-42. Yusuf Khoury, *al-Sahafa al-'Arabiyya fi Filastin, 1876-1948* [The Arab press in Palestine, 1876-1948], Beirut: Institute for Palestine Studies, 1976, pp. 3-26 provides a comprehensive listing of Arabic newspapers in Palestine before 1914.

18. Figures for missionary schools in Anon. [As'ad Daghir], *Thawrat al-'Arab*, Cairo: n.p., 1916, p. 133; for Beirut *vilayet* in Muhammad Bahjat and Rafiq al-Tamimi, Wilayet Bayrut [Beirut vilayet], Beirut: Iqbal, 1917, vol. II, pp. 152-3; for Palestine in A.L. Tibawi, *Arab Education in Palestine: A Study of Three Decades of British Administration* (London: Luzac, 1956), p. 20. For a discussion of education under 'Abd al-Hamid see A.L. Tibawi, *A Modern History of Syria including Lebanon and Palestine* (London: Macmillan, 1969), pp. 194-6.

19. Hisham Sharabi, *Arab Intellectuals and the West: The Formative Years, 1875-1914* (Baltimore: Johns Hopkins Press, 1970), p. 3.

20. Mandel, *The Arabs and Zionism*, p. xvii.

21. *Ibid.*, p. xxiv; Porath, *Emergence*, p. 17. Since, in Mandel's words, 'as many as one in every two immigrants may have departed again', and a proportion of the Jewish population were therefore transients, these figures may be inflated. Ottoman figures for 1914 for the *sanjag* of Jerusalem (cited in Kamal Karpat, *Ottoman Population 1830–1914* [Madison: University of Wisconsin Press, 1985], pp. 184-5) show 21,259 Jews in a total population of 328,168, but these numbers, which do not cover northern Palestine, are in turn probably low in not counting many immigrants who retained European nationalities rather than become Ottoman subjects.

22. E.g., that in Mandel, *The Arabs and Zionism*, p. xv.

23. Porath, 'Mrs Peters's Palestine', p. 37, summarizes the process of Arab natural population growth; extensive details, including shifts in population to the lowlands, are provided in Schölch, 'Demographic Development of Palestine'.

24. Mandel, *The Arabs and Zionism, pp. 36-7.*

25. *Ibid.*, pp. 34-9. For details on the changes resulting from the second *'aliya* see Alex Bein, *The Return to the Soil: A History of Jewish Settlement in Israel* (Jerusalem: Youth and Hechalutz Department of the Zionist Organization, 1952), pp. 36ff.

26. *Kol Kotve Ahad Ha-am*, p. 23. Summing up this period, Mandel writes: 'Most members of the New Yishuv were genuinely taken aback to find Palestine inhabited by so many Arabs', *The Arabs and Zionism*, p. 31.

27. A Ruppin, 'The Arab Population in Israel', *Arakhim*, 3, 1971, p. 10. This was done from the very beginning. A contemporary of Ahad Ha-am, Yitzhak

Epstein, described in 1907 how the lands of the villagers of Ras al-Zawiyya and Mefulla were bought out from under them from absentee landlords in 1882 and 1896 in order to found the settlements of Rosh Pinna and Mefullah: 'Shela Neelema' [A hidden question] *Hashiloah*, XV, (1907), p. 193ff.

28. Neville Barbour, *Palestine: Star or Crescent?* (New York: Odyssey Press, 1947), pp. 133-4. The details on land ownership are taken from a table on p. 111 of a manuscript by Rwhi al-Khalidi, deputy for Jerusalem in the Ottoman Parliament, entitled 'al-Sionism aw al-mas'ala al-sihyuniyya' [Zionism, or the Zionist question], left completed but unpublished at the author's death in 1913, and now in the possession of the family. This work is the first original book-length treatment of Zionism by an Arab author.

29. Details drawn from the table cited in al-Khalidi, Barbour, *Palestine*, p. 134, and Bein, *The Return to the Soil*, p. 31. For the background tô this incident, and later clashes, see Mandel, *The Arabs and Zionism*, pp. 67-70.

30. For more on the awakening of Arab feeling in the Ottoman Empire at this time see R. Khalidi, *British Policy*, ch. 4; Rashid Khalidi, 'Arab Nationalism in Syria: The Formative Years', in W. Haddad and W. Ochsenwald, eds, *Nationalism in a Non-National State: The Dissolution of the Ottoman Empire* (Columbus: Ohio University Press, 1977), pp. 207-37; R. Khalidi, 'The Press as a Source', and Rashid Khalidi, 'Ottomanism and Arabism in Syria before 1914: A Reassessment', in R. Khalidi *et al.*, eds, *Early Arab Nationalism* (New York: Columbia University Press), forthcoming.

31. Barbour, *Palestine*, p. 134.

32. R. Khalidi, 'The Role of the Press', deals extensively with this subject, as does Mandel, *The Arabs and Zionism*.

33. *Ibid*, p. 67.

34. Yigal Allon, *The Making of Israel's Army* (London: Valentine, Mitchell, 1970), p. 4; there is a 1904 photo of *Hashomer* guards in Galilee facing p. 20. See also Ze'ev Schiff, *A History of the Israeli Army, 1874 to the Present*, 2nd ed. (New York, Macmillan, 1985), pp. 1-3, and 1909 photo of twenty-three members of the group facing p. 86.

35. Bein, *The Return*, pp. 44, 77.

36. Granott, *The Land System*, pp. 80-1. The 1883 figure was obtained by Laurence Oliphant from Alfred Susuq himself, who complained that it cost him $50,000 to transport his crops to Haifa and Acre for export: *Haifa: or Life in Modern Palestine* (Edinburgh: Wm. Blackwood, 1887), pp. 42, 60.

37. Mandel, *The Arabs and Zionism*, p. 103.

38. R. Khalidi, 'The Role of the Press', pp. 116-17 covers the impact of al-'Asali, and gives references to the specific issues of the newspapers in which the articles appeared.

39. Bein, *The Return*, p. 78. Bein places the 'natural resentment of the former cultivators' third in a list of reasons for their attacks, which is headed by their desire 'to steal', and their dislike of 'the intrusion of Jews into what was a purely Arab neighborhood'. In this account, as in so much else written about the earliest clashes between Jews and Arabs in Palestine, there is a blindness to the weight of this resentment, with the results often written off as 'Arab marauding'.

40. Mandel, *The Arabs and Zionism*, pp. 112, 106-7, covers the 'Afula affair, and on pp. 112ff assesses al-'Asali's impact in the Ottoman Parliament.

41. *al-Ittihad al-'Uthmani* (Beirut), no. 737, 21 February 1911, p. 2.

42. *al-Muqtabas* (Damascus), no. 740, 29 July 1911, p. 2, and no. 748, 7 August 1911, p. 2.

43. *al-Karmil* (Haifa), no. 153, 23 June 1911, p. 3.

44. *al-Karmil*, no. 151, 9 June 1911, p. 3.

45. *al-Ittihad al-'Uthmani*, no. 737, 21 February 1911, p. 2.

46. See e.g., *al-Karmil*, no. 171, 25 August 1911, p. 1 editorial; *al-Muqtabas*, no. 767, 29 August 1911, p. 3; no. 771, 3 September 1911, p. 2; no. 782, 16 September 1911, p. 2; no. 784, 18 September 1911, p. 2; *al-Haqiqa* (Beirut), no. 373, 24 August 1911, p. 1 editorial; *al-Ahram* (Cairo), no.10167, 21 August 1911, p. 1; no. 10172, 25 August 1911, p. 1.

47. Kenneth Stein, *The Land Question in Palestine, 1917-1939* (Chapel Hill: University of North Carolina Press, 1984), pp. 226-7 gives a table drawn from the Central Zionist Archives listing registered Jewish land purchases in Palestine to 1945 with a total of 1.39 million dunums. Granott's table (*The Land System*, p. 277, table 32) thus represents about 50 per cent of this total.

48. *Ibid.*

49. Ruhi al-Khalidi, 'al-Sionism', p. 111. The table listing Jewish settlements and the sellers of the land they are located on is based in part on a list published on 11 March 1911 in *Le Jeune Turc*, a French-language Istanbul paper, but includes many additions, especially regarding vendors of land, which are not in the original and appear to be the results of Ruhi al-Khalidi's own research.

50. Stein, *The Land Question*, p. 218.

51. *Ibid.*, p. 59.

52. *Ibid.*, p. 226.

53. The importance of al-Qassam is underlined in works such as those by 'Allush and Kayyali cited in note 14, and Ghassan Kanafani, 'Thawrat 1936-1939 fi Filastin: Khalfiyya, tafasil wa tahlil' [The 1936-1939 Revolution in Palestine: Background, Details and Analysis], *Shu'un Filistiniyya*, 6 (January 1972), pp. 45-77. The writings of 'Allush, Kayyali, and Kanafani, who were all politically active (the latter two before their assassinations in 1972 and 1980 respectively), played a major part in shaping modern perceptions of this period.

54. S. Abdullah Schleifer, 'The Life and Thought of 'Izz-id-Din al Qassam', *The Islamic Quarterly*, XXII, 2 (1979), p. 61-81.

55. *Ibid.*, p. 70.

56. For contemporary documentation of al-Qassam's importance, see Akram Zu'aytir, *Al-haraka al-wataniyya al-filastiniyya 1935-1939: Yawmiyyat Arkram Zu'aytir* [The Palestinian national movement 1935-1939: The diaries of Akram Zu'aytir] (Beirut, Institute for Palestine Studies, 1980), pp. 27ff; and *Watha'ig al-haraka al-wataniyya al-filastiniyya 1918-1939: Min awaq Akram Zui'aytir* [Documents of the Palestinian national movement 1918-1939: From the papers of Akram Zu'aytir] (Beirut: Institute for Palestine Studies, 1979), pp. 397-401.

57. E.g., Uzi Benziman, *Sharon: An Israeli Caesar*, NY: Adama, 1985, p. 2: 'At first, the conflict took the form of criminal assaults on Jews and Jewish property by Arab marauders'; and Allon, *The Making of Israel's Army*, p. 11, who writes of the first Jewish settlers practicing 'self-defense against robbery, theft, marauding, murder and rape. These for the most part were non-political in nature.'

11

A Profile of the Palestinian People

Edward W. Said
Ibrahim Abu-Lughod
Janet L. Abu-Lughod
Muhammad Hallaj
Elia Zureik

History and Political Development

Early History

The land of Palestine gave rise to one of the most ancient of all civilizations. Centuries before the first Hebrew tribes migrated to the area 'Palestine gave birth to a unique culture. In this period in Palestine, as far as we know, the earliest permanent villages in the world were built.' Palestine is also the birthplace of urban life. It is 'the only place in the world where a town is known to date back nine thousand years'. Jericho is the oldest continuously inhabited city in the world, being 'four thousand years older than any other urban settlement known at present.'[1] It is one of the greatest ironies of history that in the middle of the twentieth century – in the golden age of peoples' rights to self-determination – Palestine was dropped from the map of the world.

Palestine became predominantly Arab and Islamic by the end of the seventh century. Its boundaries and its characteristics – including its name in Arabic, Filastin – soon became known to the entire Islamic world, as much for its fertility and beauty as for its religious significance. In the late tenth century, for example, we find this passage in Arabic:

Filastin is the westernmost of the provinces of Syria. In its greatest length from Rafah to the boundary of Al Lajjun (Legio) it would take a rider two days to travel over; and the like time to cross the province in its breadth from Yafa (Jaffa) to Riha (Jericho). Zugar (Segor, Zoar) and the country of Lot's People (Diyar Qawm Lot), Al Jibal (the mountains of Edom) and Ash Sharah as far as Ailah – Al Jibal and Ash Sharah being two separate provinces, but lying contiguous one to the other – are included in Filastin, and belong to its government.

Filastin is watered by the rains and the dew. Its trees and its ploughed lands do not need artificial irrigation; and it is only in Nablus that you find the running waters applied to this purpose. Filastin is the most fertile of the Syrian provinces. Its capital and largest town is Ar Ramlah, but the Holy City (of Jerusalem) comes very near this last in size. In the province of Filastin, despite its small extent, there are about twenty mosques, with pulpits for the Friday prayer.[2]

In 1516, Palestine became a province of the Ottoman Empire. Through the years it retained its fertility, as well as its Arab and Islamic character. In 1615 the English poet George Sandys spoke of it as 'a land that flowed with milk and honey; in the midst as it were of the habitable world, and under a temperate clime; adorned with beautiful mountains and luxurious vallies; the rocks producing excellent waters; and no part empty of delight or profit.'[3] Such reports persist in profusion through the eighteenth and nineteenth centuries, not only in travelers' accounts but, by the end of the nineteenth century, in scholarly quarterly reports published by the (British) Palestine Exploration Fund.

Despite the steady arrival in Palestine of Jewish colonists after 1882, it is important to realize that not until the few weeks immediately preceding the establishment of Israel in the spring of 1948 was there ever anything other than a large Arab majority. For example, the Jewish population in 1931 was 174,606 against a total of 1,033,314; in 1936, Jewish numbers had gone up to 384,078 and the total to 1,366,692; in 1946 there were were 608,225 Jews in a total of 1,913,112.[4] In all these statistics, 'natives' were easily distinguishable from the arriving colonists. But who were these natives?

Most of them were Sunni Muslims, although a minority among them were Christians, Druze, and Shi'ite Muslims. All of them spoke Arabic and considered themselves Arabs. Approximately 65 per cent of the Palestinian Arabs were agriculturalists, living in some five hundred villages where grains as well as fruits and vegetables were grown. The principal Palestinian cities – Nablus, Jerusalem, Nazareth, Acre, Jaffa, Jericho, Ramlah, Hebron, and Haifa – were built in the main by Palestinian Arabs who continued to live in them, even after the expanding Zionist colonies encroached upon them. Also in existence by that time were: a respectable Palestinian intellectual and professional class, the beginnings of modern industry, and a highly developed national consciousness. Modern Palestinian social, economic and cultural life was organized around the same issues of independence and anti-colonialism prevalent in the region, but the Palestinians had to contend with the legacy of Ottoman rule, then the Zionist colonization, then British mandatory authority (after World War I) – more or less all together. Almost without exception, Arab Palestinians felt themselves to be part of the great Arab awakening stirring since the last years of the nineteenth century, and it is this feeling that gave encouragement and coherence to an otherwise disruptive modern history. Palestinian writers and intellectuals such as Muhammad Izzat Darwazeh, Khalil Sakakini, Khalil Baydas, and Najib Nassar; political organizations such as the Futtuwa and Najjada, the Arab Higher Committees; and the League of National Liberation (which argued that the Palestinian question could only be solved by Arabs and Jews together)[5] – all these formed great national blocs among the population, directed the energies of the 'non-Jewish' Palestinian community, and created a Palestinian identity opposed equally to British rule and to Jewish colonization; an identity strengthened by a sense of belonging to a distinct national group with a language (the Palestinian Arab dialect) and a specific communal sense (threatened particularly by Zionism) of its own.

This Palestinian society was dismantled and dispersed. Even the historic fact of Palestine's prior existence as an entity and of the Palestinians as a people was questioned and portrayed as an apparition of doubtful authenticity.

It is often forgotten how recent the destruction of Palestine has been. Professor Janet Abu-Lughod has described both the uniqueness and proximity of this tragedy. Of the dismantlement of Palestinian society she writes:

> Except for the extermination of the Tasmanians, modern history knows no cases in which the virtually complete supplanting of the indigenous population of a country by an alien stock has been achieved in as little as two generations. Yet this, in fact, is what has been attempted in Palestine since the beginning of the twentieth century.

She warns against the danger of forgetting the 'startling recency' of the destruction of Palestine: 'Our natural tendency to assume that what exists today has always been, may afford us psychic peace but only at the terrible cost of denying reality. And once historical reality has been denied, our capacity to understand and react meaningfully to the present is similarly destroyed.'[6]

Zionism

The destruction of Palestine was not the unintended consequence of unforeseen events. It was, and still is, an essential part of the Zionist plan to transform Palestine into 'Eretz Yisrael'. When a young Israeli soldier participating in the invasion of Lebanon in the summer of 1982 said 'I would like to see all the Palestinians dead because they are a sickness wherever they go',[7] he was giving crude expression to a long-standing theme within the Zionist movement. This attitude was widely shared, as was reported by the King-Crane commission, whose investigations in Palestine in 1919 led it to conclude that 'the Zionists look forward to a practically complete dispossession' of the Palestinian people.[8]

Most histories of the question of Palestine focus on the Zionist effort to create a Jewish presence in Palestine. For that reason, they leave a misleading impression of a totally constructive effort. There is no question that Zionist immigrants brought to Palestine in the interwar period skilled manpower and capital, and built villages and factories. What is equally true, but less familiar, is the fact that because the Zionist movement was committed to the transformation of Palestine into a 'mono-religious' Jewish state,[9] its success required it to be as intent on the destruction of the indigenous Arab society as it was on the construction of a Jewish life in Palestine. As the late Dr Fayez A. Sayegh once put it:

> Just as the heart-beat consists of two rhythmic operations – pumping-in and pumping-out – so too the program of Zionism consists of two interrelated operations, each of which is essential for the heart-beat of Zionism and neither of which is dispensable: The detachment of Jews from their respective countries and their mass transfer to Palestine, and the detachment of the indigenous Palestinian Arabs and their mass transfer from Palestine.[10]

For this 'pumping-in and pumping-out' operation to succeed, Palestinian society had to be undermined because, as Professor Nathan Weinstock put it, the Palestinian people 'were scheduled to become aliens in their own country – assuming they were to be allowed to remain where they were'.[11]

The Palestinian Arabs were not intended 'to remain where they were', however, because 'Zionist enterprise represents a *deviant pattern of colonialism*'.[12] It sought not only to exploit but also to displace. That is why, from the beginning, the Zionists saw their conflict with the Palestinians as a zero sum game. Creation of Israel meant of necessity the destruction of Palestine. As R. Weitz, who was for many years head of the Jewish Agency's colonization department, said:

> Between ourselves it must be clear that there is no room for both peoples together in this country ... there is no other way than to transfer the Arabs from here to neighboring countries, to transfer all of them: Not one village, not one tribe, should be left.[13]

The Zionist leaders realized from the beginning that the biggest obstacle to the objective of transforming Palestine into 'Eretz Yisrael' would be the fact that it was already someone else's homeland. The reality of the situation hampered the Zionist effort to mobilize Jewish and non-Jewish support. Ahad Ha'am (Asher Ginsberg), one of the best known Jewish literary figures in the early part of this century, who traveled to Palestine and witnessed the destructive impact of Zionist colonization on Arab society, remarked that the Zionists 'treat the Arabs with hostility and cruelty, deprive them of their rights, offend them without cause, and even boast of these deeds'. He was so repelled that he said of Zionism: 'If this is the "Messiah", then I do not wish to see his coming'.[14]

Similarly, when the Zionists sought the endorsement and support of Asian nationalist leaders in the 1930s and 1940s, they were rebuffed precisely because of the destructive impact of Zionism on Palestinian society. Gandhi told a Zionist emissary who sought his support that 'you want to convert the Arab majority into a minority'. And Nehru was driven by Zionist disregard for the rights and well-being of the indigenous Arab community to observe that the Zionists 'neglected one not unimportant fact ... Palestine was not a wilderness or an empty, uninhabited place. It was already somebody else's home'.[15]

Recent research utilizing early Zionist archives makes it clear that members of the Zionist movement were not unaware of the existence of the Palestinian people and were in fact preoccupied with what was referred to as the Arab question.[16] Palestine was not only an ancient land, but the populous homeland of a contemporary society as well. In 1922, at the outset of serious Zionist colonization, 'the population density in Palestine was 72 persons per square mile – a high figure if compared with the countries of the region and those outside of it'.[17] Neither was Palestine a neglected land. Lawrence Oliphant visited Palestine in 1887 and wrote in his book *Haifa, or Life in Modern Palestine* that the valley of Esdraelon was 'a huge green lake of waving wheat, with its village crowned mounds rising from it like islands; and it presents one of the most striking pictures of luxuriant fertility which it is possible to conceive'.[18] It served Zionist purposes to deny this reality and, as Professor John Ruedy argues, 'it was convenient for Zionists and their supporters to picture Palestine as a wasteland before they came.'

However, to each other they admitted otherwise. In a letter to a Zionist colleague, Arthur Ruppin, director of the Zionist settlement department, said that 'there is hardly any land which is worth cultivating that is not already being cultivated'.[19] It is interesting to note that in their zeal to advertise the beneficial impact of Zionist colonization, symbolized by the well-known slogan about making the desert bloom, the Zionists not only downgraded the Arab achievement in Palestine but also consciously exaggerated their own. In his first visit to Palestine in 1898, Theodore Herzl admitted that he lied for this purpose. One little story will perhaps serve to illustrate the point. In an entry in his diary, dated 31 October 1898, after visiting a Jewish hospital in Jerusalem, he wrote: 'Misery and squalor. Nevertheless I was obliged, for appearance's sake, to testify in the visitors' book to its cleanliness. This is how lies originate.'[20]

As it was expedient for Zionists to picture Palestine as a neglected wasteland, it was also expedient to picture it as an empty, deserted land – from the start, the movement used the slogan 'land without people, for a people without land'. Initially, the Zionists apparently intended this slogan to be accepted in its literal meaning. The story is told of Max Nordau, Herzl's second in command, exclaiming to Herzl on first learning of the existence of the Palestinian Arabs: 'I never realized this – we are committing an injustice.'[21]

The curious thing about this Zionist view of the non-existence of the Palestinian people is how persistently they sought to maintain it. A Zionist emissary to Gandhi in the 1930s brazenly asserted that 'Palestine itself was a waste space when we went there. . . No one else wanted it'.[22] Even after they completed the conquest of Palestine in 1967, Zionist leaders continued to reassert the view: in 1969, Golda Meir, then Israel's prime minister, said of the Palestine people that 'they did not exist'.[23]

When Zionists found it untenable to maintain the myth of Palestinian non-existence in its crude and literal meaning, they sought to diminish the significance of Palestinian existence. When asked by a journalist in 1969 if he did not agree that the Palestinians, like the Israelis, were entitled to a homeland, Levi Eshkol responded: 'What are Palestinians? When I came here – there were 250,000 non-Jews – mainly Arabs and Bedouins. It was desert – more than underdeveloped. Nothing'.[24] Vladimir Jabotinsky, Menachem Begin's mentor, described the Arabs as 'a yelling rabble dressed up in gaudy, savage rags'.[25] And Ber Borochov, an early Zionist theoretician, believed that the Palestinian Arabs 'lacked any culture of their own and did not have any outstanding national characteristics'.[26]

By denying the existence of the Palestinian people, and by dehumanizing them, Zionists meant to hide from the world the intended victims of their colonization. They paraded before world public opinion as the national liberation movement of the Jewish people, but they could not do so if the fact were known that they were destroying an indigenous Asian community struggling to be free. Maxime Rodinson attributes this engrossing tendency to the European heritage of the leadership of the Zionist movement. The European view of the late nineteenth century, he said, held that 'every territory situated outside that world (Europe) was considered empty – not of inhabitants, of course, but constituting a kind of cultural vacuum, and therefore suitable for colonization'.[27] Another writer has suggested that this Zionist attitude was necessary to justify Zionist settlement, noting that

> The dehumanized image of the Palestinians which the Zionists developed and propagated was instrumental in displacing the moral issue and establishing an aura of legal justification around Zionist goals and activity.[28]

Menachem Begin in effect admitted the validity of this view. In 1969 he warned an Israeli audience of the danger of conceding 'the concept of Palestine'. He said: 'If this is Palestine and not the land of Israel, then you are conquerors and not tillers of the land. You are invaders. If this is Palestine, then it belongs to a people who lived here before you came.'[29]

For both ideological and practical reasons, therefore, the Palestinian Arabs had to be cleared from the Zionist path. In preparation for clearing the Palestinians, a task largely accomplished under the cover of war in 1948, Palestinian society had to be shaken and undermined. This the Zionists proceeded to do under the cover of the British Mandate and its 'national home' policy.

The British Mandate

The national home policy was officially inaugurated by the Balfour Declaration of 1917, which espoused the twin Zionist objectives of building up Jewish presence while undermining Arab presence in Palestine. In one brief paragraph it spoke of a commitment to establishing a Jewish national home in Palestine and made the Arabs who constituted more than ninety per cent of the population at the time inconsequential by calling them the 'non-Jewish communities'.[30] This doctrinal annihilation of the Palestinian people was reinforced by a system of colonial government that belittled the Palestinian people demographically, economically, and culturally, in effect making them aliens in their own homeland. The Mandate for Palestine (1922-48) required the mandatory power not only to facilitate Jewish immigration and the transfer of land, but also to place 'the country under such political, administrative and economic conditions as will secure the establishment of the Jewish national home'.[31] Article 4 of the Mandate authorized a Jewish Agency to share in the administration of the country.

The translation of these provisions into policies during the nearly thirty years of British Mandate over Palestine brought about the tragic and unique mutation that eventually turned Palestine into Israel. Demographically, Jewish immigration, imposed without the consent and against the explicit opposition of the indigenous community by a foreign colonial power, increased the ratio of alien settlers from one in ten in 1918 to one in two in 1947. The proportion of native population rapidly diminished from an overwhelming majority to a much smaller and continually dwindling one. In 1948, the Zionists took advantage of the outbreak of war and completed the process, thus achieving their long-standing aim of creating a Jewish majority in the country. Arab Palestine became Jewish Israel as a consequence of a 'demographic purge' of a kind unique in modern history. By the end of the following year (1949), only 130,000 Palestinian Arabs remained in the territory controlled by Israel within the 'Armistice Lines'; some 780,000 had become displaced persons either in residual parts of Palestine where they joined their compatriots, or in the immediately adjacent host countries of Lebanon, Syria, and Jordan.

As Palestine was subjected to this process of demographic transformation, it suffered under a cognate economic mutation. The transfer of land to Zionist settlers was always (and still is) a major objective of the Zionist movement. This was necessary not only to accommodate the massive immigration of Jewish settlers but also to ensure the destruction of the economic foundations of a predominantly agrarian Arab society. The Zionist policy of land acquisition was transforming Palestinian society into a community of landless peasants.

The deterioration of the quality of life available to the Palestinian Arabs as a direct consequence of Zionist colonization was documented and reported as early as 1930 by Sir John Hope Simpson, who was sent by the British government to Palestine to study its economic conditions. He found that Zionist land policy involved the acquisition of even more land than was needed for the settlement of Jewish immigrants. The policy thus led not only to the displacement of Arab farmers but also to the neglect and deterioration of much of the country's agricultural land. As an example, Simpson cited a one-time fertile plain in northern Palestine now become 'a sea of thorns' ravaged by field mice, because the Zionists had acquired more land than they needed or were able to cultivate.[32]

The Zionist movement not only deprived the Palestinian Arab of his land, it deprived Jewish farms as well as commercial and industrial establishments of Arab produce and labor. Contracts given by Zionist agencies that owned most of the Jewish-acquired land stipulated that only Jews could be employed. As Simpson noted in his report:

> Actually the result of the purchase of land in Palestine by the Jewish National Fund has been that land became extra territorial. It ceases to be land from which the Arab can gain any advantage either now or at any time in the future. Not only can he never hope to lease or cultivate it, but, by the stringent provisions of the lease of the Jewish National Fund, he is deprived forever from employment on that land.

He concluded that Arab fears of the destructive impact of Zionist colonization were well-founded, and thus called for controls:

> It is impossible to view with equanimity the extension of an enclave in Palestine from which the Arabs are excluded. The Arab population

already regards the transfer of lands to Zionist hands with dismay and alarm. These cannot be dismissed as baseless in light of the Zionist policy which is described above.[33]

The report goes on to point out that because the Zionist labor policy, which the Jewish Federation of Labor (Histadrut) helped to enforce, extended to all Jewish enterprises, the displaced Arab farmer could not even find non-agricultural employment, making the problem of unemployment among the Arabs 'serious and widespread'. Simpson refuted the perennial Zionist contention that the Arab worker benefited from Jewish immigration by saying:

> The policy of the Jewish Labour Federation is successful in impeding the employment of Arabs in Jewish colonies and in Jewish enterprises of every kind. There is therefore no relief to be anticipated from an extension of Jewish enterprise unless some departure from existing practice is effected.[34]

Jewish immigration was threatening the numerical superiority of the indigenous Arab community, and Zionist colonization was shaking its economic foundations. The Arab community was deprived of the capacity to safeguard its future in the country by the fact that throughout the British Mandate, Palestine was denied any measure of self-government. The Zionist movement threw its whole weight against the emergence of any democratic institutions in Palestine to prevent the Arab community from acquiring the capacity for political self-defence. This moved Nehru to say that the Zionists 'preferred to take sides with the foreign ruling power, and have thus helped it to keep back freedom from the majority of the people.'[35] In fact, the Zionists were so totally opposed to Palestinian rights that Chaim Weizmann, normally considered a moderate Zionist leader, thought that inclusion in the Balfour Declaration of a provision regarding the 'civil and religious' rights of the Arabs a 'painful recession' from earlier drafts supported by the Zionists, and argued that such a provision 'can be interpreted to mean such limitations on our work as completely to cripple it.'[36]

If the Zionist movement thought that safeguarding the civil and religious rights of the Palestinian people would cripple the Zionist project, it obviously thought it fatal to permit them to enjoy political rights outright. That is why, when the British government toyed with the idea of establishing a legislative council for Palestine in the 1930s, the political committee of the Zionist Congress rejected it categorically as being 'contrary to the spirit of the Mandate'.[37] Zionist enmity to the application of any degree of self-government in Palestine was so strong that Weizmann, who accomplished more gains for the Zionist movement than any other person with the possible exception of David Ben-Gurion, was viciously attacked when he showed willingness to consider the idea of a legislative council, even though the Arab majority was to have only minority representation on it. Recalling this episode later he said that on that occasion he came under 'the bitterest attacks to which I have ever been subjected'. He was called an 'appeaser' and a 'British agent'.[38] Occasionally Zionist writers used explicit colonialist logic to justify their opposition to self-government, even under British rule, in Palestine. A book which appeared in 1936 argued that the establishment of a legislative council would be a violation of British colonial traditions, which did not permit the native populations to share in the management of the country.[39]

Judah Magnes, president of Hebrew University in Jerusalem, was so troubled by this suffocating impact of Zionist colonization that he thought it an unbearable burden upon the Jewish conscience. In 1930 he wrote that self-government was being introduced in the neighbouring countries. 'Why not then in Palestine?' he asked. 'Because the Jews are here? The Jewish conscience will not bear this for long'.[40] Until the mandate expired in 1948, however, Palestine continued to lack any measure of self-government. Consequently, Palestinian Arab society was helpless to prevent its demographic erosion and the continual undermining of the material conditions for its viability and survival. Palestine was made ripe for the physical destruction it finally experienced in the war for partition.

Political Status and Organization of Palestinians Today

In the world today there are slightly more than 4.5 million Palestinians – those born in Palestine and their offspring born there or in other areas after dispersion. Nowhere do these people enjoy or exercise any political rights as Palestinians. Yet they are deeply committed to attainment of a normal political status. They are committed to a struggle for national self-determination, including the right to independence and sovereignty in Palestine, the right of return, and the right to national identity. Over the past four decades, the Palestinians have largely succeeded in maintaining that identity and in designating their own representative, the

Palestine Liberation Organization, despite concerted attempts to obliterate both.[41]

The present situation of the Palestinian people has its roots in a concrete historical event – the dismemberment of Palestine in May 1948. Israel's emergence then on a portion of Palestine had two consequences. First, Palestinians were expelled from areas that came under Israel's control and jurisdiction; this population henceforth became known to the world community as the Palestinian refugees. They numbered about seven hundred and eighty thousand originally; they are now more than two million. The social, educational, and economic development of the refugees became the shared responsibility of the United Nations Relief and Works Agency (UNRWA – created by the UN in 1950), the 'host' Arab States, and later on, the Palestine Liberation Organization. Second, there was the juridical and administrative incorporation of the remaining areas of Palestine by Jordan and Egypt. That part of Palestine that came under Jordan's control was eventually legitimized by an act of the Jordanian parliament in 1950, and became known thereafter as the West Bank; the southern part of Palestine came under Egypt's control and administration and is referred to as the Gaza Strip. Both parts came under Israeli occupation in 1967. Thus the entire area of Mandate Palestine is now exclusively controlled by Israel.

Between 1948 and 1967, Palestine ceased to exist as a political and administrative entity. Only in the Gaza Strip was it possible to use the term Palestine without incurring political opprobrium or punishment. Israel displaced its portion of Palestine, and Jordan gradually phased out the term – a decree issued by its postal administration in 1950 prohibited use of the word Palestine to refer to those portions under its jurisdiction, substituting for it the term West Bank. The cessation of the use of the term Palestine had a corresponding political, juridical and social meaning. Palestinians who continued to reside in Mandate Palestine acquired, by a series of Israeli decrees, a new legal designation. By its nationality and naturalization law, Israel made it possible for Palestinians who were physically present in their normal resi-dences when the first Israeli census was conducted in 1949 to acquire Israeli national status. These individuals, together with their descendants, are today's Israeli Arabs. A large number of Palestinians who were physically present on the territory incor-porated by Israel, but who were not in their normal residences at the time of the census, became known in Israeli law and politics as 'absentee-present' persons. Palestinians living on the West Bank, irrespective of place of origin, were naturalized in accordance with Jordanian law; similarly, Palestinians who found refuge on the east bank of the Jordan River were given the same privilege. Those who remained in the Gaza Strip or found refuge in Syria, Lebanon, Iraq, and Egypt became stateless but under the control, and subject to the rules, of the countries in which they resided. A limited number of individuals in this last category succeeded eventually in acquiring the nationality of the country in which they lived. But today the vast majority of this category of Palestinian – probably numbering over a million – remains stateless.

As a result of this fragmentation and dispersion, the Palestinian people have ceased to possess any real authority to guide, direct, and sustain a national life. They have no control over their cultural, social, and economic institutions; any rights they may have follow from their new status rather than from an integrated Palestinian polity.[42]

In political terms, Palestinians residing anywhere except in the Gaza Strip until 1967 were not allowed to organize themselves into political parties or to campaign on a Palestinian political platform, and thus were denied any sanctioned channels for development of a political leadership that would speak for or represent the entirety of the Palestinian political community. Even today, with the assumption by the Palestine Liberation Organization of the leadership of the Palestinian people, political activity specifically designed to enhance Palestinian social, economic, or cultural rights is proscribed in most states where Palestinians reside. Because of these external constraints, Palestinians, when wishing to organize themselves for national Palestinian endeavor, have had to do so in semi-legal or illegal fashion. Today, the Palestinian movements comprehended by the Palestine National Council and generally identified as the constituting elements of the Palestine Liberation Organization are primarily organized for the specific purpose of liberating Palestine. Of necessity, they exist on the margin of legality in the states wherein they function. In Israeli-occupied Palestine any association with a specifically Palestinian organization or national goal conforming to the Palestine National Charter is contrary to Israeli law or to the decrees of the Israeli military occupation of the West Bank and the Gaza Strip.

These difficulties have not prevented the Palestinians from engaging in political activity, activity primarily motivated by two broad imperatives: first, to continue the struggle to regain national rights; second, to direct existing political opportunities toward improvement of social, economic and educational conditions. These overriding concerns have led to the emergence of two types of political organization: first, those representative of Palestinians everywhere; second, those more specific to the countries in which Palestinians lived.

Palestinian National Organization

Since the dismemberment of Palestine, Palestinians have striven to forge an authority capable of addressing itself to the issue of the inherent national rights of their people. Three such authorities can be identified here. First was the Arab Higher Committee; it functioned on Palestinian soil particularly since 1946 and in theory is still extant, though ineffective. This committee, chaired by Palestine's national leader, Hajj Amin al-Hussaini, represented the Palestinian Arab national consensus, had the backing of the Palestinian political parties that functioned in Palestine, and was recognized in some form by Arab governments as the voice of the Palestinian people, until the Palestine Liberation Organization acquired its representative character. The Arab Higher Committee maintains two offices, manned by older associates of the Mufti of Jerusalem, one in Saudi Arabia, another in New York, but it has had little practical effect since the emergence of the Palestine Liberation Organization. Perhaps its main function was that it kept Palestinian hopes alive in a world that seemed indifferent. During the Palestinian political interregnum from 1948 to 1964, its principal office in Cairo issued memoranda on the question of Palestine, documented Israeli violations of Palestinian rights, and tried to raise the consciousness of the Arab States by stressing their historic responsibility to the Palestinian people. On a more subjective level, the Arab Higher Committee remained a symbol for the dispersed and fragmented Palestinian people of the commitment to Palestine.

One of the dubious achievements of the Arab Higher Committee was the forging, as Palestine was being divided among non-Palestinian authorities, of the Government of All Palestine. Partly in anticipation of the Jordanian-sponsored Jericho Conference of 1948, which was to endorse the principle of Jordanian incorporation of what became the West Bank, the Arab Higher Committee organized a Palestinian national congress held in Gaza. Among other things, the congress announced the formation of the Government of All Palestine, and appointed a cabinet. Both the congress and the cabinet had the blessing of the Egyptian administration. The cabinet was intended to govern, but it was, in fact, unable to exercise jurisdiction even in the Gaza Strip. Its functions dwindled until its only responsibility was the issue of passports to the Palestinian inhabitants of the Gaza Strip. These passports were recognized by the government of Egypt, and with considerable difficulty holders could travel as far as Egypt. Formally the government never ceased to exist, but in actuality its life came to an end with the death of its prime minister, Mr Ahmad Hilmi Abd al-Baqi, in 1957.[43]

The last national political organization to emerge from the wreckage of Palestinian life was the Palestine Liberation Organization. This occurred in 1964, in the wake of the Palestine National Congress held in May in Jerusalem. Convened largely on the initiative of Mr Ahmad Shukairi, a previously active Palestinian national leader, and blessed by the government of Egypt (then led by the late Jamal Abd al-Nasir), the Congress resolved to establish the Palestine Liberation Organization and gave it a mandate to mobilize the Palestinian people for the task of liberating Palestine. From a very simple beginning, the Palestine Liberation Organization in due course acquired legitimacy from the consensus of the Palestinian people. At the Rabat Summit Conference in 1974 the Arab States recognized the PLO as the legitimate representative of the Palestinian people. The PLO eventually obtained similar recognition from the majority of world states. In the same year, the General Assembly passed a resolution inviting the PLO to participate in the United Nations as an observer, and it acquired a parallel status in all specialized agenices of the UN. At present, the PLO maintains diplomatic-informational missions in all UN agencies and in the capitals of some ninety countries.

Political Activity in Countries of Residence and Dispersion

The impetus to forge a national political organization arose directly from the Palestinian political activities of the interregnum. The need for such activity – always proscribed as such and therefore fragmentary and inchoate before 1964 – was always clear and pressing. Active discrimination against Palestinians everywhere; abject social and economic conditions within Israel and in exile; routine control and manipulation of Palestinian politics by 'host' country security agencies (usually operating under such seemingly innocuous auspices as those of departments of Palestine or refugee affairs, or ministries of the interior or of social affairs): these were the major factors shaping the Palestinian political will, sharpening the desire to regain national rights – a desire increasingly expressed in militant terms. But before the mid-1960s, Palestinian political activity found forms that did not directly refer to Palestinian national aspirations. In Israel, for example, Palestinians who acquired Israeli national status often participated in the oppositional politics of the communist movement. The movement accepted the principle of Israeli sovereignty, but its program historically called for the establishment of two states in Palestine, one Arab and other Jewish. Moreover, the Israeli communist movement has viewed Zionism as an instrument of colonialism which, in practice, has discriminated against national minorities and the poor. Palestinian Arabs who remained in Israel – and who were thus controlled by its military regime and proscribed from engaging in specifically Palestinian political parties – found ready refuge for their political energies and aspirations in the program and activities of the communist movement. Support for communist candidates thus became one important way of asserting a claim to national political rights. The sole Palestinian attempt to organize a specifically Arab political party in Israel – the Ard (land) movement – was declared illegal by the Israeli Supreme Court, and its adherents were penalized by the Israeli state.

Elsewhere, it was only in Jordan that Palestinians were able to participate legally in politics, where they did so as Jordanians. The Jordanian political system allowed the Palestinian area of the West Bank its share of representation, at least when parliament functioned, and Palestinians had an equal share with Jordanians in the upper house (which was mostly appointed by the crown). Political volatility within the Jordanian system, however, made parliamentary life unstable and unpredictable. In any case, two things are important to observe in this regard: until 1967, Palestinians within the Jordanian system neither created specifically Palestinian political parties nor did they engage actively in dissenting ethnic politics. What dissent existed was informed by Jordanian, not Palestinian, issues.

In no other Arab country did the Palestinians have the right to engage in political activity of any kind. But the historical record indicates quite clearly that Palestinians did engage in politics in these countries. Generally speaking they participated in political movements that were Pan-Arab in character, that were reformist, and that were committed to the liberation of Palestine as well as to the liquidation of imperialism in the Arab region. Thus Palestinians in Syria, Lebanon, Jordan, and Iraq were active in the formation and development of the Baath party, and through that party and similar ones assumed positions of national prominence. But it should be noted that despite their eminence they neither sought nor were they given citizenship in these countries. As Palestinians in increasing numbers were attracted by the new opportunities of development in the Arab Gulf region, the Palestinian presence there did not produce a corresponding political weight. Both their foreign status and the somewhat constricted kind of political life itself in these countries discouraged active Palestinian participation in politics.

On a different level, public organizations based upon ethnic Palestinian principles were similarly proscribed either explicitly or implicitly in all such areas. Thus Palestinians were not permitted to organize specific Palestinian labor organizations, nor to found such groups as teachers' and writers' unions. Any such groups that did form were informally organized and generally functioned without state approval.

The only exception was found in the Gaza Strip. There, Palestinians had the freedom to assert national identity, and they did so organizationally and politically throughout the period from 1948 to 1967. The Egyptian administration neither questioned the national identity of the inhabitants of the Gaza Strip, nor did it view their national aspirations as inconsistent with Egypt's national policy. The outcome of this congruence was the eventual emergence of a Palestinian Legislative Assembly that represented the population – original inhabitants *and* refugees – of the Gaza Strip. Similarly, Palestinians there were permitted to organize themselves professionally and syndically, in accordance with legislation enacted for that purpose.[44]

From within this context of active participation in dissenting politics – and with a growing awareness of the difficulties besetting effective support by Arab States of Palestinian aspirations – a Palestinian national consciousness began eventually to consolidate itself with the creation of the Palestinian Liberation Organization. For about three years after its emergence, the PLO struggled to define itself and to press its program on its dispersed Palestinian constituency, on the Arab region, and on the world. In those years the challenge to its legitimacy came essentially from three different sources. Obviously it came from Israel, which saw in it the reincarnation of the old Palestinian people it thought had vanished. It came from Jordan, too, which perceived a threat to its political system and a challenge to its incorporation of the West Bank, should the Palestinians there identify too closely with the

PLO. The third challenge to the PLO came from Palestinian militants, who had been organizing underground for national liberation, and who viewed the organization and its leaders as instruments of the Pan-Arab politics of Egypt and neither sufficiently militant nor independent in decision making. All of these challenges to the legitimacy of the PLO were transformed in the wake of Israel's defeat of the Arab States in the 1967 June war.

Effect of the 1967 War

The first consequence of the war was the military occupation of the West Bank and the Gaza Strip by Israel. Thus the entirety of Mandate Palestine came under Israel's control. That occupation meant, in human terms, the expulsion of about three hundred thousand Palestinians from the West Bank and the subjection of over one million additional Palestinians, thus bringing a total of approximately 1.4 million Palestinian Arabs under Israel's total control.[45] Since 1967, Israel's occupation has systematically worked to the detriment of the Palestinian people. First, a process of expulsion of Palestinians from the occupied areas was initiated quite early; various political and economic pressures, as well as the direct expulsion of politically committed elements among the Palestinians, resulted in serious population attrition. (See table 7. Second, Israel's policy of building colonial settlements on the West Bank and Gaza (over 110 such settlements have been built) meant confiscation of Palestinian lands, annexation of Jerusalem, and settling of about one hundred thousand Israeli Jews therein. Thus far, over fifty per cent of the land of the West Bank and Gaza has been confiscated by Israel. Third, Israel has systematically diverted the precious water resources of the West Bank to provide for its settlements, thus causing severe drought in Arab villages and compelling Palestinian farmers to abandon their only means of livelihood. Fourth, Israel's occupation has brought about extreme economic dislocation and large-scale unemployment, so that Palestinians in Israel must work for minimal wages under harsh conditions. Palestinians have become a source of cheap labor for the Israeli economy. Finally, Israel found in the West Bank and Gaza outlets for its manufactured goods; in a relatively short time, these areas became the second 'trading partner' of Israel. Israel's exploitation of this captive market has crippled the economic base of the Palestinians in the West Bank and Gaza.

These and similar policies on social, cultural and economic levels are intended to replace the oppressive system of colonial military occupation with a system of apartheid for the Palestinian population under Israeli rule. As has been noted, practically all of Israel's policies in the West Bank and Gaza have been drawn from the long history, dating back to the early days of Zionism, of ignoring or denigrating the Palestinian Arabs. While the ultimate intention of Israel with regard to the West Bank and Gaza is still debated, it is virtually certain that, with or without *de jure* annexation, Israel intends to expel Palestinians and transform those remaining under its control into a permanently subordinate population.

Towards that end, Israel has from the beginning systematically violated the human rights of the Palestinian people under its occupation. It has exercised strict controls over cultural institutions, has refused to observe the various provisions of the Geneva convention on occupied areas, and has disregarded all UN resolutions that call for such observance. Thousands of Palestinians have been arrested, charged with opposition to the military occupation; thousands of their homes have been demolished. The violation of Palestinian human rights culminated in the dismissal, by Israel's military governor of the West Bank and Gaza, of the elected mayors of practically all major Palestinian towns and cities, in an attempt to forestall any expression of political support for Palestinian self-determination, even in its attenuated form as envisioned in the Camp David accords or hinted at in President Reagan's statement of 1 September 1982.[46]

The occupation of the West Bank and Gaza was one consequence of the June War of 1967. A second and unintended consequence was the transformation of the Palestine Liberation Organization into an effective, militant, and independent expression of the Palestinian drive to liberation. In part, this was in response to the weakness of the Arab states, as demonstrated by their easy defeat by Israel; that defeat served to discredit Arab policies of confronting Israel and also to discredit previous Arab state tutelage of the Palestinians. Thus the militant Palestinian organizations prevailed in the PLO and assumed its leadership. Palestinian militants who were organized in underground and semi-legal organizations such as Fatah, the Popular Front for the Liberation of Palestine, and so on, had questioned the ability of the PLO, while under the hegemony of the Arab states, to carry out the program of Palestinian national liberation. Thus the Israeli defeat of the Arab states meant also the defeat of that part of the

Palestinian leadership that pursued policies consistent with those of the Arab states. When the Palestine National Council met in Cairo in 1969, it allowed the militants to assume the mantle of leadership of the PLO. From that time onward, no discussion of the question of Palestine could credibly proceed without the active participation of an independent PLO and without close consideration of the premises and vision projected by the transformed organization.

The PLO After the 1967 War

Political Aims

The Palestine National Charter adopted in 1964 by the Palestine National Congress outlined the general principles and ideas that should guide Palestinian action. It also delineated, although with considerable ambiguity, the path to the realization of the formulated goal of the liberation of Palestine (which then meant only pre-1967, post-1948 Israel). The National Council of 1968 and its later amplifications projected a solution to the question of Palestine consistent not only with Palestinian self-determination but also with the reality of an Israeli Jewish presence in Palestine-Israel. The projected solution dealt forthrightly with the anomalous status of both the West Bank and Gaza. The highly organized militant groups of the PLO proposed a vision of a democratic secular polity for Palestine, in which sectarian or national influences would play no part. Both Zionism and Arab nationalism were thus rejected as a basis for the future Palestinian state. Underlying that vision was the awareness of the existence of two peoples on the same land, one Palestinian Arab, the other Israeli Jewish. The national affiliation of Palestinians with the Arab people was of no consequence to the political organization of the projected Palestine; similarly the religious affinity of Israelis with Jews elsewhere was to entail no special political right or obligation. The vision of the democratic secular polity was not of one consisting of two separate and hostile communities, but of persons whose individual rights were primary and equal. This concept challenged both Israeli Jews and Palestinian Arabs to accept coexistence in the same polity on the basis of full equality.

It was fully realized that this goal conflicted with Zionism and its embodiment in Israel. Additionally, the movement viewed Israel as an extension of European-American imperialism which therefore would marshal its resources to resist the new formulation.

Achievement of the first principle – establishment of a democratic secular polity in Palestine – could not be realized except by adherence to a second principle – the necessity for armed struggle by the Palestinian masses. Towards that end, the PLO undertook to mobilize and organize the Palestinians, and it subsequently recruited militant cadres and obtained material and political support for that program. As it did so, the PLO succeeded in organizing and in focusing the loyalty of the Palestinian people, as well as in challenging the legitimacy of the Arab states' exercise of control over Palestinians within their domain. The PLO additionally understood that Israel's control of the West Bank and Gaza must be challenged by all means including militant ·action, and it therefore rendered material, political, and economic support to Palestinians there to resist Israel's occupation. Finally, as representative of the Palestinian people everywhere, the PLO viewed its functions as including a duty to organize the Palestinian communities everywhere and to provide them with support, security and welfare.

Structure of the PLO

Today, the Palestine Liberation Organization represents the embryonic Palestinian state and government. Its constituency is the entirety of the Palestinian people. Over the years the Palestinians, no matter how subjugated or displaced, have retained a distinct and durable consciousness of themselves as a national community; in response the PLO has developed a structure capable of addressing the needs and aspirations of its constituency.

The Palestine National Council is the highest policy-making body of the Palestine Liberation Organization. At present, the council is composed of 428 members presumed to represent all sectors of the Palestinian people, geographically and culturally. (The council has allotted certain seats to Palestinians in the occupied areas, but Israeli control has prevented those members from attending the sessions of the council.) The membership of the council is drawn from three separate categories: the militant organizations (Fatah, Popular Front for the Liberation of Palestine, Popular Democratic Front, etc.) in proportion to their actual or presumed strength; popular associations such as teachers' unions, women's unions, students' unions, writers' or workers' unions, and so on; and independents. Although representation is not solely premised on geographic principles of distribution, geography does play an important role in designating members of the council. Thus members drawn from the three categories mentioned are usually drawn from the geographic spread of the Palestinian people. In short, function, geography, and politics play important roles in the designation of the membership in the council. Looked at in a different way, the council, as a representative of the Palestinian people, symbolizes Palestinian pluralism. It is a multi-party council and reflects all political tendencies present in the Palestinian political community.

The council debates all Palestinian issues at its annual meetings. Usually these meetings last about one week, at the end of which two sets of actions are adopted. One' deals with the policies that the executive is to pursue in the coming period, policies relating to such matters as finance, military activities, political strategy, or bureaucratic functions, such as the creation of various departments – education, social welfare, culture, etc. It is perhaps appropriate to point out that major political programs become binding on the executive only when so mandated by the council. For example, the modification of the Palestinian program aiming at the creation of a democratic secular state took place within the council, which adopted a Provisional Program that accepted *de facto* Palestinian authority over the West Bank and Gaza should Israel withdraw; this was subsequently amended in 1977 to demand an Independent Palestinian State under the control of the Palestine Liberation Organization. It was in the pursuit of that modified program that the Executive Committee made its appeal in the United Nations in 1981 to support the establishment of an Independent Palestinian State specifically in the West Bank and Gaza.

The second action of the council is the election of the Executive Committee and its chairman. Thus far the practice has been to elect by secret ballot fifteen persons who for all practical purposes act as the Palestinian cabinet. The Executive Committee is responsible for implementing the policies the Council had adopted. The Council elects its chairman; for the past eighteen years, Mr Yasir Arafat has filled that post. Essentially the chairman assumes the functions of president and prime minister; each member of the Executive Committee is responsible for a particular functional department. These departments are charged with advancement of the political, diplomatic, social, economic, cultural, educational and military interests of the Palestinian people; over the years, they have fostered the development of a distinct Palestinian bureaucracy which is subject to rules and regulations of service approved by the Palestine National Council.

In 1982 the PLO civil service – excluding the military cadres – numbered some eight thousand persons.

The council has also created additional governmental authorities. It has established higher councils for education, for culture, for literacy, for economic development, a Palestine National Fund (combining treasury and commerce), a Palestine Red Crescent Society (public health), and so forth. It has granted recognition to syndicalist and professional associations. The organization chart (fig. 2) illustrates the structural components of the PLO.[47]

Effect of Israeli Assault on Lebanon

These structures supply a network of Palestinian national institutions for the benefit of Palestinians everywhere. Through them, the PLO can assist the dispersed Palestinian communities in obtaining jobs, in placing students at institutions of higher learning in the host societies, in manning educational establishments, in enhancing Palestinian cultural and economic growth. The most striking success of this institutional growth and development took place in Lebanon, where the estimated four hundred thousand Palestinians began to form an embryonic Palestinian society free from the constraints of either Israeli occupation or total control by a host government. It was in Lebanon that a good proportion of the Palestinian bureaucracy was to be found; it was in Lebanon that Palestinian cultural, economic, and social institutions were to develop; and it was in Lebanon that the Palestinian identity began really to re-coalesce. All this was accomplished with considerable difficulty and without the full cooperation of the Lebanese government. But the healthy development of the Palestinian community in Lebanon made it inevitable that Israel should see it as a challenge, and attempt its destruction.

On 4 June 1982, Israel carried out massive air raids against Palestinian areas in Beirut; it continued these raids on Beirut and the entirety of south Lebanon on the fifth of June. On the sixth, its army, an estimated one hundred thousand men backed by the air force and navy, marched on Lebanon with the public objective of obtaining 'Peace for Galilee'. Israel later admitted that its objective was to destroy the PLO and its infrastructure in Lebanon.

In the course of two-and-a-half months Israel's vastly destructive campaign took the lives of as many as forty thousand Palestinians and Lebanese, seriously injured over one hundred thousand persons and left over one-half million homeless. Israel succeeded in destroying the major part of Palestinian political and

Figure 2 PLO Structure

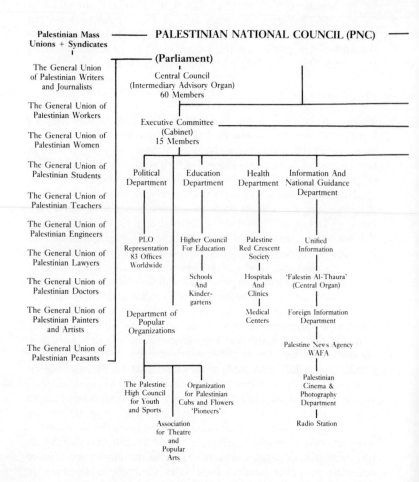

Palestinian Mass ——— **PALESTINIAN NATIONAL COUNCIL (PNC)** ——
Unions + Syndicates

The General Union
of Palestinian Writers
and Journalists

The General Union of
Palestinian Workers

The General Union of
Palestinian Women

The General Union of
Palestinian Students

The General Union of
Palestinian Teachers

The General Union of
Palestinian Engineers

The General Union of
Palestinian Lawyers

The General Union of
Palestinian Doctors

The General Union of
Palestinian Painters
and Artists

The General Union of
Palestinian Peasants

(Parliament)

Central Council
(Intermediary Advisory Organ)
60 Members

Executive Committee
(Cabinet)
15 Members

| Political Department | Education Department | Health Department | Information And National Guidance Department |

PLO Representation 83 Offices Worldwide

Higher Council For Education

Palestine Red Crescent Society

Unified Information

Schools And Kinder-gartens

Hospitals And Clinics

'Falestin Al-Thaura' (Central Organ)

Department of Popular Organizations

Medical Centers

Foreign Information Department

Palestine News Agency WAFA

The Palestine High Council for Youth and Sports

Organization for Palestinian Cubs and Flowers 'Pioneers'

Palestinian Cinema & Photography Department

Association for Theatre and Popular Arts

Radio Station

(Adapted from AMEU, The Link, XV, 3, 1982)

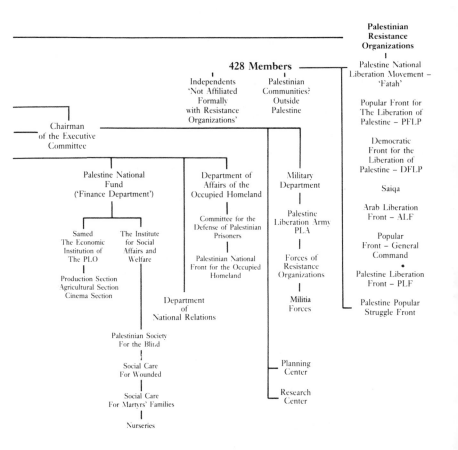

Palestinian Resistance Organizations

Palestine National Liberation Movement – 'Fatah'

Popular Front for The Liberation of Palestine – PFLP

Democratic Front for the Liberation of Palestine – DFLP

Saiqa

Arab Liberation Front – ALF

Popular Front – General Command

Palestine Liberation Front – PLF

Palestine Popular Struggle Front

428 Members

Independents 'Not Affiliated Formally with Resistance Organizations'

Palestinian Communities? Outside Palestine

Chairman of the Executive Committee

Palestine National Fund ('Finance Department')

Department of Affairs of the Occupied Homeland

Military Department

Samed The Economic Institution of The PLO

The Institute for Social Affairs and Welfare

Committee for the Defense of Palestinian Prisoners

Palestine Liberation Army PLA

Production Section
Agricultural Section
Cinema Section

Palestinian National Front for the Occupied Homeland

Forces of Resistance Organizations

Department of National Relations

Militia Forces

Palestinian Society For the Blind

Social Care For Wounded

Social Care For Martyrs' Families

Nurseries

Planning Center

Research Center

social institutions in Lebanon. The entire Palestinian health program and facilities were destroyed; economic enterprises (SAMED, for example) were wiped out; communication systems – radio, newspapers, and publishing houses – were either looted or destroyed. Palestinian settlements in Lebanon from Rashidiyya in the south to the Fakhani district of West Beirut were reduced to rubble. The only Palestinian community to have raised itself from the wreckage of Palestine in 1948, and to have achieved a condition of relative autonomy, was wilfully destroyed. Thousands of Palestinians were expelled from Lebanon and those that remained have endured enormous political, economic, and social hardships, and continue to do so.

As a result of Israel's assault on Lebanon and the Palestinians residing there, the overall Palestinian situation has become considerably more complex. Not only is the Palestinian liberation effort temporarily weakened but the goal of independence for the West Bank and Gaza – something that would ameliorate the Palestinian plight significantly and that is fully supported by international consensus as expressed by the United Nations – continues to be problematic. The Palestinian hope for return to Palestine, as mandated by the United Nations, has grown much dimmer with the daily influx of those expelled from both occupied Palestine and occupied Lebanon who drift into neighboring countries such as Syria and Jordan. Without question the loss of the Lebanese offices and land base has complicated PLO operations and reduced its ability to enhance the welfare and security of the Palestinian people. But as the PLO reorganized and mapped out alternative strategies to carry on its mandate, it did so fully confident of the backing of a Palestinian national consensus. No matter the jurisdiction exercised over them, no matter the conditions under which they suffer, the more than 4.5 million Palestinians continue to press for their return to an independent Palestinian state. In that effort they have the growing support of the world community.

Demographic Circumstances

Palestinians are, ironically, displaced persons, whether they live 'at home' or 'abroad'. Each passing year since 1948 has taken them farther from their homeland. Because they are denied political rights, each passing year since 1967 has brought more oppression and injustice. Yet Palestinians do not forget ther heritage – they continue to identify with their native towns or villages, even though they may never have seen them. Although the older generation with vivid memories of Palestine is fast dying off, now that thirty-five years have elapsed since the first expulsion sent seven hundred and eighty thousand Palestinians into exile, younger Palestinians are no less attached to the idea, if not the substance, of Palestine. The successive wars that have racked the region and the growing toll of death and destruction have served to intensify, rather than to diminish, that attachment.

Who are the Palestinians? Where do they live? How did they come to be so scattered? And what does the immediate future hold?

Present Demography

Palestinians now number over 4.5 million persons. These include the survivors of the 1.4 million Palestinian Arabs alive in 1948, together with their children and their children's children. This figure is neither totally accurate nor simply unreliable – it is approximately correct, plus or minus some few hundred thousand. The fact that it has been impossible to make a true count of Palestinians is symptomatic of their plight, for in few places where Palestinians live are they enumerated as Palestinians in national censuses. Ironically, it is only inside the borders of Palestine, now completely occupied by Israel, that it is possible to obtain a relatively firm estimate of their number, although in Israeli statistical sources they are referred to as 'non-Jews'.

In 1984, according to our best estimates, some 1,974,300 Palestinians (or about 42.5 per cent) were still living within the borders of Palestine. Of these, about 579,200 were treated as 'citizens' of Israel, another 896,000 (including the population in East Jerusalem and vicinity, 'annexed' to Israel) were nominally Jordanian nationals with the status of conquered people, and the rest (about 499,100) were residents of Gaza, similarly conquered but (depending upon one's point of view) either stateless or Palestinian citizens, since they carried Palestinian identity papers but no universally recognized passport.[48] A very large proportion of the Palestinians still in Palestine are not living in their communities of origin.

In addition to these 'in-country' displaced persons, there are now some 2,639,700 Palestinians (or close to 60 per cent) who currently reside outside the boundaries of historical Palestine. Of these, most still live in the adjacent countries of Jordan, Syria, and

Lebanon, although over the years this proportion has been dropping. In 1984 we estimate that about 1,756,200 Palestinians lived in the core countries next to Palestine: about 245,000 in Syria, perhaps 275,000 in Lebanon and about 1,236,200 on the east bank in the Hashemite Kingdom of Jordan.[49] It is difficult to determine any of these numbers with precision because most Palestinians living in exile hold other nationalities (since there is no such thing today as Palestinian nationality) and, in their countries of residence, censuses have not distinguished persons of Palestinian origin from others.

Next to Palestine itself, the Hashemite Kingdom of Jordan (east bank) contains the largest number of persons of Palestinian birth or descent. In 1949, Palestinians on the so-called West Bank as well as refugees on the east bank were given Jordanian citizenship. In 1979 a census was conducted in Jordan (east bank only); at that time questions designed to elicit information on (Palestinian) place of birth and descent were suggested for inclusion but were dropped because of the politically sensitive nature of the distinction, which Jordan officially does not make among its citizens. Informed analysts suggest that approximately half of the two plus million residents on the east bank are actually of Palestinian origin.

In Syria, Palestinians were not automatically given citizenship, although some unknown number were eventually naturalized. Although Syria does not gather census data on persons of Palestinian origin, it does keep a register of Palestinians. According to the statistical abstract of Syria (1979) there were about 226,000 Palestinian refugees registered in Syria in 1978. By 1984 these would have increased to some 245,000.[50]

The number of Palestinians who were in Lebanon at the time of the Israeli invasion in June 1982 is a matter of conjecture. Some estimates place that figure as high as one-half million, although most analysts believe it was under 400,000.[51] Lebanon has not conducted a full census since 1932. In the sample census in 1971, Palestinians living in camps were not actually enumerated but were estimated by the Palestine Liberation Organization at 130,000. By 1982 the United National Relief and Works Agency (UNRWA) had about 230,000 Palestinians listed on its register, not all of whom lived in camps. Informed observers suggest that since 1948 about 50,000 Palestinians gained Lebanese citizenship and many Jordanians of Palestinian origin were permanently residing in the country. After the expulsion of the Palestine resistance from Jordan in 1970, there was considerable illegal entry into Lebanon;

possibly as many as 15,000 to 30,000 Palestinians relocated there. Against these additions we must weigh an exodus of Palestinian middle- and upper-class persons, pulled by the post-1973 prosperity in the Gulf states and pushed by the tension of the Lebanese civil war of 1975-76 and the aftermath of the Israeli invation of 1982.

Over time, however, Palestinians were forced by circumstances into ever-widening dispersion. In recent years, the Arab countries of the Gulf have absorbed an increasing number. Including the relatively small communities that settled initially in Egypt and Iraq and the relatively small community that eventually went to Libya, the total number of Palestinians now living in the non-core countries of the Arab world was estimated, as of June 1984, at slightly under 633,500 or about 13.6 per cent of the total. The largest community in a country of 'second settlement' is found in Kuwait, to which Palestinians began moving in the 1950s.[52] Saudi Arabia contains the next largest community. According to the Saudi census of 1974, there were only some 76,000 Palestinians in that country (about half carrying Palestinian identity papers, about half Jordanian passports) but the numbers have more than quadrupled since then.[53] Other countries of the Gulf – the United Arab Emirates, Qatar, Bahrain, Oman, etc. – all contain some Palestinians. Again, it is impossible to give exact figures because of the nationality problem. Palestinians from Lebanon, Syria, and Gaza who have not taken on another citizenship are identifiable by nationality. However, 90 per cent of all Jordanians in the Gulf are estimated to be of Palestinian origin, and some of the Lebanese migrants are also of Palestinian descent.

Whereas in 1948 there were almost no Palestinians living outside the Arab world, over the years this has become less and less true. While we lack firm figures for the dispersion of Palestinians outside the Arab world, we have estimated their total at about 250,000 as of 1984.

Table 6 shows the distribution of Palestinians as of the end of 1979, and as updated to 1984. Two questions must be posed. First, how did the Palestinian community come to be so fragmented? And second, how have the recent events in Lebanon contributed to their further dispersion?

Fragmentation of the Palestinian Community

More significant than the precise number of Palestinians is the fact of their continual displacement. The Israeli invasion of

Table 6 Estimated Size and Distribution of the Palestinian Population as of End 1979 and Beginning June 1984

Palestinians by Current Place of Residence	December 1979		June 1984	
	Number	%	Number	%
TOTAL (estimated)	4,000,000	100.0	4,614,000	100.0
Palestinians Living inside Palestine	1,715,00	42.9	1,974,300	42.5
Pre-1967 Israel[1]	(520,000)[4]	(13.0)	579,200	(12.46)[2]
West Bank including Jerusalem	(791,000)	(19.8)	896,000	(19.27)[3]
Gaza, excluding Sinai	(404,000)	(10.1)	499,100	(10.73)
Palestinians Living outside Palestine	2,285,000	57.1	2,639,700	59.2
Adjacent Arab states	1,540,000	38.5	1,756,200	37.8
(Syria)	(210,000)	(5.3)	(245,000)	(5.3)
(Jordan, East Bank)	(1,000,000)	(25.0)	(1,236,000)	(26.6)
(Lebanon)	(330,000)	(8.2)	(275,000)[5]	(5.9)
Other Arab states	584,000	14.6	633,500	(13.6)
Rest of world	160,000	4.0	250,000	(5.23)

Source: The 1979 figures are taken from Janet Abu-Lughod, 'Demographic Characteristics of the Palestinian Population', Annex I, part II, *Palestine Open University Feasibility Study* (UNESCO: Paris, 30 June 1980), especially table-VI, p. 29. This detailed document was based upon examination of all relevant government sources and demographic dissertations, and used a complex method of projections cross-checked against aggregative figures for sequential data points to reach what we consider to be the most authoritative, although certainly not 'precise' estimates of total population and its distribution. The original document should be consulted for detailed description of methods, data base, and assumptions. The only adjustment made for this table for 1979 was to remove the Palestinian population living in 'annexed' East Jerusalem from Israel and reclassify it with the West Bank. The 1984 figures are based upon projections from the 1980 figures shown in the most recent *Statistical Abstract of Israel* (1982), suitably adjusted for Jerusalem and vicinity, and best 'guestimates' by the author for the period of time between end 1979 and beginning 1984.

[1] Jerusalem and vicinity, merged with Israeli 'non-Jews' in official documents, has been excluded.
[2] There have been recent drops in fertility recorded for the Palestinian population in Israel. Projection is based upon lower natural increase.
[3] Includes an estimated 120,000 Palestinians in East Jerusalem and vicinity, which may be too high. Had natural increase not been counteracted by expulsions and emigration, this figure should have reached well in excess of 1,200,000 by 1984.
[4] Parenthetical figures represent subtotals.
[5] Includes Palestinians in the armed forces.

Lebanon during the summer of 1982 was only the most recent episode in a series of cataclysms that progressively denuded Palestine of its indigenous population and forced Palestinians to find refuge in places increasingly remote from Palestine.

In 1948, before the Palestine bicommunal war and the unilateral establishment of the State of Israel, there were 1.4 million Muslim and Christian Arabs in the country. As a result of the war and the *de facto* partition of Palestine, approximately nine hundred thousand persons were declared 'refugees'. Of these, 780,000 were physically uprooted; the remainder lost their lands and therefore their livelihoods.[54] By 1952, when the total number of Palestinians approached 1.6 million, only 11 per cent (179,300) were living inside the armistice line of Israel, 18 per cent (nearly 300,000) were crowded into the Gaza Strip, while 47 per cent (some 742,300) lived in the remaining portion of Palestine that had been annexed by Jordan and renamed the West Bank. Thus, most Palestinians (76 per cent) still clung to the soil of Palestine, albeit either as refugees or as 'hosts' to refugees. Almost all of the remaining 380,000 waited in neighbouring countries for their chance to go home. Some 114,000 (7 per cent) were in Lebanon, close to 83,000 (5 per cent) in Syria, and about 150,000 (9 per cent) in Jordan on the east side of the river. No more than 2 per cent of all Palestinians were scattered beyond this radius.

In the 1950s, as Palestinians sought to recover from the financial as well as political consequences of the 1948 war, they began to move to areas offering some way to make a living. The east bank of Jordan was particularly hospitable because, as citizens, Palestinians of the West Bank were entitled to live there. Others gained entry into economically more prosperous areas, such as Libya and Kuwait, which were benefiting from oil, and Lebanon, then the most viable state in the region.

By 1961 evidence of dispersal was already apparent. Only 65 per cent of the estimated 2.1 to 2.2 million Palestinians were still living on Palestinian soil (11 per cent in Israel, 17 per cent in Gaza, and 37 per cent on the West Bank). By then, over one-third of the Palestinians were in exile, with the east bank of Jordan the major recipient (about 380,000 persons of Palestinian origin or 17 per cent of the total). Lebanon hosted about 183,000 (8 per cent), Syria another 116,400 (5 per cent), while about 100,000 (under 5 per cent) were scattered farther from home.[55]

These trends continued into the 1960s, with a sizeable exodus of breadwinners from the east and west banks of the Jordan moving to Kuwait in response to the expanding demand for skilled

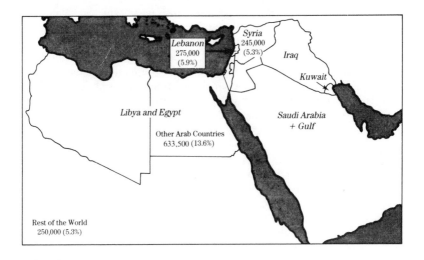

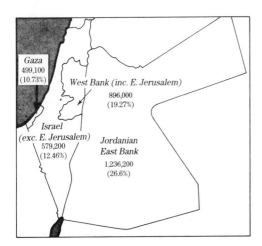

Figure 3 Distribution of Palestinian Populations in 1984

manpower. However, on the eve of the June 1967 war, the distribution of Palestinians was not very different from what it had been at the beginning of the decade. By then, 63 per cent of the estimated 2.65 million Palestinians were still in Palestine. Extremely high rates of natural increase had raised the percentage inside Israel to 12 and that in the Gaza Strip to 18. However, net out-migration from the West Bank counteracted natural increase, so that only 900,00 (or 34 per cent of the total) remained there.

The 1967 war, during which Israel invaded and conquered all remaining segments of Palestine as well as parts of Syria and Egypt, had catastrophic effects on the Palestinian population. In the immediate aftermath of the war no less than 300,000 Palestinians who had been living on the West Bank or in Gaza were exiled, while a sizeable number of Gaza residents who were temporarily absent from their homes or had retreated with the Egyptian army were not allowed to return. Most fleeing West Bank residents relocated on the east bank, although some of these displaced persons continued on to second settlement areas, mostly in Kuwait but also in Lebanon.

Whereas just before the war some 63 per cent of all Palestinians still lived in Palestine, by the end of 1967 this percentage had dropped precipitously to only 50. The losses were experienced primarily on the West Bank and secondarily in Gaza. The proportion of Palestinians living in pre-1967 occupied Palestine (Israel) remained constant at 12. However, the percentage on the West Bank dropped from 34 to 24.7;[56] the percentage in the Gaza Strip dropped from 18 to 15. Table 7 shows the immediate effects of the 1967 war in increasing the dispersion of the Palestinian population. While the east bank of the Jordan received the largest number of new expellees, about 5 per cent of the population scattered even farther, into the Arab countries of the Gulf, into Libya, Egypt, and the rest of the world.

Gradually, between 1968 and 1982, further erosions and displacements took place. An Israeli policy of deportation, harsh military rule, physical harassment and economic control and deprivation (such as through exclusion from water resources and confiscation of land) was carried out systematically in the so-called 'Administered Territories' of the West Bank and Gaza.[57] The effects of that policy were clearly reflected in the declining proportion of Palestinians able to remain within pre-1948 Palestine. The proportion of all Palestinians living inside Palestine declined from 50 in 1967 after the war to 46 per cent by 1970, to 45.5 by 1975; by the end of 1979, it had dropped to 42.9. By the

Table 7 Probable Distribution of Palestinians Just Before and After the War Begun on 5 June 1967

Region or Country of Residence	Estimate as of 1 June 1967		Estimate as of December 1967	
	Number	%	Number	%
TOTAL PALESTINIANS	2,650,000	100.0	2,700,000	100.0
Palestinians Living inside Palestine	1,668,200	63.0	1,338,338	50.0
Pre-1967 Israel	318,200	12.0	325,700	12.0
West Bank including Jerusalem	900,000	34.0	666,377	24.7
Gaza	450,000	18.0	346,261[1]	13.0
Palestinians Living outside Palestine	981,800	37.0	1,361,662	50.0
(Lebanon)	(200,000)[2]	(8.0)	(225,000)	(8.0)
(East Bank)	(466,000)	(17.5)	(730,600)	(27.0)
(Syria)	(140,300)	(5.0)	(143,000)	(5.0)
(Kuwait)	(91,000)	(3.0)	(101,000)	(4.0)
(Gulf, Saudi Arabia, Libya and Iraq)	(37,000)	(1.0)	(82,162)	(3.0)
(Egypt)	(10,000)	(0.0)	(33,000)	(1.0)
(rest of world)	(37,500)	(1.0)	(47,600)	(2.0)

Source: UNESCO report, cited in table 6. See original for full explanations, and detailed sources.

[1] Excludes Egyptian Sinai.
[2] Parenthetical figures represent subtotals.

beginning of June 1982, we estimate the proportion had further eroded to only 40.8 per cent.

Particularly after the oil 'boom' that began as part of the Arab strategy in the 1973 war, and especially after the Arab defeat in that war which signalled to Palestinians that liberation of the occupied areas was not imminent, dispersal became more marked. Not only did emigration continue from the West Bank and Gaza but many of the Palestinians from the east bank of Jordan also began to migrate in search of employment in the economically expanding countries of the Arab Gulf. The proportion of all Palestinians residing in east bank Jordan dropped from its high point of 30 per cent in 1970 to about 27.5 per cent by 1975, 25 per cent by 1979, and to only 24 per cent by June 1982. Some small portion of that drop was attributable to the expulsion of Palestinian forces after their defeat in September of 1970, but most was due to the stagnation of the east bank economy, as contrasted with the job opportunities in the Gulf.

The Israeli invasion of Lebanon, which began with an unprovoked bombing raid on Beirut on 4 June, 1982, followed by a well-planned attack from assembled ground forces, appeared to have two demographic objectives. One was directed toward the Palestinian population in Lebanon, the other toward the Palestinian population in the occupied areas of Gaza and the West Bank. Both objectives continued the dual policy designed first to 'cleanse' Palestine of its non-Jewish population and to make room for further settlements and eventual annexation and, second, to 'empty' areas bordering Israeli-held territory of populations that might threaten her expansion. The Camp David accords reached with Egypt had succeeded in removing any contest for Gaza and in demilitarizing all Egyptian territory near it. The unilateral annexation of the Golan Heights in December 1981 similarly 'validated' a *cordon sanitaire* at the Syrian frontier. The remaining adjacent states were Jordan and Lebanon. Both were historic objects of Zionist ambition, but a logical sequence dictated attention first to Lebanon.

The Palestinian population in Lebanon consisted primarily of survivors and descendants of the one hundred thousand Palestinians who had been driven out of northern Palestine in the war of 1948. By 1982, these persons were located in three main concentrations: in and around the southern Lebanese cities of Tyre and Sidon; in certain neighborhoods of West Beirut and on the outskirts of Beirut, chiefly south of the city where they had regrouped in the course of the Lebanese civil war and the continuing Israeli invasions of southern Lebanon; and in northern Lebanon in the vicinity of the predominantly Muslim city of Tripoli. In addition to descendants of the original 'refugee' population, Lebanon also hosted Palestinian members of the PLO armed forces and political cadres that had been expelled from Jordan in 1970, and Palestinians serving in the Syrian forces that had been invited to help restore peace after the Lebanese civil war of 1975-6. Furthermore, a Palestinian community of businessmen, professionals, and intellectuals had grown up in Beirut over the years, drawn by the sophistication and entrepreneurial opportunities of the capital.

The objective of the Israeli invasion was to eliminate the Palestinian presence in Lebanon. This became increasingly clear in the course of the war, which began with destruction of Palestinian areas in southern Lebanon, passed through a stage of bombing of Palestinian neighborhoods and camps in and around Beirut, saw some of its objectives achieved with the expulsion of PLO troops and political cadres by the end of August, and culminated in the Israeli-assisted massacres of thousands of Palestinians (chiefly women, children and old men) in Sabra and Shatila and the incarceration of several thousand Palestinian males of 'military age' (that is, between 12 and 60) from the 'conquered' territory.

It is still too early to assess the extent to which the goal of eliminating a Palestinian presence in Lebanon has been achieved. Indeed, the continued Israeli occupation of Lebanon indicates that the end of the process is not yet in sight. Palestinians have been eliminated from Lebanon in three ways: by death and incapacitation, by expulsion, and by incarceration. We would estimate that thus far the Palestinian presence in Lebanon has been 'reduced' by about 75,000, or by 20 per cent. And there are indications that additional forced uprootings of Palestinians are planned and will be carried out, unless prevented by the international community.

The Lebanese official estimate of the number of deaths that occurred as a result of the Israeli invasion and bombing and shelling indicates that the figure may run as high as 40,000 of whom possibly 25,000 to 30,000 (including those at Sabra and Shatila) were Palestinians. Two to three times that number were seriously injured, of whom perhaps half are incapacitated by loss of limbs, burns, etc. This number does not appear to be an exaggeration, given the few records we have been able to assemble. Table 8 shows a summary of some of the medical services rendered by Palestine Red Crescent hospitals between 6 June and 15 August in West Beirut alone.

Table 8 Medical Services Rendered by Palestine Red Crescent Hospitals in West Beirut, 6 June – 15 August 1982

Kind of Case	Civilians Treated		Fighters Treated		Total Number	% Total by Type
	Number	% of Total	Number	% of Total		
Deaths	2,739	81.2	636	18.8	3,375	12.4
Amputations, Serious Injuries, Serious Burns	6,518	80.3	1,599	19.7	8,117	29.9
Light Injuries, Light Burns, Fractures, Compound Fractures, Other	13,539	86.2	2,175	13.8	15,714	57.7
TOTAL CASES	22,796	83.8	4,410	16.2	27,206	100.0

Source: Records retrieved by administrator of PRCS who was there during the Beirut attack.

If we consider first that a large number of those killed never reached any hospital (and among the fighters this proportion was higher than among civilians); second, that other hospitals (Barbir, the American University of Beirut, etc.) were also operating; third, that the data end on 15 August before the massacres in Sabra and Shatila; and fourth, that the entire southern portion of Lebanon has not been included, an estimate of 20,000 to 40,000 dead, 100,000 seriously injured, and close to 200,000 traumatized is not unreasonable. These figures, of course, include Lebanese as well as Palestinian victims.

The number of Palestinians deported from Lebanon or 'fleeing' from Israeli house-to-house searches in West Beirut is similarly impossible to determine with strict accuracy. By the latter part of August, some 12,000 soldiers and members of the political cadres of the PLO had been 'redeployed' to other parts of the Arab World, and civilian Palestinians who had been unable to leave due to the blockade also departed. However, since that time an undetermined number have returned. We would estimate, however, that about 25,000 Palestinian civilians, including those with permanent residence or Lebanese citizenship, have not yet resumed residence, and some may never do so.

Most Palestinians in Lebanon, however, are neither fighters nor equipped with sufficient funds or papers to travel. Those who have survived will remain in place unless forced to leave. The destruction and levelling of their homes in the 'refugee camps' (a misnomer since these quarters had long since become permanent neighborhoods) of southern and central Lebanon is one of the forces being applied. Without homes and with many of their male providers either dead, incarcerated or deported, those survivors face enormous hardships, hardships that can no longer be ameliorated by the PLO's infrastructure of pensions, orphan-widow relief, free medical service, etc. Furthermore, fears stimulated first by the Phalangist massacre in 1976 at Tel al-Zattar and then intensified by subsequent massacres during the summer and fall of 1982-6 in Damur, Sabra, and Shatila, add to the air of uncertainty.

Finally, from the opening days of the invasion, Israeli troops have rounded up Palestinian males and shipped them to detention camps in southern Lebanon and to interrogation centers in Israel. In the joint Israel-Phalangist 'clean-up' in West Beirut, additional thousands were detained; some without papers were expelled from the country, others with papers were imprisoned. Israel has guarded its detention camps and interrogation centers from outside observers, but it is estimated that many thousands are still incarcerated. What does the future hold for them? We do not know.

Nor do we know what price will be paid by the Palestinian community of Lebanon for 'settling' the dispute between Israel and Lebanon, that is, for inducing a withdrawal of Israeli forces. There remain unconfirmed reports that Lebanon hopes to move many of its Palestinian residents to Syria. If so, the proportion of Palestinians in Lebanon will decrease considerably, but they will only have been relocated to another 'border' with Israel.

Thus far, outright military campaigns have not been waged against either the nearly 1.3 million Palestinians in the post-1967 occupied areas or the more than one million Palestinians on the east bank of the Jordan. During the summer of 1982, military control over the former was tightened, as armed troops and vigilante Jewish 'settlers' battled unarmed, rock-throwing Palestinian protesters. It is still too early to assess the full impact of this tightening of control over the conquered population, but the campaign shows no sign of ending. Israel continues to pursue its 'settlement' policy and implements it by the 'iron fist'.

We can therefore expect continued attrition of the Palestinian population in Palestine, a steady drain occasionally accelerated by violent events. If Israel finds this process too slow, it will undoubtedly redouble its combined pressures of economic strangulation and violent suppression to speed the exodus of Palestinians.[58]

Clearly, the path out of the country for residents of the West Bank remains eastward across the Jordan River. That is why no military campaign against Jordan can yet be mounted. Once the number of Palestinians within the conquered territories has been reduced to a desired level (not too large to permit control but not so small as to deprive the Israeli economy of cheap labor), then it is possible that the Jordan Valley will be invaded and 'cleansed' of Palestinians, and it is even conceivable that the 'stronghold' of Amman will receive the same treatment as West Beirut. While this remains conjecture, it would not be an illogical continuation of the thirty-eight-year process of expulsion and dispersal of the native population of Palestine.

Socio-economic Circumstances

Throughout this century the history of Palestine has been the history of its successive occupation: first the collapse of Turkish rule, followed by British incursion, and ultimately Zionist colonization. The latter has been the most decisive factor in shaping the Palestinian experience. It is possible to characterize the recent history of Palestine in the context of Zionist colonization into four distinct stages, each stage manifesting a specific form of control, but all leading to the ultimate goal of the national dispossession of the Palestinians (see Table 9).

Methods of Control

Administrative and juridical control over Palestinians differs according to the differing circumstances of the Palestinians themselves. Those under Israeli rule, who happen to be citizens of Israel, face methods of control specific to their location; these differ from the methods of control over Palestinians in the occupied territories. Nonetheless, as will be shown below, there are important common denominators that characterize Zionist attitudes toward the Palestinians as a whole, irrespective of location.

Similarly, Palestinians in the Arab world face differing circumstances which must be understood not only in terms of the political complexions of the host societies (republican or monarchical, so-called radical or conservative regimes) but more importantly in terms of the specific sphere of activity in which the Palestinians engage. For example, the methods of economic control exercised over Palestinians in the Arab world differ from those in the political sphere.

To begin with, it is important to bear in mind that the largest concentration of Palestinians within one geopolitical region remains in historical Palestine, where 50 per cent of them continue to reside. As in other societies subjected to conquest, the Palestinian social structure, be it in pre-1967 Israel or in the occupied territories, reflects a distorted pattern of development characteristic of native societies in colonial-settler regimes.

In his comparative study, *Race and State in Capitalist Development*, Stanley Greenberg analyzes patterns of domination in four settler regimes: Israel, Alabama, South Africa, and Northern Ireland. He reaches the conclusion that capitalist growth in settler regimes does not eliminate or lessen the extent of class exploitation and racial domination; rather, it intensifies it. In Alabama and South Africa domination over black workers is accelerated by capitalist expansion and penetration. The situation of Palestine before and after 1948 is described as follows:

Table 9 Stages of Twentieth-Century Palestinian History

Stages	Period	Salient Features
Dual society (Zionist colonization)	pre-1948	Asymmetrical power relationships mediated by the British presence; exclusivist Zionist institutions; stunting of Arab economic development; Zionist hegemony and eventual Palestinian dispersion.
Internal Colonialism (pre-1967 Israel)	1948-67	Marginalization of Palestinian peasants; land confiscation; political manipulation; economic stagnation; residential and occupational segregation; duality of economic and social relations.
Dependency of West Bank and Gaza on Jordan and Egypt	1948-67	Economic and political dependency on Jordan and Egypt; co-optation and political suppression.
Accelerated forms of internal colonialism in Israel; colonial dependency of West Bank and Gaza on Israel	1967-present	Further proletarianization of Palestinians in Israel; economic penetration of West Bank and Gaza accompanied by land confiscation and encouragement of Palestinian emigration; political suppression and denial of Palestinian rights.
Total Control by Israel	Future trend	Depopulation of Palestinians through expulsion and emigration; ultimate goal is Zionization of historical Palestine, and, if possible, resettlement of Palestinians in Arab countries.

In Israel the pattern of mixed capitalist and collective economic development under ascendancy of the Jewish labour movement, brought the intensification of discrimination against the Arab population. In the Palestine period, the Histadrut had sought to limit employment in the Jewish sector and in British mandatory agencies; it had attempted to create quotas and 'civilized' wage rates for Jewish employment; it excluded Arabs from the Jewish trade unions and labour exchanges. But after partition and with the establishment of the Jewish state, the Histadrut's petty discrimination became state discrimination on a large scale. The state takeover of the labour exchanges and state economic development policies ensured that Arabs would remain outside the developing sector of the economy and within an institutionalized, secondary labour market.[59]

The methods of control exercised by Israel over the Palestinians fall into two categories: segmentation and co-optation and dependence.[60]

Segmentation is attained through the physical and residential segregation of Palestinians, enhanced by an elaborate institutional separation between Arabs and Jews. The Jewish National Fund, the army, Histadrut, and various Zionist political parties, as well as cultural organs which had their genesis in the pre-1948 period, have continued to buttress Zionist hegemony in society. More importantly, the vast financial and economic resources available to the state from outside sources are directed exclusively to the needs of Jewish citizens under the pretext that these are not, strictly speaking, state institutions, and so do not fall under state law. The Jewish National Fund is an excellent example, for the millions of dollars that are solicited abroad every year are exclusively used to 'dispossess Palestinians of their land and accommodate Zionist settlers in their place.

Co-optation is another method of control and is made possible through continued economic dependency of the Arabs on the Jewish sector. A system of patronage and side-payments had been developed, according to which Arabs seeking jobs and economic rewards must show proof of loyalty and submission to the authorities.

Analysts note that while for the coming ten to fifteen years Israel is likely to maintain its control over the Palestinians, the system will become too costly to maintain in the future. Increasing politicization of the Palestinians will lead to increasing difficulties for the Israeli authorities. If this occurs, it is within the realm of possibility that the regime will resort to outright expulsion of Palestinians. Although the Likud leadership may have been most open to this option, it should be remembered that it was in 1976, under the auspices of the Labor government, that Israel Koenig, a senior official in the Ministry of Interior, prepared the blueprint plan for systematic reduction of the indigenous Arab population through expulsion and the imposition of additional obstacles to the development of the already stagnant Arab sector, which would result in further emigration of Palestinians.

Palestinian social structure under Israeli rule can be viewed as the outcome of a system of internal colonialism, resulting in a distorted class structure, a peasantry that is alienated from its land, and, in the cities, a pattern of development dependent upon and peripheral to the dominant Zionist society.

Economic Circumstances

No society can control its own destiny without control over its economic environment. Palestinian society offers a case in point. It lacks both a productive professional middle class and a corresponding industrial working class.

The bulk of the Arab labor force in both Israel and the occupied territories is concentrated in the lowest wage-earning segment. In 1978, this lowest segment accounted for 63 per cent of all Arab wage earners, in contrast to 30 per cent of all Jewish wage earners. The pattern of economic relations reveals the nature of 'the dual labor market': a primary labor market connected with the more strategic military industry, open only to Jewish citizens; and a secondary labor market connected with the consumer goods industry, open to Arab citizens.[61] The outcome has been increased occupational segregation. Table 10 delineates the patterns of occupational status among Palestinian males in various countries.

In examining the data on Palestinian workers who are Israeli citizens, it is clear that they are concentrated in semiskilled and skilled manual, non-supervisory forms of labor-intensive work, whereas the Jews dominate the skilled, supervised, technical positions. Moreover, the Arab industrial workers are to be found in the non-strategic goods producing sector, whereas Jews are concentrated in the managerial, industrial, and strategic sectors of the economy, such as the diamond, military, electronic and associated industries. Twenty-eight per cent of all Israeli citizens employed in construction are Arabs, compared to seven per cent of those who are employed in industry. For the Arabs in the labor force the leading 'industrial' sector is furniture making, woodworking and upholstery. Faced with labour shortages in the

Table 10 Occupational Distribution of Palestinians (Males) in Selected Countries and Regions

Percentage in Occupational Categories by Descending Status

Country or Region of Resident	Prof./ Techn.	Admin./ Manager	Sales/ Clerical	Commercial	Indus./ Trans./ Util.	Serv. (pers.)	Agric./ Fish./ Mining
Saudi Arabia (1974) of which:	51.5	2.9	6.0	3.2	28.9	3.3	4.3
Jordanians	63.0	3.1	6.1	3.1	20.1	1.9	2.1
Palestinians	36.9	2.6	5.7	3.3	39.3	5.0	7.1
Kuwait (1975)	20.8	1.3	17.8	8.6	41.1	8.4	2.1
Jordan East Bank (1975 Amman)	9.7		7.0	11.8	45.4	11.2	14.5
Syria (1970)	10.8	0.7	8.2	8.9	57.0	6.6	7.9
Israel (1980)	7.8	*	2.2	5.9	58.8	10.0	15.0
West Bank (1980)	6.1	0.9	2.7	12.0	53.4	7.3	17.6
Gaza (1980)	4.3	0.8	2.3	11.7	53.8	8.6	18.5
Lebanon camps (1971)	3.7		1.4	15.3	46.1	8.9	24.7

Sources: Derived from Janet Abu-Lughod, 'Demographic Characteristics of the Palestinian Population', Annex 1, part II of *Palestine Open University Feasibility Study* (Paris: UNESCO, 1980), p. 61; *Statistical Abstract of Israel*, No. 32, 1981, tables XVII/21, XII/17; *Palestine Statistical Abstract* (Damascus: Palestine National Fund, 1980).

technical, industrial sector where specialized training is needed, and in conformity with the duality imposed on the labor market, Israel is turning to the importation of foreign skilled workers.

Two opposing forces operating in the Israeli economy have far-reaching consequences for the Palestinian working class. First, the reorientation of Israeli industry to export markets has created a shift in the demand for Arab labor. Construction, until recently a major economic activity of Zionist colonizers in Palestine, has reached a saturation point, and the closure of the African and Iranian markets has led to a significant shift to the South African and, more recently, to the Egyptian market. In both cases, cheap, unskilled labor is secured from the labor force of the destined markets, thus causing a significant decline in the demand for unskilled Palestinian labor in local construction.

The second factor of consequence to Palestinian workers in Israel is the gradual integration of the military-industrial complex into the civilian sector. There has been a tremendous expansion towards export markets in the arms and high technology industries. This has necessitated induction, however reluctant and selective, of Palestinians into military-related industries. But here too the duality of the Israeli labor market seems to operate. Arabs are hired to work in non-sensitive, routine, often hazardous jobs. High technology and 'chip' industries are expanding into areas close to Arab concentrations such as the Galilee, where a cheap, abundant labor supply is available.[62]

The restrictions and constraints placed upon Palestinians living in Israel have forced many of them into migratory labor, with all the dislocation this kind of work entails. Most industrial enterprises are located in the Jewish sector, so Arab workers have had to travel long distances from their villages to places of employment. It is estimated that around 70 per cent of Palestinian workers commute to work places outside their villages; the figure approaches 90 per cent among workers aged fifteen to twenty-five. Of Arab youths working in Jewish centers, one observer noted:

> Their working conditions are extremely hard, with no legal super-vision. They work ten to twelve hours a day, six or seven days a week; most of them get their weekly or monthly wages in cash, without any pay-slip as a proof of their employment. Only a few are registered with the income tax and national insurance authorities. Employers prefer to dodge taxes and to avoid assuring them social benefits. Someone injured at work instead of receiving paid leave and compensation is often ignored and dismissed from his job.[63]

Since 1967, Arab women have been entering the labor force in increasing numbers. Their experience parallels that of the men. They are employed in canning factories, as fruit pickers, and as seamstresses on a subcontract basis.

Jewish economic dominance in the country and the near absence of any viable Palestinian industrial sector have had two effects. First, it has been impossible to develop the capital needed to establish Arab industries. Arabs have been forced to remain dependent upon the Jewish economy, providing it with a cheap labor supply yet unable to reap the benefits of the surplus value created by the sweat of their labor. Second, the Arab sector remains structurally stagnant and unable to compete wth the more technologically advanced Jewish industrial sector. The impacts of recessions and economic crises will continue to fall most heavily on Arab workers, who tend to be laid off first in any decline in economic activity.

The low occupational profile of the Palestinians is reflected in their incomes. Official figures provided by the Israeli government regarding income distribution are confined to urban employees only. These figures show that by the middle of the 1970s the gross annual income of an Arab employee amounted to 84 per cent of that of a Jewish employee. It must be remembered, however, that because of larger families among Arabs and the smaller size of the Arab labor force to begin with, the calculated *per capita* income of an Arab is significantly lower than that of a Jewish citizen – approximately one-half.[64] Furthermore, one Israeli analyst admits that 'while there are no systematic studies of trends in the socio-economic gap between Arabs and Jews, there are no reasons to believe that the gap has narrowed. Since the proportionately greater investments are made in the Jewish sector, it is possible that the gap has grown even wider over the years.'[65] If income distribution in the rural sector were taken into account, the differences between Arabs and Jews would be even more striking. Table 11 gives 1980 income data per urban household.

In all estimates of standards of living, the Arabs are consistently worse off than Jews. Arabs spend in proportional terms more on food and shelter than Jews; the latter spend substantially more on durable goods such as cars, telephones, televisions, etc. The most dramatic contrast must be in the area of housing. Increases in family size and continued confiscation of Arab land have caused the population density in the Arab sector to reach an all-time high level. Upper Nazareth, a Jewish settlement with around seventeen thousand inhabitants, has a population density of 548 square

Table 11 Average Monthly Income for Urban
Households in Israeli Shekels (1980)

Group	Shekel	Arab as per cent of
Arabs	2,285	–
Israeli-born Jews	4,424	51.0
European-American Jews	3,341	68.0
African-Asian Jews	3,083	74.0

Source: Statistical Abstract of Israel, no. 32, 1981, table XI/1.

meters per capita, compared to 178 square meters per capita for
Arab Nazareth, with a population of more than 40,000 people.[66]
The situation is no better in other neighbouring Arab villages in
the Galilee. Data for 1980 show that there are twice as many
persons per room in the Arab as in the Jewish sector. Overall
housing density distribution is presented in Table 12.

The position of the Israeli government with regard to the
occupied territories is set forth by describing them as a
'supplementary market for Israeli goods and services on the one
hand, and a source of factors of production, especially unskilled
labor for the Israeli economy on the other'.[67] All the current
indicators demonstrate that this policy has been faithfully
implemented. Whereas in 1968, 4.2 per cent of Palestinian
workers from Gaza and the West Bank worked in Israel, the ratio
climbed to 32.4 per cent in 1975 to 40 per cent in 1980, and is
expected to reach the fifty per cent level by the late 1980s.[68]

Table 12 Percent of Arab and Jewish
Households at Different Densities (1980)

Persons Per Room	Arabs	Jews
Up to one person	15.0	58.6
1-2	20.3	29.7
2-3	29.6	10.0
3-4+	35.1	1.6
Total	100.0	100.0

Source: Statistical Abstract of Israel, no. 32, 1981, table XI/21.

Moreover, due to the stagnant nature of the West Bank and Gaza economies, they cannot absorb the workers entering the labor force, thus making the occupied territories more susceptible to higher unemployment rates and further economic integration with Israel.

At the present time close to forty per cent of the West Bank, including its most fertile land, is either controlled or destined to be 'Judaized' through settlements and military zones.[69] It is worth noting that the settlements themselves are located in areas densely populated with Arabs. The illegal annexation of East Jerusalem and the separation of Arab population concentrations through a grid of roads and settlements, a process that is a perfect replica of an earlier process implemented in the predominantly Arab Galilee, are intended as an obstacle to the emergence of a future Palestinian state and to the meaningful integration of Arab towns, with East Jerusalem as the main urban center. The Arab population of the West Bank has even been deprived of control over its water resources. It is not surprising to find out that the area of cultivated land on the West Bank has declined by one hundred thousand acres since 1967, a significant loss when it is realized that the total land under cultivation there is only five hundred thousand acres.[70]

Land confiscation, expulsion of Palestinians, and daily harassments, not to mention outright terrorism by such groups as the Gush Emunim Zionist vigilantes, who are armed and protected by the government, have been the essential mechanisms adopted by the Zionists in their colonization plans for the West Bank and Gaza.

An International Labor Organization (ILO) Commission investigating labor conditions on the West Bank noted that since 1975 there was a yearly net outflow of about 20,000 persons from the occupied territories; two-thirds of this loss originated in the West Bank.[71] Prior to the period singled out by the ILO Commission, it is estimated that 9,000 persons left the West Bank annually between 1968 and 1975. What is significant about this emigration, which is directed mainly to the Gulf countries, is that it is depriving the West Bank of its professional and educated strata. It is estimated that, of a total of seventy thousand Palestinians with university degrees, no more than 10 per cent work in occupied Palestine.[72]

A 1979 report by the Inter-Agency Task Force carried out under the auspices of the United Nations Development Program supported the above findings, and noted further developments on the economic and industrial fronts. The main finding[73] of the report concerns the stagnant and dependent nature of West Bank economic and industrial developments *vis-à-vis* Israel. Official Israeli statistics note that close to 90 per cent of West Bank imports come from Israel; the main 'export' of the West Bank to Israel has been unskilled labour, mainly labourers destined to work in the construction and service sectors of Israel, doing jobs that are shunned by Israelis. The Palestinians have been reduced to hewers of wood and drawers of water in the Zionist state. By the middle of the 1970s, 16 per cent of Israeli exports went to the occupied territories, compared to 2.6 per cent in 1967. According to official Israeli statistics, the surplus of imports over exports stands at 92 million Israeli pounds, whereas in 1971 the surplus stood at 1.68 million Israeli pounds. In 1977, the ratio of exports to imports between the West Bank and Israel amounted to 3.7:1.0. And 'figures for the year 1978 show that Israeli exports to the West Bank and Gaza, including East Jerusalem, exceeded 25 per cent of all Israeli export market, ranking even before the United States.'[74]

The increasing economic and political domination of the West Bank has led to the following consequences. First, many Palestinian farmers are abandoning their land in pursuit of higher paying jobs in the Israeli unskilled labor market. As a result of this there was, between 1970 and 1978, an overall reduction of six thousand jobs in the occupied areas while the population increased by 35,000. Taking into account those legally employed through Israeli Labor Exchanges and those illegally employed, it is estimated there are now more than eighty thousand Palestinian workers from the occupied territories employed in Israel; 20 per cent of the workers are under the age of 17, most of them school dropouts. The labor shortage in the West Bank has had a negative impact on the agricultural sector and the housing market.

Second, the growth of industrial activity in the West Bank has declined from 8 per cent to 5.4 per cent between 1968 and 1976. The same is true of tourism, which used to be a flourishing activity in the West Bank. The increase in gross national product, a propaganda item much touted by Israeli officials, is accounted for not by real industrial growth but by earnings brought into the West Bank by Palestinian emigrés and workers in Israel. According to one observer, industrial activity in the West Bank and Gaza is best described as 'primitive in character and there are no discernible beginnings of an industrialization process'.[75] More than 10 per cent of industrial establishments on the West Bank and Gaza consist of workshops employing less than ten persons. If recession hits the Israeli economy, its effects are likely to be most devastating in the occupied territories where according to the ILO report, the workers are not insured against unemployment. Israeli economists admit that if the current economic recession is not turned around, it is expected that by the middle and late 1980s there will be a decline by as many as fifty thousand in the number of workers from the occupied territories in Israel. This trend is apparent from a comparison of the 1979 and 1980 figures which shows a 15 per cent drop in the number of workers employed in Israel.[76]

Third, the cost of living has skyrocketed in the occupied territories under Israeli domination. Whereas the average level of prices in Israel went up by 400 per cent between 1970 and 1977, the rise averaged 500 per cent in the West Bank and 600 per cent in Gaza during the same period. This trend is even more significant if one notes the discrepancy in wages received by Arab and Jewish workers. Palestinians from the occupied territories who work in Israel receive 40 per cent of the average Israeli wage. Similarly, Palestinian workers on the West Bank and Gaza earn between 60 and 90 per cent less than their Palestinian counterparts who work in Israel.

Finally, Israeli domination has resulted in violations of basic human rights in the economic sphere, violations documented by such organizations as Amnesty International, the ILO, and other international bodies. Any attempts on the part of Palestinian workers to organize to protect their rights and strengthen their unions are met by restrictions and opposition from the military government. Three factors help to account for the precarious position of Palestinian unions. First, 40 per cent of Palestinian workers in the West Bank and Gaza work in Israel; unions in the occupied territories do not represent their interests and cannot attract them to join.[77] Second, in February 1980 the occupation authorities amended the Jordanian Labor Law so as to limit union activity and restrict election to union offices to those individuals approved by the occupation authorities. Third, it was decided to extend Histadrut activity to the occupied territories – this must lead to further weakening of Palestinian unions as possible vehicles to counter further Zionist incursion into the economic life of the West Bank and Gaza.

Data on the Palestinians living outside historical Palestine are outdated and unreliable. In certain cases, such as in Lebanon, systematic data on the close to 400,000 Palestinians are totally lacking. But based on the data presented in table 10, broad conclusions may be drawn. First, the occupational distribution of the Palestinians by status shows a clear difference in ranking by country. Saudi Arabia, followed by Kuwait, have the largest concentrations of Palestinians in professional and technical jobs. Syria and Jordan rank next. Except for Lebanon, where the sample is based on camp residents, the Palestinians under Israeli control (particularly those living in Gaza) show the lowest representation in the professional groups. Second, although economic status varies from country to country, the fact remains that the bulk of the Palestinians, no matter where they live, are in jobs with the lowest status.

No thorough understanding of the Palestinian predicament in the Arab world is possible without examining the situation in the refugee camps. Here it is important to note that no comprehensive studies of Palestinian camp life exist. What we have is a series of case studies.

There is no doubt that the displaced Palestinians who live in refugee camps act as the most visible symbol of Palestinian suffering. It is the Palestinians of the camps, mostly of rural background, who continue to provide the Palestinian revolution with its fighting cadres. They are the ones who, more than any other group, have paid with their lives for the Palestinian cause – the recent Zionist-Phalange collaboration in the slaughter of Palestinian refugees in Lebanon is a grim example of the vulnerable position of these Palestinians.

Refugee camps have nevertheless managed to keep families together in the face of adversity and sustain a sense of solidarity instrumental to maintaining Palestinian identity. Yet one must not romanticize what is essentially a harsh, uprooted style of life which was forced upon them.

The state of existence in the camps has led to a feeling of dependency and despair. With the passage of time, this dependency on the United States Relief and Work Agency (UNRWA) system has been extended to those Arab host countries on whom the Palestinians have had to rely for employment, education, and other social amenities. The refugee status has meant the denial of basic human rights, such as the right to organize, to assemble, and to move freely across international boundaries.

No doubt one of the requirements of normal social and psychological well-being is that adequate standards of public and even personal health be met. The numerous surveys conducted by UNRWA, the World Health Organization, and the Palestinians themselves testify to inadequate health standards in the camps, a situation which must have deteriorated drastically as a result of the recent Israeli devastation. For example, prior to the latest round of fighting, surveys have shown that a camp physician on the average examines sixty-five cases per day; a dentist treats thirty patients per day; anaemia is prevalent among 20 per cent of Palestinian children up to thirty-six months of age, while another 50 per cent 'are maintaining a precarious marginal level', the UNRWA report concluded. Malnutrition, which affects one of every five children, may lead to permanent damage of the intellectual and physical abilities of the young Palestinians in the camps.[78]

Education

Palestinian education in Israel has been governed all along, and continues to be governed, by a set of political criteria which the Palestinians had no say in formulating. Controlled by a separate unit within the Ministry of Education, Arab educational policies have continually been the product of the ministry's Zionist bureaucrats and party functionaries, rather than of trained educators sensitive to the needs of the Palestinians. That Israeli educational policy is premised on an exclusivist Zionist ideal is demonstrated by detailed evidence on the nature of government-sponsored curricula at the primary and secondary school levels. Arab pupils must spend many class hours in the study of Zionist culture and history and the Hebrew language, whereas Jewish pupils have little exposure to Arab history and language. An academic researcher on the state of Palestinian education in Israel concluded recently that 'the denial and deprivation of relevant curricula for Arab students seems to be escalating'.[79] It is apparent that for Palestinian youth living in Israel, the educational system functions as an agency of social and political control and not as an institution whose purpose is to develop in the young a democratic personality, enriched creativity, and critical thought.

The most optimistic analysts estimate the number of Palestinian university students in Israel institutions of higher education at around 3.5 per cent of the total student population – this in spite of the fact that Palestinians constitute more than 15 per cent of the total population. The cumulative proportion of university graduates within the Arab sector is around 0.1 per cent, whereas it is about 1.32 per cent for the Jewish population – a thirteen-fold difference.[80]

Many factors contribute to this low enrolment of university

students among the more than one-half million Palestinians in Israel. There are few adequate teaching facilities and properly equipped classrooms at the primary and secondary levels, and few properly trained and qualified teachers in the Arab sector. (About 50 per cent of the teachers in Arab schools were classified as unqualified.) The teaching method in Arab schools perpetuates the traditional system of rote learning and memorization, thus handicapping Arab students in matriculation examinations demanding training in analytical thinking. Many qualified high school graduates turn away from a university education because they feel they will not gain any benefits from it in Israeli society. There is also continuing discrimination in university admission policies to key science faculties (electronics, nuclear physics, aeronautics, etc.) for 'security' reasons, which forces an increased number of prospective science students to turn to the humanities and the social sciences – areas in which job prospects are limited.

In contrast, Palestinians outside direct Israeli jurisdiction have consistently attained educational levels higher than those of

Table 13 University Enrolment of Palestinians by Region

Region	University Population (78/79)	Total Population (1979)	Rate per 100,000
Israel	1,900	600,000	316
West Bank	3,193	688,000	464
East Bank	6,000	1,000,000	660
Lebanon[1]	15,000	330,000	4,545
Syria	4,000	210,000	1,904
Kuwait	1,200	250,000	488
Saudi Arabia	1,280	180,000	711
Europe/America[1]	12,500	100,000	7,812

Source: Derived from tables in Baha Abu-Laban, 'The Palestine Open University and the Educational Needs of the Palestinian People outside of Occupied Palestine', in *Palestine Open University Study* (Paris: UNESCO, 1980), Annex II; Khalil Nakleh, 'Palestinians under Israel's Jurisdiction in Post-Secondary Education'. *Ibid.* Annex III; and Janet Abu-Lughod, 'Demographic Characteristics of the Palestinian People'. *Ibid.*, Annex I, part II.

[1] The rather high rates per 100,000 for Lebanon and Europe/America are misleading. The number of registered students in both cases includes a large number of Palestinians from other regions.

Palestinians who have been under Israeli control since 1948, as is evident from table 13.

Palestinians in the occupied territories face different problems from those encountered by Palestinians in Israel. Basically, these fall into two main areas. First, the structure of higher education on the West Bank is not congruent with the social and national needs of the Palestinians. A recent analysis uses Bir Zeit University to illustrate the educational predicament:

> Bir Zeit shares with other institutions in the Arab World a deficiency in technical and vocational training courses and programs for their students. For example, the curriculum at West Bank universities, including Bir Zeit, places little emphasis on the acquisition of skills relevant to rural planning and development, whereas 70% of the area's residents live in centres where the population is less than 5,000 inhabitants. Agricultural production itself accounts for 30% of the West Bank's GNP. The net result of this situation is that many students graduates and find difficulty adapting their skills and academic training to the social and economic development needs and employment realities of the West Bank. Subsequently, they emigrate and market their skills in a wider Middle East labour market at the expense of the West Bank.[81]

The Zionist goal of depopulating historical Palestine of its indigenous Arab population is well served by the continuous outflow of professional Palestinians from the West Bank. The conclusion of the ILO report referred to earlier is instructive in this regard, for it concluded that even technically skilled graduates of pre-university technical training programs such as those implemented by UNRWA find it difficult to secure jobs on the West Bank due to the industrial backwardness of the region, brought about in large measure by Israeli occupation resulting in economic dependency on Israel.

The second problem, one likely to have serious repercussions for the future education of Palestinians on the West Bank, is the induction of minors into the Israeli labor market to perform unskilled, seasonal jobs. It is estimated that 20 per cent of irregular workers from the occupied territories are minors who entered the labor market prior to high-school graduation.

The educational experience of the Palestinians is characterized by fragmentation in educational values, depending on the type of institution to which the Palestinian is exposed. But the most serious threat to Palestinian education comes from the lack of academic freedom on the West Bank and Gaza as a result of

Israeli interference. A 1977 UNESCO report concluded that 'Arabic books which pass the censor are often of doubtful value, e.g., a great many crime novels, popular science books', and that 'the censorship as presently practised restricts the prospects of young Palestinians in the occupied territories by giving them a distorted image of their cultural heritage'.[82]

The lack of coherence inherent in Israeli educational policy towards Arabs culminates, in the occupied territories, in direct interference in the affairs of the schools. On more than one occasion schools at all levels have been shut down by Zionist forces to silence student opposition to occupation. On more than one occasion Palestinian youths have been beaten, arrested wthout trial, and even murdered by forces of occupation. Bir Zeit has been shut down several times; in 1982 for almost the entire academic year and most recently in spring/summer 1987. Book censorship and refusal of Zionist authorities to renew and/or grant work permits to Palestinian and foreign professors to teach at Bir Zeit has attracted critical world attention. In 1983, the military governor refused to renew the work permits of foreign and Arab university professors who would not sign pledges stating that they do not recognize the Palestine Liberation Organization as the representative of the Palestinian people – this at a time when the overwhelming majority of Palestinians in the West Bank and Gaza identified the PLO as their representative.[83]

Conclusion

The present situation of the Palestinian people then is funda-mentally and seriously anomalous. The Palestinians have all the attributes of nationhood – a common history, language, and set of traditions, a national culture, national institutions, a national representative, the Palestine Liberation Organization, recognized universally by every segment of the Palestinian population as well as by a large majority of the world's states, a common framework of aspirations and values – but they do not control Palestine, the natural site of their projected independent state. The United States has been very clear on the imperatives for Palestinian national self-determination, and so too have the Islamic Con-ference, the Movement of the Non-Aligned, the Organization of African Unity, as well as various important European, Asian and Latin American states. Yet still, the inexorable processes continue by which the Palestinian people has been alienated both from its natal territory and its cultural patrimony. Today, more Palestinians than ever before are born in exile and face the prospect of continued exile. In the Occupied Territories, more Israeli settlements, more Israeli violence and collective punishment attempt to break the Palestinian national will: the aims of Israel are clear, for, as Zionist and Israeli leaders have been saying candidly for several generations, Palestinian national claims are neither admissible nor valid. As for Israel's chief ally, the United States of America, while Presidents Carter and Reagan have gone as far as admitting the existence of a question of Palestine, even to the extent of speaking guardedly about the need for a Palestinian homeland of some sort, the US has not accepted the premises of Palestinian nationalism. With Israel, the US has resolutely opposed the idea of national self-determination, and insofar as it foresees the need for a solution to the question of Palestine, it does so in terms that firmly opt for not accepting the Palestinian and international consensus definition of an acceptable solution.

The sufferings consequently imposed upon a people in its dispersion and political difficulties are legion. All these sufferings derive, however, from the complete *inability* of every Palestinian man, woman, and child to exercise a fundamental set of inalienable rights. No Palestinian has a Palestinian passport, no Palestinian has Palestinian nationality, no Palestinian can vote in a national election as a Palestinian, no Palestinian can voluntarily return to Palestine and take up residence there. In most places, the very word 'Palestine' is either denied or in some way made the object of particular (usually injurious) juridical, political, social and cultural discrimination. Thus, for example, there has never been a Palestinian census, nor, for that matter, a referendum. The anomaly of course is that, as a people, the Palestinians are among the most advanced in the world so far as their political consciousness is concerned. Every Palestinian shares with all other Palestinians a history of dispossession and, no less important, a history of determined struggle. For the profoundest truth about the Palestinians today is not that they are exiled, dispersed and punished, but that they have advanced so far beyond these negative attributes as to have articulated a positive vision of the future. Unmistakably and collectively, the Palestinian people has formulated its own sense of itself and of its future as intending the establishment of an independent Palestinian state on their historical national soil.

This inalienable right can neither be denied nor can it be reduced to a set of substitutes. Palestine is not Jordan, any more than it is a corner of Eretz Yisrael. And indeed, it is something to be remarked, that alone among the inhabitants of Palestine, the Palestinian people has spoken of its national destiny collectively in terms accommodating the fundamental human rights of others. The Palestinian people – which has had its society destroyed by a movement claiming to achieve national liberation, paradoxically, in the form of settler colonialism – wishes no negative form of self-determination or liberation for itself. Its bitter national experience has bred in it a respect for civil and human rights abrogated by others. The Palestinian vision therefore is predicated upon democracy and justice, upon dignity and community. It is neither about conquest nor about a narrowly defined ethnic nationalism. This is why the question of Palestine has found supporters everywhere among the oppressed people of the world, those with a colonial past and those who oppose colonial injustice today, as well as those in the West who are courageous espousers of truth, justice and human freedom.

World public opinion has at last come around to understanding and, in no uncertain way, supporting the claims of the Palestinian people to national self-determination. It is no longer possible to say that there are no Palestinians, or that Palestine is a historical fiction. The moral and political challenge facing the international community today is a clear one. Since the Palestinian national will cannot at this point be rolled back or reduced to zero, how long can the attainment of inalienable Palestinian rights be postponed? How many more Palestinians must die, be incarcerated, or expelled from their land before this people's identity is acknowledged and its national purpose consummated in an independent and sovereign state? For unless there is a positive response to these questions, then the future portends violence and human waste on a scale and with an intensity truly to be avoided at all costs. For its part the Palestinian people wishes for no more than peace and justice, and because its unhappy fate was forced on it, there has arisen a congruent desire to end, rather than perpetuate, the anomalies of displacement, dispossession and exile. This desire is profoundly benign and positive: so too must be the international community's response, and its determination to implement that response.

Notes

1. Emmanuel Anati, *Palestine Before the Hebrews* (New York: Knopf, 1963), pp. 7, 241-2.

2. Quoted from Istakhri and Ibn Hawkal, in Guy Le Strange, *Palestine under*

the Moslems: A Description of Syria and the Holy Land from AD 650 to 1500 Translated from the Works of the Medieval Arab Geographers (1890; reprinted Beirut: Khayat, 1965), p. 28.

3. Quoted in Richard Bevis, 'Making the Desert Bloom: An Historical Picture of Pre-Zionist Palestine', *The Middle East Newsletter* (Feb.-Mar. 1971), 5(2): 4.

4. *The Anglo-Palestine Yearbook 1947-8* (London: Anglo-Palestine Publications, 1948), p. 33.

5. See Adnan Abu-Ghazaleh, *Arab Cultural Nationalism in Palestine* (Beirut: Institute for Palestine Studies, 1973).

6. Janet Abu-Lughod, 'The Demographic Transformation of Palestine', in Ibrahim Abu-Lughod, ed., *The Transformation of Palestine* (Evanston, Ill.: Northwestern University Press, 1971), p. 139.

7. *The Times* (London), 17 June 1982.

8. King-Crane Commission's recommendations, text in George Antonius, *The Arab Awakening* (London: Hamish Hamilton, 1938), p. 448.

9. Quoted in Simha Flapan, *Zionism and the Palestinians* (London: Croom Helm, 1979), p. 56.

10. Fayez A. Sayegh, *Zionism: A Form of Racism and Racial Discrimination* (New York: Office of the Permanent Observer of the Palestine Liberation Organization to the United Nations, 1976), p. 7. This text was originally delivered as a speech before the Third Committee of the UN General Assembly on 17 October 1975.

11. Nathan Weinstock, 'The Impact of Zionist Colonization on Palestinian Arab Society Before 1948', *Journal of Palestine Studies*, 2, p. 51 (Winter 1973).

12. *Ibid.*, p. 50.

13. Quoted in Arie Bober, ed., *The Other Israel* (New York: Doubleday, 1972), p. 13.

14. From his article, 'The Truth from the Land of Israel', quoted in Alan R. Taylor, *The Zionist Mind* (Beirut: Institute for Palestine Studies, 1974), p. 103.

15. Quoted in G.H. Jansen, *Zionism, Israel and Asian Nationalism* (Beirut: Institute for Palestine Studies,1971), pp. 178, 182.

16. See Flapan, *Zionism*, and Neil Caplan, *Palestine Jewry and the Arab Question, 1917-1925* (London: Frank Cass, 1978).

17. George Kossaifi, 'Demographic Characteristics of the Arab Palestinian People', in Khalil Nakhleh and Elia Zureik, eds, *The Sociology of the Palestinians* (London: Croom Helm, 1980), p. 16.

18. Quoted in John Ruedy, 'Dynamics of Land Alienation', in I. Abu-Lughod, ed., *Transformation of Palestine*, p. 126, n.20.

19. Quoted in Flapan, *Zionism*, p. 172.

20. Quoted in Bober, *The Other Israel*. p. 37.

21. *Ibid.*, p. 38.

22. Quoted in Jansen, *Zionism, Israel and Asian Nationalism*, p. 177.

23. *The Sunday Times* (London) 15 June 1969.

24. *Newsweek*, 17 February 1969.

25. Quoted in Taylor, *Zionist Mind*, p. 96.

26. Quoted in Bober, *The Other Israel*, p. 37.

27. Maxime Rodinson, *Israel and the Arabs* (New York: Random House, 1968), p. 14.

28. Taylor, *Zionist Mind*, p. 48.

29. *Yediot Aharanot*, 17 October 1969; also quoted in Bober, *The Other Israel*, p. 77.

30. Text in J.C. Hurewitz, *Diplomacy in the Near and Middle East* (Princeton, NJ: Von Nostrand, 1956), vol. 2, p. 26.

31. Great Britain, *Parliamentary Papers, 1922, Cmd. 1785*, pp. 107-11.

32. Sir John Hope Simpson, *Palestine: Report on Immigration, Land Settlement, and Development* (London: His Majesty's Stationery Office, 1930, *Cmd. 3686*), p. 17.

33. *Palestine: Report*, pp. 56, 133, 135.

34. *Ibid.*, p. 133.

35. Quoted in Robert John and Sami Hadawi, *The Palestine Diary, 1914-1945* (New York: New World Press, 1970), vol. 1, p. 226.

36. Chaim Weizmann, *Trial and Error* (New York: Harper, 1949), p. 207.

37. Quoted in Jansen, *Zionism, Israel and Asian Nationalism*, p. 183.

38. Weizmann, *Trial and Error*, p. 381.

39. J.M. Machover, *Governing Palestine: The Case against a Parliament* (London: P.S. King, 1936), p. 21.

40. Quoted in Flapan, *Zionism*, p. 170.

41. See Edward Said, *The Question of Palestine* (New York Times Books: 1980) and I. Abu-Lughod, 'Retrieving Palestinian National Rights', paper given at the UN Seminar on the Question of Palestine, Havana, Cuba, 31 August – 4 September 1981, reprinted in Ibrahim Abu-Lughod, ed., *Palestinian Rights* (Wilmette, Ill.: Medina Press, 1982), pp. 3-10.

42. The following works are very helpful in delineating the status of Palestinians and Palestinian areas: Sabri Jiryis, *The Arabs in Israel* (New York: Monthly Review Press, 1976); E. Zureik, *The Palestinians in Israel* (London: Routledge and Kegan Paul, 1978); and Ma'had al-Buhuth wa-Dirasat al-Arabiyya, *Al-Filastiniyyun fi al-Watan al-Arabi* (Cairo: 1978), esp. pp. 579-604.

43. See, among others, Barry Rubin, *The Arab States and the Palestine Conflict* (Syracuse: 1981), pp. 206-7, and Izzat Tannous, *Al-Filastiniyyun* (Beirut: 1983), pp. 513-25.

44. See Husayn Abu al-Naml, *Quita' Ghazza, 1948-1967* (Beirut: 1979).

45. Figures based on Janet Abu-Lughod, *Palestine Open University Feasibility Study*, Annex I, part II (Paris: UNESCO, 1980), p. 23.

46. See, among others, United Nations General Assembly documents, *Report of the Special Committee to Investigate Israeli Practices Affecting the Human Rights of the Population of the Occupied Territories*, especially for the years 1980-82; *Report on the Living Conditions of the Population in the Occupied Arab Territories* (A/35/533, Oct. 1980); Michael Adams, 'The Universal Declaration of Human Rights and the Israeli Occupation of the West Bank and Gaza', in I. Abu-Lughod, ed., *Palestinian Rights* (originally presented at the UN Seminar on Question of Palestine held in Vienna, August 1980).

47. A. A. Rahman and R. Hamid, 'The Palestine Liberation Organization: Past, Present and Future', UN Seminar on Question of Palestine held in Arusha, Tanzania, July 1980; Cheryl Rubenberg, *The Palestine Liberation Organization* (Belmont, Mass.: Institute of Arab Studies, 1983).

48. *Statistical Abstract of Israel 1981* (Israel Central Bureau of Statistics, 1982) estimates the 'non-Jewish' population in the subregions of Palestine as of 1980. We have projected these to mid-1982 and have made certain adjustments to conform to jurisdictional realities. Israeli sources include the Arab population of East Jerusalem and its environs with Israel. Our analysis reapportions this population and classifies it with the occupied area known as the West Bank, more accurately designated as occupied eastern Palestine.

49. This section on the demography of the Palestinians draws heavily upon Janet Abu-Lughod, 'Demographic Characteristics of the Palestinian Population', Annex I, part II of the *Palestine Open University Feasibility Study* (mimeo. Pariš UNESCO, 30 June 1980). This document employs a complex set of demographic

methods to triangulate from natural increase and known (but incomplete) parameters to reach an estimate of the size and distribution of Palestinians in the world as of 1979. In the present documents, the base 1979 data have been projected to June 1982, taking into account relevant new census and migration information.

50. Syrian Arab Republic, Ministry of Planning, Directorate of Statistics, *Statistical Abstract of Syria, 1978* (published 1979).

51. Estimates as high as 500,000 have been widely quoted in newspaper and other accounts but these seem to us to be exceedingly high. In 1948 approximately 100,000 Palestinians sought refuge in Lebanon, and their number had increased to perhaps 115,000 by 1952, taking into account natural increase. Even at high rates of natural increase and with no net emigration, this base population could have grown to no more than 330,000 by 1982.

52. The figures for Kuwait are based upon relatively accurate census returns. We have assumed that more than 90 per cent of the Jordanian citizens resident in Kuwait are Palestinians, as are all persons listed as Palestinians (those emigrating from Gaza, Lebanon, and Syria).

53. This figure is conjecture. As of 1979, using data on Palestinian and Jordanian school enrolment in Saudi Arabia and estimating total population from these school enrolment figures, we concluded that there were approximately 150,000 persons of Palestinian descent living in Saudi Arabia. Since that time, we can presume a doubling of this population but must admit that no hard data exist on this point.

54. See Janet Abu-Lughod, 'The Demographic Transformation of Palestine', in Ibrahim Abu-Lughod, ed., *The Transformation of Palestine* (Evanston, Ill.: Northwestern University Press, 1971), pp., 139-63, esp. 153-61, for estimate of displaced persons and refugees from the 1947-49 period.

55. 'Demographic Characteristics of the Palestinian Population', UNESCO, esp. Table IV, pp.20-1, which gives full references to the data sources and evaluates their relative reliability.

56. We have included here the 65,000 to 67,000 Palestinian residents of East Jerusalem and vicinity who lived in the zone Israel illegally annexed; as noted, Israeli statistical sources list these with the 'non-Jews' of Israel rather than as residents of the 'Administered Territories'.

57. This policy has been verified and recounted in 'Report of the Special Committee to Investigate Israeli Practices Affecting the Human Rights of the Population of the Occupied Territories', (United National General Assembly, Document A/35/425: 6 October 1980).

58. See Janet Abu-Lughod, 'Israeli Settlements in Occupied Arab Lands: From Conquest to Colony', presented to The Fourth United Nations, Seminar on the Question of Palestine, held in Havana, Cuba, September 1980, reprinted in *The Journal of Palestine Studies* (Winter 1982), pp. 16-54, and also in I. Abu-Lughod, ed., *Palestinian Rights: Affirmation and Denial* (Wilmette, Ill.: Medina Press, 1982).

59. Stanley Greenberg, *Race and State in Capitalist Development: Comparative Perspectives* (New Haven: Yale University Press, 1980), pp. 397-8.

60. See Ian Lustick, *Arabs in the Jewish State: Israel's Control of a National Minority* (Austin and London: University of Texas Press, 1980).

61. Najwa Makhoul, 'Changes in the Employment Structure of Arabs in Israel', *Journal of Palestine Studies* (1981), 10(2), p. 84.

62. See Makhoul, 'Changes in Employment', pp. 91-5.

63. Cited in Elia T. Zureik, *The Palestinians in Israel: A Study in Internal Colonialism* (London: Routledge and Kegan Paul, 1979), p. 99.

64. *Ibid.*, pp. 126-7.

65. Cited in *ibid.*, p. 128.

66. Zureik, *Palestinians in Israel*, p. 130.

67. Cited in Abbas Alnasrawi, 'Palestinian Manpower Needs and the Palestine Open University', in *Palestine Open University Feasibility Study*, Part II, Annex VI, (Paris: UNESCO, 1980), p. 12.

68. *Ibid.*, p. 14.

69. *New York Times*, 12 September 1982, p. 14.

70. M. K. Budeiri, 'Changes in the Economic Structure of the West Bank and the Gaza Strip under Israeli Occupation', *Labour, Capital and Society* (1982), 1:47-63.

71. *Report of the Mission Sent by the Director-General of the ILO to Examine the Situation of the Workers in the Occupied Territories*, (Geneva: International Labour Office, 1979).

72. Cited in *New York Times*, 12 September 1982.

73. *United Nations Development Program: Report of the Inter-Agency Task Force on Assistance to the Palestinian People*, 1979.

74. Budeiri, 'Changes in Economic Structure', p. 58.

75. *Ibid.*, p. 56.

76. Cited in *Ibid.*, p. 57.

77. *Ibid*, pp. 58-63.

78. See Elia T. Zureick, 'The Learner's Environment', in *Palestine Open University Feasibility Study*, Annex 4, (Paris: UNESCO, 1980).

79. Sami Mar'i, *Arab Education in Israel* (Syracuse: Syracuse University Press, 1978), p. 89.

80. Zureik, *Palestinians in Israel, p. 153*.

81. Philip E. Davies, *'The Educated West Bank Palestinians', Journal of Palestine Studies*, 3 (1978), p. 69.

82. Jacqueline Henin, *Report to the Director-General of UNESCO on Multi Purpose Centres for Research and Creative Work in the Arab Territories Occupied by Israel since 1967*, Annex IV, 104, Ex/52, p. 5.

83. See, for example, *Boston Globe*, 17 November 1982; *New York Times*, 20 November 1982.